Somebody Down Here Likes Me Too

Somebody Down Here Likes Me Too

by

Rocky Graziano

with Ralph Corsel

STEIN & DAY/*Publishers*/New York

To my life-long love, my stand-up Norma, and to Vicki and Ralph Corsel, the guys who helped me make this book happen.

First published in 1981
Copyright © 1981 by Rocky Graziano and Ralph Corsel
All rights reserved
Designed by Judith E. Dalzell
Printed in the United States of America
STEIN & DAY/*Publishers*
Scarborough House
Briarcliff Manor, N.Y. 10510

Library of Congress Cataloging in Publication Data
Graziano, Rocky, 1921-
    Somebody down here likes me, too.
    1. Graziano, Rocky, 1921-   2. Boxers
(Sports)—United States—Biography.   I. Corsel,
Ralph.   II. Title.
GV1132.G62A29   796.8′3′0924 [B]   81-40332
ISBN 0-8128-2828-3   AACR2

CONTENTS

Illustrations

(between pages 108 and 109)

Rocky in training
Trainer Whitey Bimstein puts Rocky through paces
Tony Zale takes a hard right
Outside Stillman's Gym
With Jack Healy and George Raft
Teaching Paul Newman how to play Rocky
As Martha Raye's television boyfriend
With Frank Sinatra
Esquire cover with Jack Palance and Raquel Welch
With "Little Caesar," Edward G. Robinson
With Zsa Zsa Gabor
Martha Raye separates Rocky and "The Raging Bull," Jake La Motta
In costume for "Miami Undercover"
Doing a fruit drink ad
With Liza Minelli
With Sugar Ray Robinson
Rocky and wife Norma
Making a pizza commercial
Making a commercial for an auto transmission repair firm
With Terence Cardinal Cooke
Rocky the artist
With New York's Governor Carey
Campaigning for President Reagan

PREFACE

I vividly recall the first time I met Rocky Graziano. The year was 1945. Rocky was twenty-three then and busily building a reputation as a boxer who, from the opening bell, never stopped throwing murderous punches until his opponent was out cold on the canvas.

At that time I was a hustler, a gambler of sorts, working occasionally as a bartender.

On that particular day I was walking along Forty Ninth Street, off Broadway, with Joe La Motta, another pugilist and brother of Jake (The Raging Bull), when we noticed Rocky approaching with an entourage of "Dead End Kid" types in tow.

I had been to many of Rocky's fights, bet money on him, and had yelled a lot of encouragement to him from my seat near the ring.

It was a special treat to see him stop and talk with Joe, whom he knew well.

I was surprised that he was so handsome, his nose straight, and his eyes bright and clear. He didn't have the punched-up face of the average boxer, even though he had been fighting wildly, in and out of the ring, practically all his life. His body was lean and strong-looking. He wore a light-colored zoot suit with high-waisted pegged pants but no tie. Lying flat on his head, with up-turned brim was a pork-pie hat, another youth style of the time. A small shock of reddish-brown hair peaked downward over his forehead.

"I see you got your mob with you," Joe said.

"My boys," Rocky answered pointing a thumb in their direction as they shuffled in a semicircle around him.

Joe introduced me as his friend Ralph, and Rocky assessed me with a glance, as he took my hand and mumbled a greeting. He turned to Joe, and as they spoke of fighters, managers, and the gym Rocky would turn to spit out through a narrow space between two of his front teeth, a sign of the tough-guy days of his youth.

Rocky's boyhood was a maze of bleak days and lonely nights. The roach- and rat-infested tenement he grew up in was in constant turmoil. From the day he learned to walk, Rocky bore the brunt of a father's frustrations—a bitter father, whose dream of happiness, if he ever had one, had crumbled in the reality of the rock-bottom Depression. Rocky's father had failed in his own boxing career, a career that put some seventy professional fights under his belt, all of which had taken their toll.

In the streets where Rocky grew up, adeptness as a petty thief and two flashing fists became his key to survival. He and members of his youthful gangs worshipped only at the shrine of and basked only in the reflected glory of "heroic" mobsters.

Rocky dropped out of school, after repeated absences, at a very early age. Today, when asked what he took in school he answers with a grin, "I took chairs, typewriters, pencils, lamps, loose change, anything I could get my hands on."

However, Rocky didn't restrict his ventures to the schoolhouse. He reeled in radios by their aerial wires from tenement rooftops, looted parked cars, broke into vending machines, and later graduated to "breaking and entering."

Arrest finally landed him in a reformatory, where he sought out excitement in the only way he knew, with his fists in the gymnasium boxing ring. On subsequent enforced visits to one institution or another, Rocky would again work out his frustrations in the ring. Physically undefeated but mentally calloused, he would return after a term to the streets of his poor neighborhood. There, discontent and disillusionment would drive him back to the poolroom hangout and back to his old friends and habits, following closely in the footsteps of a racketeer uncle called Danny Bob, who was found lying in a lot one morning, his chest full of lead.

While Rocky Graziano was growing up in the Italian neighborhood in the Lower East Side of Manhattan, I had a similar Italian upbringing from a "Little Italy" in the South Bronx. My own youth was similarly plagued with juvenile delinquency, reform school, and all the ills that seem to befall so many who suffer deprivation.

During my youth I fought in amateur boxing contests, as did Rocky. He had that killer instinct that made him the great fighter he became, while I, without anger, contented myself with boxing as a sport.

One of the great turning points in Rocky Graziano's life came when two neighborhood boxers talked him into entering a Metropolitan A.A.U. boxing tournament, which earned him a gold medal as the New York Welterweight A.A.U. Champion.

Up to the time I met Rocky, I knew little about his past. There was hardly a week that went by when Rocky wasn't being written about in the newspapers and sports magazines, but at that time the articles were all about his skills in prize-ring combat. Even today, *Ring* Magazine and other sports periodicals continue to put pictures of Rocky on their covers and write glowing testimonies about his days in the ring. In fact, through the years, there has hardly been an issue of *Ring* in which Rocky hasn't been mentioned.

I saw as many of Rocky's fights as I could, right up to the

championship and beyond. Violence was his middle name and he smashed a violent path through his opponents. As Joe Louis once said of his own opponents, "They could run but they can't hide."

During his ring career, Rocky fought eighty-three bouts, winning fifty-two by knockouts. In 1972 this record finally earned him his rightful place in the Boxing Hall of Fame.

I became Rocky's friend, joined his entourage and clamored to have my picture taken with him like everyone else. Our friendship grew, and we've spent a lot of pleasant times together and with others, laughing and carousing in the harmless, boisterous way that even grown men do.

Rocky's speech sometimes sounds as if it had been drawn across coarse sandpaper, but an honest warmth always comes through.

Over the years, I've studied Rocky with something more than passing interest. It was as if I knew I would one day write about him. With great joy I watched his climb to the top as one of the greatest fighters of all time. I've been amazed at his success in show business. In wonderment, I've watched this kid rise from the slums to friendly association with presidents of the United States. His associations with other important personalities are too numerous to recount here, but you'll read of many of them a little later in the book. Rocky's magnetism for the great and for average Joes alike lies in his indomitable joy of life.

Today, Rocky's favorite game is golf; he plays it well, and with many of these same personalities. A natural at golf as he was in boxing, he has played in dozens of tournaments, winning many with scores in the low seventies. His home is adorned with trophies.

As Middleweight Champion of the World, Rocky Graziano became exposed to a life that had always been foreign to him. Doors unknown or closed suddenly opened. Celebrities clamored to meet him, and offers to make personal appearances on radio, television, and before public gatherings launched him on a new and prosperous career as an entertainer. He is now one of the most sought-after personalities to make television commercials and is reputed to be earning well into six figures. However, when asked about his earnings, Rocky answers, "I do real good." His unpretentious yet charismatic personality is probably making him more money outside the ring than any prize fighter in history.

Today Rocky devotes all the time he can to visiting schools and institutions, making speeches to wayward boys in the same predicament in which he once found himself. The head that Rocky's father once said wore devil's horns is now adorned with a halo.

Rocky has a keen sense of humor that enables him to laugh at himself as exuberantly as he laughs at others. He loves being recognized. When strangers stop him and ask, "Aren't you Rocky Graziano?" he answers, "Yeah, but I can't help it."

In the mid-1950s, Rocky, with the help of writer Rowland Barber, wrote *Somebody Up There Likes Me.* The book, a great commercial success, was later nominated for the Pulitzer Prize. It was also made into a big money-making film starring Paul Newman and Pier Angeli. Paul Newman's portrayal of Rocky was a superb job that put him on the road to stardom. The film *Somebody Up There Likes Me* is now a classic and appears regularly on television all over the country.

A second book, *The Rocky Road to Physical Fitness,* a spoof on exercising, was published in 1968. A reviewer observed with wit that this one had also been translated by Rowland Barber.

I've come to several conclusions about Rocky. Over the years there've been times when I could sense turbulence in his thoughts, of early boyhood frustrations that still plague him, and an inability to expose or clearly express true feelings. Though he could not express himself in the best King's English, the honesty was always there for me and others to recognize.

Rocky is a nervous mass of energy; he's always on the move. When not working, one can find him running from one well-known watering-hole to another, making phone calls or in search of friends. His hangouts are places like J. B. Tipton, P. J. Clarke's, Friar Tuck, La Maganette, Elmer's, and others. Rocky can't stand the formality of an office and so arranges his appointments in these bars. The words, "Excuse me, I have to call my office," are not in his vocabulary. He carries his office in his pocket, worn business cards and scraps of paper tied up with a rubber band.

Rocky has always had a need to be surrounded by men. He searches constantly for an unself-conscious comradeship that only the closest of rough men can know. It's as if he were on an endless search for something he missed in childhood, for a guy to put an arm around his shoulder in a gesture of true affection—as if he were spending his life looking for a father unlike the one who never knew that what his son needed and craved most as a boy was a father's love and understanding.

Since those days thirty-six years ago both Rocky and I have had our share of acclaim, I as a writer and he as a boxer/entertainer. We have also both made our fortunes, he in his field and I in mine.

Behind Rocky's sometimes half-articulate, ruptured English lies a keen perception of the world. If he is not a seer, he does show insight. "A lotta people think I'm stupid, Ralph, but I'll tell you somethin, I know how to count money," or "You know why I like to hang around with millionaires, Ralph?" No, why? "They never ask you for money."

Yet with all Rocky's fondness for male companionship, one instantly suspects that Rocky loves his wife, Norma, more than life itself. It is always the strongest impression that one senses in their company. A soft look from her has the power to melt him.

Rocky Graziano has been happily married to the same woman since the four-round-fight days of his struggling youth. Besides tending to their beautiful home, Norma involves herself with many projects and keeps up with Rocky, who's usually up and running by seven in the morning. Their two married daughters are very secure with beautiful families of their own. Wife Norma, a petite, attractive blonde, lives with her Rocky in a luxurious penthouse apartment in the Sutton Place area of Manhattan. Their home is decorated almost entirely in white. On entering, one can immediately see that Rocky appreciates and is a patron of the arts. He is once again on canvas but this time in the form of numerous professional looking paintings hung on his walls. Most depict fights and related scenes. Rocky modestly admits that he painted these himself in his spare time. Their spacious terrace is an aboretum of small trees, flowers, and even basil and tomato plants. Rocky grows them to remind himself of the "Little Italy" in which he grew up.

During a recent talk, President Ronald Reagan spoke of the circumstances that gave rise to success stories like Rocky's. He spoke of "a spirit that drives us to dream and dare and take great risks for good.

It's the spirit of millions who may have been born poor, but who would not be denied their day in the sun."

I offered Rocky my help in putting together a book expressing, in his own words, his remembrances of some of the most important people in his life, and the events that led to his days in the sun—a sun that still shines brightly. This is that book.

Ralph Corsel

Somebody Down Here Likes Me Too

O N E

When I was a kid my mom, Ida, always called me her poor little baby, while my pop, Nick, rocked me with punches and called me the devil hisself. Before I hit my twenty-first birthday, I had spent almost half of those twenty-one years in reform schools, jails, an prisons, and then one day all that fuckin misery and bitter anger started comin out through my fists, an it took me right up to the Middleweight Championship of the world. Two more careers follow after that, and durin my life I get to meet, shake hands, an have my picture took, starting with Harry S. Truman, with eight presidents of the United States. It had to start with one day when somebody up there must've looked me up an down, an said, "Let's give this kid a couple-a more chances."

I know somebody down here gotta like me too. And, when I go down for that last count, what else can they remember me as but the luckiest bum that ever lived?

One of the things I gotta tell you is the kinda lumps I catch in my throat when I think about all the heartaches I bring my mom during those sad years an the buckets of tears she fill, running in an out of police stations or on some long trip she take to visit me in some stinkin can. I never forget the way she look in the visiting room in her cheap, beat-up clothes when she says, "I couldn't bring you nothin. I didn't have no money left after I raise the fare to get here."

My poor mom useta run around all day an night tryin to get somebody to come up with bail money to spring me out of the stinkin can. It was as little as two hunnerd bucks but every bookie an racket guy in the neighborhood turn her down, but she hit up everybody, stores, relatives, peddlers, pushcarts, five bucks here, ten there, till she get it all and come spring me.

I'd say, don't worry, ma. I pay back every penny. But like it was crazy, me and the times. I clear that beef an break her heart with another. Things like I steal, a bunch of shit, typewriters, addin machines outa a school, odds and ends offn a truck, an then we hock or sell the whole swag for something like four cents.

I can't tell you how many times I promise my mom, who's cryin hysteric, that I be good an how many times the crazy, broke, unhappy guy inside me make me break my promise.

All my mom's prayin with the priests in our parish, beggin, askin they make God straighten me out, nothin, no-how, did no good.

When I watched my mom cryin from the other side of a glass or chicken-wire window, in a visitors' room it was like the worse beatin I ever took in my life, but all it done was made me wanna go out an kill anybody who got in my way, just to break her and me even. I'd grit my teeth to stop myself from bustin out cryin, an I say, "Don't worry mom. Someday, just wait till someday!" And I never know then that there really was gonna come a someday for me. And that someday was gonna start with boxin, the one thing I hated more than anything else in the world when I was a kid.

Like they say, never complain an never explain, but if I go this route how the hell am I going to tell you my story? Don't get me wrong, complainin is the last thing I do, so when I tell you about my life an how I feel, it's because I want you to know how I crawled up out of the cellar to where I got today.

Like I said about my pop, in his eyes I was the devil but in my eyes the only thing that shown was a hate that made me wanna kill him. But then, if he wasn't the mean kind of a guy he was I'd never grown up like I done and become Middleweight Champ of the World an have all those great things happen afterwards.

Some of the things I remember best about my pop was his being outa work a lot, an whenever he scrounged up a extra buck or two he blew it on wine. He yelled a lot, beat up on us kids, and made my mom sick. It was like somebody musta t'rown the horns in on our house before I was born. Even a guy who works down in a city sewer gotta look up some time, but my pop had no place to look. An what I didn't know in those days was what done it to him.

My pop was a boxer, long before I come along. He fought under the name of Fighting Nick Bob, and he put about seventy pro fights under his belt before he was forced to hang up his gloves. When he hung em up it musta killed something inside the guy, that was his whole life. He hung the gloves right on a wall in the small front room, under a picture of hisself posed in boxing trunks and wearin gloves. Musta been years they was hangin there because all the leather was peeling off them. From what I useta hear, my pop was a pretty fair welterweight who held his own in the ring, but nothin ever happen except what happen inside his head.

I remember my pop bringin home other ex-fighters and they sit around the kitchen drinkin wine an talkin about the old days, and fighters like Dempsey, Stanley Ketchel, Mickey Walker, and Benny Leonard. My mom just look on an moan things, like whatcha gonna do?

I was about five years old when my pop started forcing me to fight with my brother Joe, who was not only three years older but a lot heavier than me, an my pop always rooted for Joey. My old man would hold up Joey's hands and show Joe how to punch to knock me dead. All I was to my pop was Joey's punching bag.

This went on for a few years, up to the time I start runnin away from home for two, three days at the time just to try to dodge the misery. Then sometimes I come home, and maybe he come in from lookin for work on the docks or lugging crates someplace. He'd start maybe wine drinkin, put the gloves on me an Joe again, and yell out things like, "Come on, Joey boy! Let's go, champ! He's open. Send in that right to the jaw," just like he was yellin from the corner of the ring. He'd show Joe how to bob an weave, an t'row punches, just like he was trainin him to be a future champ, just like it was hisself he was gonna put back in the ring someday to finish the job to the championship. Me? I was just somethin they could wash down the sewer.

In those days, I didn't know enough to feel sorry for my pop. How could I know what was eating him inside an how it felt to be a washed-up boxer?

I remember gettin so mad I wanna kill everybody. Pop would egg Joey on, and Joe would bloody my nose or cut my lip, and I'd lunge at him like I'm gonna tear him apart. The more the tears come, the madder I get. The madder I get, the more he dance around me connectin an makin me miss. That fuckin pop of mine laughed his friggin head off watching me t'row a million punches with only a few bouncin off Joe's gloves. Then I'd jump swingin at my pop, and he grab my wrists until I stopped kickin an yellin, and he'd send me into the bedroom. As soon as the coast was clear, I disappear again for a coupla days, steal my food, an sleep in somebody's hallway or on a roof.

There's a lotta nights I useta go to bed, achin an sore, and I dream I grow up someday an flatten both Joey and my pop with just my two fists.

There was times, too, when I go out in the street and beat the shit outa some kid my size or even bigger, and maybe steal somethin from him just to break even.

Only once my pop shoulda put his arm around my shoulder and hold me close like I seen so many fathers do. Only once, he shoulda taken me to a ball game or something like that, an who knows I mighta been President. But then, who knows?

It coulda been good then, and bad today. Without even knowin it, what my pop left with me I can't even tell you what it is. I can only feel it, and you can't buy it for all the money in the world.

What I remember best about the tenement traps we lived in when I was real small, was that they was full of pets—cockroaches an rats that ran all over the hallways. The building was a steambath in the summer and ice cold in the winter. None of us was ever warm. Even about four years old, I could remember going out lookin for wood an coal in the streets so we could keep our broken-down coal stove going in winter. I musta become the biggest coal booster in the neighborhood. In those days everybody got a coal stove and every couple-a blocks there's a coal man sellin sacks of coal outa a corner cellar. I hang around near the cellar with a sack under my jacket and as soon I see him take off for a delivery I run down, grab what coal I can carry, and rush it home. We wuz always running out of coal and when we did the stove would burn up what was inside and then go out. One winter, when my mom just has new twin babies, she's always going around bundling them up and trying to keep them warm, but they must've caught bad colds anyway, and they develop pneumonia. Then, in the middle of one of the coldest nights of winter the stove went out and in the morning we find both babies dead. It's too late to do anything about the babies but as I'm growin' bigger, I'm stealin' bigger sacks and if I don't bring coal home every day we maybe all freeze to death. I heard once that some times of the year the sun competes with the cold tryin to keep your coat on or off. What happens when you ain't got a coat, which was me? Believe me, when I tell you the only thing good about bein poor is it don't cost no money, and in my house we were so poor I grew up thinking knives, forks, and spoons was jewelry.

I went around stealing from the earliest days I could remember, mostly because I was always hungry. My biggest ache in the stomach useta come when I would walk by the Italian bakery when they were baking their fresh hot bread. Man! Do I remember that smell! There'd be days and days when my stomach was always growlin, and all my mom could give us was spaghetti and nothin on it. I useta get up long before anybody else, even before it got light, an I'd go down in the street and steal food offa wagons making deliveries. Mostly I stole things like milk, bread, cakes, and fruit offa the wagons.

Everybody ate what I brought home, and everybody was warm around the stove, but my pop was always saying I was gonna wind up in the chair someday. When he got real mad he'd whip off his belt and believe me, I could still today feel the way it useta snap across my ass. While he was beating me, he'd yell out, "You're the devil! We got the devil in the house," and that's just the way I always got treated.

I learned to run pretty good too in those days, away from him and the cops, and by things I could swoop up, specially at newsstands. I'd go by the stands, grab the pennies and sail down the street like an alligator was snappin at my ass. Whatta you think of that? I was even doing roadwork then, almost like I knew it would come in handy some day for my fighting career.

The greatest calamity of that time, and everybody suffered from it, could bring on heart attacks, a stroke, or even worse. It was the payment of rent due or Christmas coming without a penny in the house. There was only one remedy and that was robbin things from those who didn't have the problem. And you gotta believe, I stole everything and anything that began with "a." A bicycle, a scooter, a pair of pants, a watch, a penknife, a pair of skates, a flashlight, and even a lady's purse, if somebody was careless enough to leave one near my reach. I was so crooked ya coulda used my arm for a corkscrew. My ma was always crying, in and out of Children's Court, because of my robbin everybody blind and playin hooky from school. She was always tellin everybody what a good boy I was, but then Al Capone's mother musta said he was a good boy, too. I wasn't a juvenile delinquent, I was just a kid with an impediment of the reach. I couldn't keep my hands in my pockets. An you'd never believe it by my mom. Always sticking up for me and ready to fight other moms who were looking to do battle because I beat up their sissy kids in a fair fistfight. I swear, my mom t'rew a better left hook than me. I oughta know, just by the whacks she caught me with when I was bad and got close enough for her to reach me.

There was whole weeks when I never went to school. If I happened to go, there was a good chance the teacher was out hooky. I spent all my time walkin the streets, dreaming of when I grow up, and lookin for somethin to steal.

Sometimes, after one of my mom's visits to Children's Court, they would useta give me to my grandma and grandpa, who live not too far away. My grandma'd hug me and love me and say she want to take me for a couple-a weeks because she knew she could straighten me out. I love her too, an I never have to steal any food when I'm with them, but already by that time even Jesus Christ can't straighten me out.

I remember the dog they useta have, and I never forget how that dog and me love each other, and until today I always have a big dog because of Walyo. That was his name, Walyo was one of those big-headed, broad-shouldered Italian bulldogs, and he only understood Italian because that's the only way they ever talk to him. They would say to the dog in Italian, "Take Rocco to school and wait for him." When I come outa school at three o'clock, there's Walyo right at the door waiting just like they tell him, and he takes me home. Durin those days Walyo was the only real friend I had.

While I'm talkin about my grandma, I gotta tell you she bought me the first suit I ever own. I was gettin pretty big then and I gotta make communion, and she can't understand how come I'm in rags, specially on Sundays. She always says on Sunday you gotta put on a suit and go to church and pray. At that time Canal Street was known as suit-huntin street. There was nothin but clothin stores there, both sides of the street. In fact, I swiped a lotta swag off the street counters on that street. There, nobody ever pay the price on the tag. You start with the tag price and bargain down. Mostly it was just immigrants shopped there. They never trusted stores like Gimbel's and Macy's because they couldn't get them down from the ticket.

I remember my grandma walking along Canal Street, an she's got me tight by the hand, and the hawkers are callin out for her to bring me in their stores. One hawker, where she stops to look in the store window, grabs her by the arm and tries to pull me inside. Man! You never heard nobody curse in Italian like my grandma curse at him. When she goes into a store an finds the suit that fit me, with a right ticket price, she starts bargaining. The guy comes down a little and she wants him to come down more. When he says he's sellin her the suit for a ridiculous figure, I wanna flatten the guy. Anyway, that's how I got my first suit. Nobody was ever so much around when I needed them like my grandpa and grandma, rest in peace.

One day my mom starts bringin in boxes and crates from the grocery and vegetable stores and packin our things, and she says, we gotta move, that's all. A guy told me once, you don't know whatcha got until you lose it. Moving meant nothing. I didn't have one fuckin thing to lose and neither did my family. We go from one roach palace into another, on Tenth Street and First Avenue, and till today this was the place I always figure for my growing up home. Maybe it's because I got into my biggest troubles with the cops there.

This pad, even though they supposed to have steam heat, go find it. Here, in the middle of winter, even the janitor banged on the pipes for heat. And, if you paid your rent on time, you could be arrested for suspicion of robbery.

First thing I do when we move there is get together a gang, and my fists made me the leader. We stole offa trucks, outa warehouses, stores, an garages, anything we could get our hands on that we could sell for a few bucks. People useta pray we didn't rob them whenever they seen me walking along with my mob, Big Gumball, Nunzi, Foongi, Mongo, Calabash, and The Rake. We made the neighborhood so tough the local Woolworth had to even sell their ten-cent toy watches outa a locked case, and Bibles got sold from under the counter. The only things free was our hands.

During those days, could you see somebody coming to me and sayin, "Don't worry, kid, in your life you're gonna become a millionaire, and you're also gonna meet eight Presidents." First thing I'da said was, "Eh, see where you gotta go." For sure I would've swore the guy had rocks in his skull. Y' mean?

Politics was a word I never heard and knew nothing about. But the word election, that was important. To me and my gang, election meant makin a buck or two, and having a lot of fun.

The neighborhood politicians useta come around with these little red, white, and blue pin buttons and circulars, with pictures of guys running for election, and they pay us a buck to pass 'em out up and down the avenue. We useta pass 'em out for a while and then dump the rest of the circulars in a garbage can. The pin buttons was another thing. We went south with them, and later we gamble for them with playing cards. It didn't make no difference which buttons we won or lost. One face was as good as another. I useta hear the voting people in our neighborhood saying politicans were all so crooked they hadda screw their hats on. Others say they ain't never gonna vote because it make no difference who was talking from the top of the stand. It was the same old bullshit about how some guy in power was robbing everybody blind. And guys running against them would yell, "Just give *me* a chance!"

When I grow up I find out these were the big days of the political bosses. The guys who hire us to pass out the stuff were the guys who get favors for deliverin the vote. I could remember talk at the Democratic Club, which was like a social club where the big guys useta play cards. They were always talking politics and about political machines and guys like Boss Tweed, Al Smith, Jimmy Walker, Vito Marcantonio, and Tammany Hall, the Tammany chief, and things like that. But it was all Greek to me.

To us, the biggest thing about election, the thing we all looked for every year, was the fire. We useta start saving up wood in an empty side-street lot days before election came along. We called the wood we saved "lection." Every guy in the neighborhood has to go out and find some, and bring in his lection.

If a guy didn't bring in his share of lection, he couldn't come around the fire when it was lit election night. Most of the wood came from vegetable crates we collected from all the pushcarts that useta line both sides of the avenue, but then we also got old furniture that people threw away.

When we got the fire started, usually in the middle-a the street, we'd start heaving the crates up to the top. Sometimes we'd get the wood up as high as the second story. Once we even threw on a telegraph pole from a backyard clothesline, and even a pushcart went. Another time, when the fire was going strong, my gang tore down the high wooden fence all around the lot and heaved that too.

The only real bad thing that ever happened is when Big Gumball t'rew a full bottle of kerosene in the fire to make it stronger. The bottle explodes and Foongi lose an eye when he got hit with flyin glass.

The blaze and smoke could be seen for blocks and blocks, and no firemen dare come near or they get mobbed.

When I was small I'd sit on the curb looking inna the fire, and I'd make all kinds of crazy dreams. I'm glad a lot didn't come true, because I useta dream of becoming a big racketeer some day so I could get rich and get my ass outa the house.

Another thing we did was roast potatoes we swiped from home. We useta put nail holes in vegetable cans, tie a cord on top, put in some char wood and a spud, and then twirl it around till the spud got cooked.

These were the things that election meant to me.

T W O

When I was twelve years old, in 1933, I had just finished my first stretch in the Catholic Protectory. Before I come home, all I could think about was straightening out my brother Joe for all the lumps he give me when I was a kid. Joe was fifteen then, but I knew I was a killer already. I had beaten up and straightened out older and tougher kids than him at the Protectory. There was a lot of gettin even for all the years Joe used me for a punchin bag.

When he came home I didn't give him a chance. I dump him all over the apartment and left him cryin on the floor against a wall. Afterwards, I thought about how everything wasn't his fault and I felt sorry. There was always something I want to say but I never know how, so I'd let my fists do the talking for me. After dumpin Joe I feel like a heel so I disappear for a couple-a days. It was like I hadda prove that if there was gonna be a killer in that house it hadda be me, no matter how old I was.

By the time I was fifteen I had already done a lot of time and I was on the lam, havin escaped over the wall from another stretch in the Protectory. Nothing ahead but more trouble. Trouble was the only thing I ever knew. It was always there waiting around any corner I turned.

My pop kept callin me the devil, an everybody said it wouldn't be long. I was headed right for the chair or a bullet in the head from a sharpshootin cop. I never wanted to be a big shot with other mob big shots. Just being a hero to the guys on the corner was all I needed to make me feel like I was somebody and not a piece of shit you flush down the bowl.

You know, in those days all us kids had idols, and through the years I had my share. My biggest idols was gangsters like Al Capone, Dillinger, Dutch Schultz, Vincent Coll, Frank Costello, guys like that, and the actors who played them in movies about their lives. But, one of my idols was nobody that big. This was Jack Healy, one of the older guys who hung out around the corner down on Tenth Street and First Avenue. Even though the name wasn't Italian, the guy was still a dago. His real name was Guisseppi Leponto, and sometimes I used to hear other Italians call him Pino. In those days a lot of Italian wise guys and Italian prizefighters took on Irish nicknames. Some guys coming up still do it today. You know what I mean?

We all respected Jack Healy because he was tough, the sharpest guy around, and he never treated us like kids. He even played a guitar and sang all the hit songs of the day. We all knew, from his tellin us, that he was some kind of a hoofer, doing shows too, in big dance halls around the city. His shoes were so shined you could see your face in them, but if a kid come up with a shine-box, Jack'd quick say, "Okay. Shine 'em up," just so he could give the kid a break.

There was a Italian restaurant across the street on First Avenue called Lanza's, still there today, and Jack an all the guys like Jack hung out there late at night, but me an my mob wasn't old enough for that action yet. All we could do late at night was look through the front window, wonder who was sittin there, and think about what big jobs they planning to knock off.

As we grow up, we figures we know the guy better an better. Jack is

Broadway through and through. We get to know a lot of things about the guy, like he's connected with the mob. Healy was also supposed to be Big Frenchie's chauffeur. One time, when Vincent Coll kidnapped Big Frenchie, Jack was with him, but they let Jack go. Jack says he shit in his pants that day. You knew that anybody who hung around a lot always sharped up, hadda be a bookie or a shylock or a number guy, or somethin like that. You just took somebody's word and never asked.

I still remember the way he useta watch me whip some bigger kid in a street fight. After that, Jack would put his arm around my shoulder, walk me into the candy store for a soda, an tell everybody I was going to be champ some day. You never seen me that I didn't have a chip on my shoulder, like it was my old man I was gettin back at for all the beatins he useta give me.

Jack Healy was always talking to me like a uncle shoulda, and he always listened to what was eatin me up.

For some reason he useta talk different to me. It wasn't like when he was talkin to the big guys he knew. When he talked with them he was always arguing, like he knew everything. He argued about horses, baseball, boxin, and all kinds of sports. He could tell you all the winners of the Kentucky Derby for years. The guy was a walkin book of knowledge, and he'd bet on anything. He'd even bet you on the weather one week away. And the guy had a short fuse with a real bad temper. Mad enough to kill a guy one minute, and laughing friendly with him the next. But he hadda be right. There was no such thing as Jack Healy being wrong. He'd argue with an electrician about electric even though he didn't know the first thing about the man's business.

To get back to us, it don't matter how he was with the big guys, yellin his ass off that he was right, we thought he was one hell of a good guy. And me, I useta wanna be like him.

He told us stories about show biz, how he started as a gigolo and how he useta dance with big guys' girls at the Cotton Club, and how one guy got jealous once and poked a forty-five in his face. He told us he was going to Hollywood some day and become a movie star, and how George Raft was one of his best friends, and someday he an Raft were gonna be making pictures together.

Sometimes, some of the guys would say "bullshit" after Jack left, but they still like to hear him. Me, I believe him one hunnerd percent, and with my mouth wide open, while he's talkin about Raft an guys like that. Jack knew all about what big lady movie star was gettin banged by some bartender, and he told us about the Fifty Second Street show girls he useta go with. The guy was a dark and very handsome guy, like a Rudolph Valentino.

I'm walking along Tenth up the block near Second Avenue one day, and Foongi comes up to me puffing an says, "I been looking for ya all over the neighborhood. George Raft is over in Lanza's Restaurant eating with Jack Healy."

I barely hear Foongi say, "Healy asked me if youse was around," because I'm already dashing up Tenth Street toward First just as fast as I could go. I run across the street to Lanza's, where a lotta neighborhood people are crowded, looking through the window, oohin an aahing. I squeeze in and look too. Man! You never know how excited I am. Here's one of my biggest heroes, right in the middle of my own neighborhood and I gotta look at 'im through a store window, an on top of it I can't see the guy good because he's got his back to the front window.

Healy spots me through the glass and he waves, come in. I'm kinda scared but I goes inside and Healy sez, "Come here, Rocky boy! I wantcha to meet my pal Georgie Raft."

"Hiya," I says, and Healy is grabbing a chair from another table and sits me down.

Raft's got a nice smile on his puss. I'm too scared to shake his hand, and I don't put mine out an he don't put his out. He just stands up, puts a hand on my shoulder, friendly like, and moves me into the chair.

Even though you can't prove class by me, I knew I was with it. He got a crease on his pants so sharp he could cut his steak with it.

"Rocky here," Healy tells Raft, "is the toughest kid in this neighborhood. I seen this kid whip guys four times his size, and right out there in the street."

I kinda blush when he keeps saying things like, "Man! You should see this kid go." He says, "I keep telling him he's gonna become a big main-event fighter some day, but he don't want nuttin to do with boxing."

They sip Lanza's espresso coffee and Raft says, "I hope you don't end up like I did." This bothers me later when I remember his saying it because I know the guy's on top of the world.

"What wouldja like to have?" Raft asks me when the waiter comes. Glassa wine, I tell him.

"How would you like me an Raft managing you when you turn pro?" Healy asks me. I don't answer the question. I'm too excited. Healy grabs me and kids around mussin my hair, while Raft's saying things like, "I can't get over how much this kid reminds me of myself when I was his age."

Goose pimples keep comin up on my arms, and I rub them like I'm cold.

Raft keeps watching me with a big smile in his eyes. Maybe he thinks he's looking at an angry screwed-up kid, and if that's what he's thinking he's right.

I guess he knows I'm scared meeting him, so he says, "You know somethin', Rocky, I was just like you. I was born and raised just a few blocks north of here, West Forty First Street in Hell's Kitchen. I slept in these same kind of hallways you got around here, and when I was thirteen I was already out on my own."

The guy was hittin me with nuttin but surprises. I turn to look out the front window an there's my whole gang out there waving like bring me in. I act like I don't see them.

Raft is sayin, "Tough road to come up, off these streets, but it makes a guy fight twice as hard to make it."

"You can say that again," Healy tells him.

"Ten kids in my family," says Raft. "I had to move out in the hallways because there wasn't enough room, and the only fun we ever got in those days was going out and stealing things."

Man, was I in the clouds just hearing Raft talk like that. Like he was talkin about me. I wanted to put myself in the guy's pocket and never leave him.

"Just like you," he says to me, "I hung out on the same kind of stoops you got in that block. We use to spend hours singing songs and talking about baseball, girls, and big-shot racketeers."

Not me, I wanted to tell 'im, I'm too busy running, but I just smile and keep watchin him like I'm afraid he's gonna disappear.

A woman brings a piece of paper and a pen and wants his autograph. He signs it and gives her a big smile, and she starts to say somethin but nuttin comes out. I can see she's more scared than me. She says, "Thanks," and goes away.

"I broke into show business right up here at the Union Square Theater on Fourteenth Street," Raft says. "That was my first shot on the vaudeville stage."

"No kiddin," I say. "I saw *Scarface* there three times."

"I had the experience before I made that picture," he tells me. Then he says to Jack, "Remember me tellin you Owney Madden was my buddy when we were kids? I still see him today. Before I went out to Hollywood, and my pockets were taking a beating, he use to give me jobs driving beer trucks and booze cars so I could pay my way."

They talk some more about old times and how they started as hoofers together in New York dance halls, and how they won dance contests before Raft got discovered and went to Hollywood. I could sometimes see a sad, sad look in Healy's face when they was talking about how lucky Raft makes it. I could see then, even if I don't understand it good, how Healy must've had the same dreams and never made it. And I know today how something could eat up your insides with a hunger no lack of food could ever put there.

When they get up to leave I look outside and feel like a guy who was in a different world. Now I gotta go back to all that shit I always have around me.

There's a limousine waitin outside. Healy an Raft say goodbye an they drive off. Even the grownups rush up to me and want to know what Raft talked about, but I'm in another world. All I do is shake my head. My gang surround me, asking questions with those "I can't believe it" looks on their faces.

All I can say is, "You see, what'd I tell you about Jack? Who's doin the bullshittin now?"

I break away with a "See you tomorrow," and I walk off down the street and I start gettin sad. Then I start thinking about the movie

Scarface Al Capone, which starred George Raft and Paul Muni. Before you know it I'm dreaming real good. I take out a coin an start flipping it like George Raft did in the movie. I put the coin away and when nobody's looking I act like I'm holding a machine gun, walking down the street spraying bullets all over the joint. Big beer trucks and bulletproof gangster cars are crashin all around me. I pass a flower shop, and with one sweep I fill the joint full of bullets, just like they got O'Banion in the movie.

After that, George Raft become my only idol, and for a few years I worship the guy an want to grow up and be like all the gangsters the guy plays in the movies.

All the dreamin in the world ain't gonna straighten me out because I go on dreamin about all the wrong things and so, by the time I'm sixteen, I make Coxsackie, the can for the big boys. I stole a car from a road inside a cemetery. When I come up before the judge and he asks me why I stole it, I tell him I figured the owner was dead and wasn't gonna need it no more.

When I get to Coxsackie, who's already there but two of my sidekicks from my East Side neighborhood. One-a them is Angelo De Sanza, who, after he gets out, turns fighter under the name Terry Young, and the other guy is Hammerhead Jake La Motta, The Raging Bull, who became middleweight champ after me.

The bit with my old man is still bad inside my head, so I don't want nothing to do with the ring. But, these two guys are working out in the prison gym all the time, banging heads, and throwing punches like they know they're gonna become future champs.

I don't stay in Coxsackie too long because I get meaner and madder every day, banging heads, cursing out guards, things like that. It's either they gotta keep me in solitary all the time or send me to another cage. So, they transfer me off to the New York Reformatory, where I spends my seventeenth birthday.

Once I hit the street again, I start hanging out in the poolroom. I spent a lot of time walkin around the neighborhood wondering what I do if I ever get my hands on a thousan dollars. I musta walked a million miles, and just around the East Side. I was always dreaming or casing jobs. Even today I can't stand still too long in one place. I gotta always be movin around, like no matter where I am I gotta be someplace else. Like I'm always looking for somebody new to talk to, somebody that's got some new action. I could never hear the same bullshit twice without the guy knowing it. It showed on my face, and I'd run to a new spot with a "See you tomorrow." I never said, "See you later," but the other guy always said it.

Terry Young was already sprung from the joint before me, so we team up an put the gang back together again. By this time my whole mob had done one or two stretches some place. One of the reasons we was always in trouble was because we were all superstitious. None of us would work on a week with a Friday in it.

After those few bits we done, we all come out feelin like pretty tough guys so we start getting rougher. Now we're out banging heads to make scores. Like, I knock out a night watchman with one punch and we grab all the swag we can haul, which we later dump for peanuts. Sometimes we just crash into a neighborhood store late at night and do everything but clean it out.

Along the way I find out my old man was also a bad guy, a *malandrine,* before he got married and I was born. I find out he hisself had done a stretch in Elmira Reformatory, and me, I'm followin right in his footsteps.

T H R E E

My gang and I are making some pretty good scores so we start
duking ourselves in fancy clothes. We all gotta look like George Raft,
right? So, we deck ourselves out in pin-striped suits and these big
bomber hats.

When I walk down the street, I make my steel heel-plates zing the
pavement so everybody knows I'm coming, and they get outa my way.
Another reason I got heel plates on is they keep the heels from wearin
too fast.

I even go see my barber, Eddie the Junkie, and get 'im to fix my mop
like Raft's. I put so much *anzonia,* grease, in my hair, some character ask
me where I left the sardines.

During those days my whole world was Tenth Street and First

Avenue, and it belonged to me, my turf, an I ruled it with my Tenth Street mob.

Terry Young also brings around his cousin Lulu Constantino who's got it in his head, like Terry, to become a champ someday. Lulu's the same age as us but he's already in the gym trainin serious. The guy never went around stealing like we did, but his cousin Terry was just like me. He would haul away a hot stove and then go back for the smoke.

The two of them, Lulu and Terry, were always trying to talk me into coming to the gym and take up training. Knowing how I threw punches in the street they called me a natural. But I never told them the reason I didn't want no part of boxing was because of what my old man did to me with my brother Joe.

I hated my pop's boxing picture which he hung up everyplace we lived and forced us to look at for years. Because of my pop and all his boxing friends, I knew all the popular fighters of the day. It was all they ever talked about. But I still wanted nothing to do with it. Don't get me wrong, I don't mean I didn't fight. I fought almost every day of my life then, but with my bare knuckles. I settled all my arguments that way. Fightin was always for protectin me or one of my gang. If a guy picked on one of us, it was just like he picked on me. I swear to God, I did more fighting in those days than I ever do in the ring.

Take today, with the guns, clubs, knives, and chains. Things were rough in my day too, but you didn't have to worry too much if a guy just said, "Put em up!" This meant get your dukes up, because it was gonna be a fair fight, like mosta the ones I always got in. When you hadda worry is when a guy says things like, "I'm gonna break off both your legs, an bite you on the t'roat until your eyes pop outta your head an then we push you through the bars in the zoo an letta lion eat youse!" Another time you hadda start running was if a tough guy catches you with his sister and he says things like, "We gonna take you down to the tracks an put your cock on the third rail," or, "We gonna chop it off an stuff it in your mouth!"

As time passes, Terry Young an Lulu get more and more serious about turning pro. They were hitting the gym almost every day, and every day they needled the hell outta me about training with them. Because they're there I'm going up to the gym a lot just to watch them an hang out, but no matter how much they needle I still ain't putting on no gloves. They work out three, four hours a day, an they're also doing a lot of roadwork.

I'm still doing roadwork too, but it ain't like theirs. I'm out on that street like a wild jungle cat, going over rooftops, through cellars and backyards where I got plenty of room to run or hide from the cops.

Terry and Lulu never let up on me. Why, you gotta be pushing your muscle in the street when you got this great club where you could work out and maybe become somebody big?

I watch Terry punchin the bag and jumping rope with a big grin on his face, like he's already on top. The guy moves so fast he's like lightning. Long as I knew the fight game I never seen another fighter move so fast.

Terry was always tellin me about his dreams, how he's gonna become Champion of the World some day. And you know somethin? I gotta admit, that's how the guy started getting to me.

One day, he catches me just right and talks me into putting on the gloves with him. As soon as I get them on, all the old venom starts pouring through my blood, all the hurt my pop give me.

I didn't mean to, but one of the first punches I t'rowed, I knock Terry down. If I'm fightin, I fight like I'm in the street. It's him or me, and I don't care who the guy is.

Terry gets up with his mouth wide open an instead of being mad, he sez, "Jesus Christ, Rocky! You're a fuckin real fighter! You know what a punch you just t'rowed? You hit me like you was a mule."

From that day, both Terry an his cousin Lulu always try to get me to go work out, and fight in the club. "You could be a pro inside a year," they tell me. "You could make a lotta big money. All the broads you want, a big car. The fuckin sky!"

I just laugh and walk away. I still never tell them how I felt about my old man and all the old-time fighters he got drunk with. Like my father an his friends were all a bunch of washed-up bums, an how my pop, and brother Joe who was supposed to someday become a pro, and how they wound up.

After a little time goes by Lulu and Terry start fighting four-round pro fights, and both of them start building a nice fight record. About this time I'm going with a girl named Josephine and I'm at a Red Range A.C. dance with her when Terry and Lulu comes up to me very serious. They tell me there's a big boxing tournament on, and the welterweight representing our neighborhood is sick and can't make it. Since I'm in that weight I gotta take his place. I tell the guys I ain't interested, an they keep tellin me how its important for the neighborhood, how it's the big city amateurs, the A.A.U. Championships, and I tell 'em I still don't care.

Since Lulu Constantino and Terry Young are now fighting four-round pro fights this counts them out.

They follow me around the neighborhood for days and I keep telling 'em they gotta be kidding. I ain't getting my head busted an my eggs scrambled for nuttin, or nobody.

Then I start hearing all over how I'm yellow. Rocky's dogging the amateurs. I wanna beat up Terry, Lulu, and the whole gang. I go see Terry an the look he gives me, disgusted like, all I can say is, "Where you want me to kill these guys?"

When the first fight comes up, I sail into this kid and I give him one shot with my right and he tries to hide behind the referee. I catch him after two minutes of the first round and flatten him cold. Only time in my life, guy scared the shit out of me. I thought I killed him. When he hit the deck he splashed on it like an egg droppin on a sidewalk from a eagle's ass.

I wanna know when I get paid, but they tell me I gotta win all the fights and I get a gold medal. I wanted to quit right there but the whole gang is in the dressin room. Terry, Lulu, Big Gumball, Mongo, Nunzi, Romulo, Calabash, The Rake, everybody. They all start pounding on my back tellin me, "What a punch! Ya gonna be a real champ someday." They're doing the fight right in the dressing room, how I swung over my right and VARROOM! the guy's on his back.

By now I'm soaking it up. Where's the next one, I wanna know.

The second guy in the tournament is a colored guy who ain't scared, but I catch him a minute an a half of the first round.

The next week, in the semifinals, it's the same colored kid I flatten before. When we touch gloves I say, "Hey, didn't I knock you out last week?" He says, "That was my twin brother." I say, "Okay, I do you the same favor." VARROOM! I put this guy on his back at exact the same time, a minute an half of the first round. They put that in Ripley's "Believe It Or Not."

They try in the worst way to get me to train for the finals. I tell 'em I never got beat in my life in a fair fight, so why I gotta train? I didn't change nuttin and come next Friday night, the one bad thing I do is I miss my opponent once with a big swing that gives 'im pneumonia and the miss knocks four teeth outa the referee's mouth. That night, Rocky, *me,* I become the Metropolitan A.A.U. Welterweight Champ, and my face ain't got a scratch on it.

I hocked the medal for six bucks an give the whole six bucks to my mom. She thought I stole the money, but she need it so she took it anyway.

My name gets in the papers for something good for a change, an everybody in the neighborhood is slapping me on the back an all kind of ghees come up to me an wanna be my manager, but I still ain't looking to become no pro fighter.

Terry and Lulu start coming around wearing new clothes and flashing a few bucks and finally this is the clincher that makes me see the light. Only, they talk me into putting a few amateur bouts under my belt to get a little experience, which I tell them I don't need, but I go along. In these I knock them all dead an I get paid off in watches which I hock for needed cash.

But, crazy me, I can't wait to get some bigger money so I'm still out there trying to rob everybody blind, so I get snaggled again and back to the joint I go.

I do a short stretch an I'm out on parole, and I turn pro. Now for the first time in my life I'm making it straight, because for the first time in my life I'm making a little legitimate loot from my first four-round professional fights. Besides that, I still got my girlfriend Josephine, who I gotta spend a buck on when I take her out. I'm up in the gym so much now that the only guys in my mob that I see are the ones in the fight game like me. Funny part of it is, I don't miss them or the crazy action. Some of my old scuffling buddies are in the can anyway.

I didn't tell you I was born on New Year's Day, did I? Yeah, New

Year's Day, 1921. So, every year when the day comes around I got two things to celebrate. Only thing is, most of the celebrations through the years was in jail.

So now it's New Year's Eve and I take out my girlfriend Josephine. Luck's going good for me for the first time in my life, and I gotta celebrate. Right? I gotta celebrate New Year's, my birthday, my good girl, not being in jail for this one, and my luck. Y'mean?

We're running around mosta the night but we ain't doing nuttin bad. We take a long wild ride with coupla friends, drink a lil beer, kiss a little, and then we go to a pizza joint where we spend hours talking about things like when we get married someday, and things like that.

You know something, when ya young time stands still, but that night it didn't for Josie an me, and before you know it it's getting daylight when I take her home. We come down the street toward her mother's joint, and we're singing in the street like the world belongs to nobody but us.

Then alla sudden we stop singin. Josie's mother is standing in front of their place with two big guys look like cops.

"Whadja do to my baby, you crook?" her ma's yelling mad in my face.

The detectives throw handcuffs on me, an Josie starts crying hysteric, while her ma's got her in a stranglehold and yelling, "He raped my daughter, he raped my little baby. You sonofabitch! I hope they bury you!"

All I could think of is, Jesus Christ! I din lay a glove on her. An down at the precinct I get charged with what they call statutory rape. An how you like that for my New Year's 1940 birthday celebration? Again, my ass got t'rowed in the can.

When the phony bit comes up in court, there's nuttin they can do but t'row it out, but they get the parole officer to take another look at my record.

Then, I find out I gotta go to court again as a possible parole violator, and who's gonna hear my case but the famous Lou Gehrig, who useta be with the Yankees. Him an Babe Ruth were my biggest baseball heroes.

Gehrig had to quit baseball because of a sickness, an right now he's got some kind of a honorary thing, like Mayor LaGuardia put him on the parole board or something.

All my buddies are telling me I got it made because I gotta go before him. "Ey, Rocky. Just tell the guy how much ya like baseball," they say. And this ain't no lie.

Then the day comes. I'm in this courtroom waiting and my chin drops four feet when he comes in. He's almost bending the crutches that get him to the desk. Somebody already tells me he's got some kinda blood disease, or something. Everytime he makes a step I could see all the pain in the guy's face and it's hurtin me worse than him. The guy's sweatin pretty good when he sits down, and then he asks me to stand up.

First thing he says is, "How old are you, Rocco?"

"Nineteen," I tell im.

"I been over your record," he says, "and it's pretty bad. You've caused a lot of grief." He talks an preaches for awhile and even asks my favorite sport. I'm waiting and pop up quick with, "Baseball!" Y'mean?

He looks me over, sad, but straight in d'eye, like he's trying to make up his mind, then he says, very slow like, "Rocco, I've got to send you back for violation of parole. You got anything you want to say?"

I was so stunned, I get put in shock and I can't say one word. All I'm thinking, this is what I get for taking my girl out on New Year's Eve to celebrate my birthday.

Lou Gehrig is getting on his crutches to leave the room, an a correction officer starts pulling my arm to get me off the spot I'm like glued on. My eyes are already flooding with tears and I yells at his back, "Fuck you, Mr. Gehrig!" The next June the guy dies and I cry all over again. This time I cry for him and me both. The only other time I remember cryin since I'm grown up is when Dillinger gets shot an killed by the F.B.I. in Chicago.

What could I tell you? That's the way the mop flopped.

They pack me off to Riker's Island, and I turn into the meanest guy in the joint. Here, when they give you a two-week vacation it means two weeks in the hole, and I bang a few heads an curse a few screws, and I was always a candidate for one of these vacations. In the hole I got nothing to think about except all the heartaches I planted on me, my mom, and everybody else. There wasn't a week went by that my knuckles wasn't skinned or bloody, maybe even broken, and it wasn't from punching guys but from yelling out like a wild caged animal and punching my cell walls with my closed fist. They useta say ya got nothing to do in the joint but dream your million dreams and they was all for free, but mine was mostly nightmares.

I gotta lot of bitter hostility in me because of this phony rap and I know I gotta get it out or I'm gonna wind up killin a con or even a guard, so when I get out of solitary again I decide to go into the prison gym and try to work it out in the ring. The one good thing about long-term cans, they all got a boxin ring, and any arguments could be settled there if the other guy ain't yellow, and if you wanna do it for a sport you might even catch the screws making a bet on who's gonna get dumped.

So once I'm in the gym I start challenging everybody who's boxing training there. Right away I'm knocking out all kinds of older wise guys with my fists. It's hard for me to make you understand, but I know I never be a kid again. My fists take over and do all my talkin for me. When I'm in that ring with another con, I curse him and go after him like I'm gonna tear him apart, bust his nose, cut 'im till he's bleeding all over, and kill 'im. The referee has to pull me off the guy, and I realize the fight's over with the guy passed out in a heap and when I see this I put my arm around the guy and wanna be his friend.

I never read like a lotta other guys do to pass the time, so I gotta do something to keep from going crazy when I ain't in the ring, so I grab hold of some crayons and start drawing pictures on my cell walls. I din even know I could draw, but I seen other things on the walls from guys before my time, so I figures to give it a shot to help pass my time. Screw come by one day and he sees it, mostly comic characters like Barney Google, and Jiggs and Maggie, and I figures trouble. Instead the guy starts telling me it's good and next day he brings me a cheap paint set like ya buy for a kid and a big pad. I don't let my can buddies see me making with the paint job because I feel like they gonna think me a sissy. But ya know somethin? I realize I gotta knack for the brush and it takes all the pressure off my ass. I don't even know I'm doing time and I work out all the animosity putting how I feel in pictures I teach myself to make. This makes time go fast and I finish the bit in my twentieth year, but I hit the streets flat busted. I gotta get some moola fast so I can buy some clothes and things, so I ask my pal Terry Young to take me to Stillman's Gym and try to line me up a fifty-dollar fight. At Stillman's they say I gotta train. I tell 'em I don't make move one less I get paid. Just line up the fight and I be there. They get me a four-rounder and I flatten the guy without even getting my hair mussed. After that I started knockin guys dead right'n left. Most of them were tough and some look like they run outta gas and there ain't no gas station no place.

From there, like they say, I go on to bigger things. Lulu Constantino and Terry Young become main-event fighters and they get me four-rounders on their programs.

Only Terry, who was always a little bit of a sick gambler, is blowin all his purses on cards and dice, and I hear he's pullin jobs on the side or booking horses on the corner. This keeps Terry always in trouble with the cops.

I run into Lulu every once in awhile, and I always catch him joggin with a bunch of kids joggin after him, callin out, "Yeah! Lulu!"

I got nothing but envy when I see this. Someday those kids'll be followin me, I say to myself. I ask Lulu about Terry and he says Terry got pinched but he's got a good chance to beat the rap.

My fights get a little bigger an I'm making good money, so I start gettin the feeling I ain't never gonna rob anything or nobody no more in my whole life. I don't want to walk down the street with my hand in my pocket, holdin on to the green, an looking over my shoulder thinking a cop's gonna grab me for stealing it someplace. Everything's rosy and I wanna love everybody and I want everybody to love me, specially my pop. Now that I begin to see it's a way out and I'm putting some good green in my pocket, I begin to change about the boxin game. I see myself going right to the top of the world, all the way to Madison Square Garden.

When I was a kid I never had any shoes. I wore torn, worn-out sneakers, mostly hand-downs from my brother Joe. I go out now and I buy six pair. The shoes I bought was those pointy Cuban-heel kind, and I put a shine on a pair every time I wore them. I swear, if anybody woulda stepped on those shoes in those days, I'da killed them. I even go out an buy a noisy junk-box Ford which I race around all over the neighborhood.

FOUR

There was a clique of good girls, around sixteen, seventeen, who hung around the ice-cream parlor and candy store, who none of us messed with. We didn't bother with them because in this clique was also a couple-a my buddies' sisters.

Anyway, since I was one of the best looking guys in the neighborhood, I catch them always diggin me.

One of these girls, girl by the name of Alice, is talking to me one day, an she mentions a girlfriend of hers, Norma, wants to meet me. Alice tells me Norma is real pretty, and she's a smart kid, who lives high-class out in Brooklyn.

I don't wanna meet or get tied up with no nice girls in those days, let alone I want no part of Brooklyn. All I'm looking to do now is fight and make money. The only kinda chicks I wanna bother with once in a while is those that put out when a guy needs a little. Y'mean?

Day or two after I knockout Frankie Falco in Ridgewood Grove in Brooklyn, I run into a set-up. Alice corners me in front of my house and says, "Rocky, this is my girlfriend Norma Unger."

I try not to look at her too good, but I notice she got a nice little shape and these big dark eyes, smiling shy-like.

I say hello and then I say so long, but Alice jumps in front of me and says, "This is my girlfriend I was tellin you about."

I don't wanna know nuttin, because, well, mainly because in those days who knows anything about how to talk to nice kids? So I just say something like, yeah, okay, I see youse. And I jump in my broken-down, junk-box Ford, which I got on the curb, and I gun it off loud like a big shot.

Then it starts happenin. I don't know why, but I can't get Alice's girlfriend outta my mind. Coulda been because she came on so shy an nervous, an she was nuttin like some of the wise-guy chicks that came around the candy store.

There's only one other good girl I useta go with up to then, but it's a long time since I see Josephine. An besides, I find out Josephine ends up marryin some neighborhood guy. This don't bother me too much because afta awhile, I know, with Josephine, we was just buddies.

Once in awhile I see Alice and I ask, "How's your girlfriend?" But then, I only make it look like I'm trying to be nice.

One night I spots Norma about to go into the subway all by herself, and before I know it I'm yellin afta her, "Hey, you going home to Brooklyn this late all alone?"

"Hiya, Rocky!" she says. "I ain't afraid."

Next thing you know I'm sayin, okay, but I see you get on the train safe. I go downstairs, put two nickels in the slot and I go out on the platform with her to wait for the train. I could see she likes me worrying about her. I go to the penny gum machine, I look in the mirror, and I try out a few punches. She wants to know if that's what they call shadow boxin an I tell her, yeah.

Next thing you know the train pulls in and I say goodnight and watch her go through the doors. Just as the doors are closing I push 'em open again and jump in too.

"Oh, Rocky," she says, worried like, "I live way out in Brooklyn. You don't have to take me all the way home."

That's okay, I tell her, and then we don't say nuttin for a long time. The train shakes bad on a curve and I use it as an excuse to take her hand. Norma just squeezed it an goose pimples come up on my arm. One time I think, ey, goof, whatta ya doing on this train? But, I know I ain't the same guy no more. Somethin's happening to me that never happen before. The feeling is even bigger than the first time I flatten a guy in the ring for money.

When we get off the subway we walk down Ocean Parkway, and we sit on a bench right near this ritzy apartment house she tells me she lives. We start talking and laughing and we're singin songs, and say how we ain't gonna tell Alice nothing, and before you know it, it's three o'clock in the mornin. She jumps up sayin, "Goodbye, Rocky, thanks, thanks for takin me home," and she runs into the big apartment house.

All the next day I couldn't get Norma outa my head. I call myself all kinds of creep for being soft and letting it hit me. Tough guys don't let things hit 'em like that. I wanna punch the shit outa every wise guy I see just to prove to myself I'm still a tough guy. But you know something? I'm just like the cow with the bell when the sun starts to go down. Right back to the barn. The train I'm riding on late that night is like a big piece of iron shootin me to that big apartment magnet way out in Brooklyn.

I go with no invitation, no nuttin, and the reason I don't go with my jalopy is my tank is dry, an that day I ain't got the price for gas.

When I get near her house I sits on the same bench waiting, maybe Norma comes out or goes in. Afta a while I get so mad at me, I punch a tree and skin all my knuckles. Y'mean?

I walk up an down, and when I see a patrol car I try to act like I belong there. I wait till twelve o'clock and I go back to the East Side.

I get all kinds of feelins that next day. One time I'm mad, an next time I'm in the clouds. I go back to Ocean Parkway and afta awhile I work up the noive to go in the hallway, maybe I ring her bell. I check all the names an there ain't no Unger. Then I really think I'm gettin goofy. Maybe I'm in the wrong house. I go back outside and sit on the bench for awhile, then I go home.

I don't sleep too good that night, so the next day I go lookin for Alice. I figure I forget being stubborn and tell her I wanna date her friend. While I'm lookin for Alice, I go by the ice-cream parlor and who do I spot inside but Norma. We have a soda together, and then I borrow a fin from a buddy to buy gas, an I drive her all over, singin, talkin, laughin, like I never laugh before.

When I take her home, I go in the same hallway with her, and I say, just like I'm looking at the bells for the first time, I say, "How come there's no Unger on the bells?

"It's Levine," she says. "I live with my stepfather. My mom got married again."

"You Jewish?" I say, but right then and there I don't care if she's Jewish, Irish, a Polack, or anything else.

She wants to know if it makes any difference, and I tell her, all I wanna know is, does she wanna be my girl.

She looks at me with those eyes of hers and she says, "If you really want me to."

I remember that day like nuttin else I remember. I wanna grab her an squeeze her and kiss her, and never let her go. But you know, I just say something like, I see you tomorrow, same time, same place, and I run outa the hallway.

Afta that we're always together, me and my girl. I take her wherever I go, and during summer we go to Coney Island and Rockaway Beach, and when I'm short we take a beat-up spread to tar beach and get our suntans there. The tar-beach rooftops were beautiful in those days and they didn't have those tall buildins to shut out the sun, and you could lay down and look at the sky and make dreams like no millionaire could ever buy. I even take Norma to the gym, but she never liked the wise guys I knew, and she didn't like fight talk an cigar smoke and the sweat stink of the gym. Most of all she couldn't stand thinking I could get hurt. Whenever I'm with my mob, she always moved over to the side, but she never liked the way I left her alone when I talked to the boys about fightin, and scores, and things like that.

My fight purses get a little bigger as I move up, and now I'm makin' seventy-five dollar purses, and we're going to dances on Fourteenth Street and across town in the Village. We even start hittin some pretty fancy spaghetti houses. I know now that I'm gonna marry Norma some day, so I just consider myself engaged, but I never tell her nothing. One day, afta a couple-a-glasses of wine in a spaghetti house, I tell her we get married as soon as I see myself clear, and you never seen a happier girl in your whole life.

Being in love is also making me a little impatient. I want to start taking on the top guys so I can get to the big money. I decide I gotta have a number-one manager so I team up with Irving Cohen, the guy who knows how to call the business shots, the guy with all the answers. I was so dumb about words in those days that when Cohen once tells me we gotta talk about expenditures, I says, "Don't worry. Sign the guy up and I knock him dead for you."

The kids are followin *me* aroun now, and Jack Healy is with me almost all the time, my biggest fan, and he personally escorts me to all my fights. He stayed right in my corner, and gets excited like you never seen. He's my Tenth Street manager and number-one fan. The guy wasn't in it for money then, he just loves me.

Jack Healy watched over me, kept the wise guys away, an knew how to steer me inta the right people. When we run into Joe Di Maggio, Joe calls him Blackie, like he knows him all his life.

I know I gotta do somethin for the guy so as soon as I start gettin some good money fights I declare Jack in for ten percent as one of my real managers, without the guy even asking.

By now he's already spending almost all his time watching over me, seeing I get everyplace on time, an making sure nobody gives me no trouble.

One day he even brought George Raft up to the gym to watch me train. I'm thrilled all over again, and everybody up there surrounds the guy, but he acts like he only wants to see me. I knew he never forgot me. Guys keep comin up tryin to say hello, and you could see in their eyes, just like me, they're all thrilled out of their skulls. You gotta know that this guy Raft was one of the biggest Hollywood killers of all time. Rest in peace.

Afta my trainin session, some photographers take pictures of Healy, Raft, and me, and we leave the gym together.

"So I'll see you," I says to Healy.

"Wait a minute," Healy says. "You're comin with us." So we get in a cab an go to Lindy's on Broadway.

Autograph hounds spot Raft, and they don't leave 'im alone.

At a table, I gotta ask him first, something been bothering me for a long time. I say, how come that time when I meetcha long ago you says something like, I hope you don't end up like me.

"I was probably talking about my boxing days," he says. "Just like you, I had my share of street battles, so one day I decide to turn pro to try to make a few bucks."

"I din know you useta be a boxer," I says.

"Yeah, a short career," he tells me. "I was only sixteen, no training, no preparation, when I went into the ring for my first pro fight. I had seventeen pro fights in all, and got knocked out seven times. My last fight was with a guy called Frankie Jerome. He broke my nose, blackened and puffed my eyes, and almost ripped off one of my ears. It needed twenty-two stiches to sew it back on. I never knew the meaning of the word defeat, and then I found out nobody could ever recognize me either, lying on my back on the canvas. For that fight I got five bucks. I could shoot a pretty good game of pool, and I realized I'd make more money hustling poolrooms, so I blew the five on a special cue stick that unscrewed in the middle. The money I made hustling pool and winning dance contests was what kept me going through a lot of hard times. That's how I met Jack here, who was doing the same thing. From there, the vaudeville stage, where I got discovered, and Boom! first thing you know, I'm in Hollywood making pictures."

The guy keeps talking my language instead of going over my head. "You know something Rocky. There's one good thing about being on the bottom. There's no place to go but up."

This is something I never forget. The guy is just an ordinary guy with a big heart, who dresses with class.

Irving Berlin and other guys from Tin Pan Alley came over to the table, and some were actors or comedians that Raft or Healy knew. Some looked like down-and-out Broadway Damon Runyon characters. Sometimes I'd spot Raft slipping one some money. No matta who comes to the table, Raft introduces me as Rocky, a great little up-'n-comin fighter. Y'mean?

The way they talk to me and make things look so easy, I wanna jump right through Lindy's window and into show business. One time Healy and Raft both catch me startin to talk to myself out loud, like I'm dreamin, and I'm sayin, "Someday . . . "

Both of them, at the same time, say "Someday, what?"

All I'm thinkin about is, here's a guy off the streets who was once a fighter, who went into show business and made it big, big, big! Why can't I? But I just laugh cause I got caught dreaming and I don't say nuttin. Here I am, sitting in famous big-shot Lindy's Restaurant, where I come for the first time in my life an I'm sitting next to my greatest hero. How could a bum like me tell you how I hadda feel rubbing elbows with a guy that knows everybody in Hollywood, and who made love, in an outa the movies, with some of the greatest Hollywood broads you ever seen? My hero knows all these people like I know my Tenth Street buddies. How could I go back to Tenth Street? But in those days there was no place else to go.

After we break up I go back to my old neighborhood, and when I can't find anybody I figure I'll go over to Eddie the Junkie's barber shop, get a haircut, and tell Eddie about Raft. I walks into the barber shop and he ain't aroun. I go in his backroom an there's Eddie the Junkie, stretched out on the floor, with his marbles wide open, staring at the ceiling, an the guy's still holding his needle. I run out scared, and I phone the cops from the candy store without saying who I am.

I watch from outside when they take the guy away in this long, closed basket and I'm thinking there's a guy who could be junked up to where his immies turn into little beads but he still give you the best George Raft gangster haircut any place on the East Side.

Jack loves this action so much he woulda paid me to let hisself follow me around. But it worked two ways. I was a stupid kid who never knew how to act an what to do with anybody in those days. Jack taught me how to act around important people. He useta say things like, "You could be bustin inside but you gotta smile, and when you smile people are gonna love you, and when you see them lovin you whatever you're bustin with goes away."

Terry Young is now my best friend and we make all the fights together. If he ain't fighting some nights, I am. And then sometimes we go see Lulu fight an it's a big thrill when they introduce us in the ring like big shots, with people screaming all over the arena.

Even the gym starts to become a lotta fun. There's all kinds of nutcrackers there, so you always get plenty of laughs. Everybody is always ribbin everybody else.

There was a fighter by the name of Al Pennino who wanted to become a singer some day, so when the guy ain't training he's always vocalizin. He sang in the toilet, in the shower, while punchin the bag, and loud. We tell him how to make his voice better. We got the guy vocalizin in a dresser drawer, out the window, and once we put him in a closet and say we listen outside the closet, and don't come out till we tell 'im. This was a dirty trick but we done it. We all went away and when we come back, three hours later. Al's still in the closet, singin his fuckin head off.

I was no different. They ribbed and kidded me just like everybody else, and I could take it except when it come to fuckin with my family. "Ey, Rock," one guy once said, "I hear your old man got pinched drunk, and when the judge says, 'You was brought before me for drinkin, your pop says, 'Okay, where's the wine?'" and they all bust out laughin.

That's when I look 'em dead 'n in the eyes and say, "If you know what's good for youse, you better leave my old man out of it, or you gonna see one crazy dago going on a rampage, and don't one fuckin guy call me no sore loser." They never joke about my pop no more.

In my first fight in Madison Square Garden I was an unknown and I'm just fighting on somebody else's ticket. I look around like I'm in choich. This is the arena where all the big ones fought. I almost feel like making the sign of the cross as I think about all the guys my pop and his friends useta talk about. Names like Mickey Walker, Benny Leonard, Barney Ross, Jimmy McLarnin, and Henry Armstrong. I could smell these guys close, all over the joint. When I go into that Madison Square Garden ring and I hear those people screaming out their lungs for me, I knock guys dead, one after another.

I start getting my pop tickets to come see my fights, and from the ring I spots him screaming out his lungs and shadow boxing the air.

I know my pop gotta now feel he had his money on the wrong kid, puttin it on Joey, who never become the battler my pop was countin on.

I'm sure now, while he's on his feet yelling toward the ring, he's seeing himself up there, knocking all these guys dead and finishing the job right to the top. When he come back to the dressing room after a fight he grin wide but look all spent like he just go ten hard rounds hisself.

I got a fight comin up with Randy Drew. This one's supposed to be a tough one, so my manager Irving Cohen tells me I gotta train for this guy.

I loved to go to the gym because I meet all my buddies there but I just didn't like to train too much, up to then. I was more interested in the laughs I got from all the characters, like the time a nut comes up to Stillman's playin a fiddle once, an Terry Young runs the guy out on Eighth Avenue for laughs. Lou Stillman says to Terry, "Obvious you never hoid of Stradervarious," an Terry wants to know who this Stradervarious ever fight. While I'm telling you this I gotta tell you about another guy we useta get laughs outa in Stillman's. This was a tough light-heavyweight boxer called Jack Brazzo. He was always showing everybody ballet jumps he was learnin in a ballet class someplace, an we kidded the shit outa him. Funny part is he gave up fighting, changed his name to Jack Palance and become an actor. I gotta tell you, I could never make Norma understand how I needed all the action with the guys and I needed her, too. She figures it should be one or the other.

The more I'm training now, the more word gets around, and the gym's always packed when I'm working out.

It was like that right up to my last fighting days. The word was that they always get a good show when I'm in the gym. That year I knock out five guys in a row, and the whole fight mob's got their eye on me.

Everything starts changing now. With those first four-rounders nobody but my handlers an my buddies from down on the lower East Side come back to the dressin room after a fight. Now, while I move up in the game and my manager keeps t'rowin me in with tougher an tougher guys, I do with them like I did with the four-rounders. I knock 'em dead too.

In between rounds I could see the excitement all around the ring, just like they would give anything to be in my place when they see my opponent getting knocked out. They yell up all kinds of curses, like, "Let me at that fucking bum!" And then there's the hecklers who heckle the other hecklers with things like, "Go ahead, wise guy. Get up in that ring with him. He's got him all softened up for you." Y'mean? An then the guys who yell toward the ring, "I'm witcha! I'm witcha!" Don't that go to show you? You never know who you're wit. Sometimes when it's over I wanna roar just like those roly-poly fight fans that roar louder than anybody else.

My Norma is up in the gym one time, and while I'm working out I spots Lou Stillman talking with her. A little later I go look for Norma and she ain't no place around. I go to Lou and I wanna know what he said to my girl. I wanna know if he chased her.

"I just told her, I hope you ain't serious about marrying this pug," he tells me.

I calls the guy a fuckin bum, packed in my training for the day, and took off.

I go back to the neighborhood and find Norma in the ice-cream parlor. I wanna know why she left the gym without waiting for me, and she says, Lou Stillman asked her, what's a nice Jewish girl like you doin with this no-good hoodlum? He told her he seen hunnerds of fighters like me and he never seen one of them turn out good. He even told her I had a record as long as yer arm, and now Norma wants to know if it's true.

I says, "Suppose it is?"

An she says, "Not now anymore?"

An I gave her my woid, and I meant it. I even swear on my mother.

She smiles and grabs me, and the whole world lights up again. I'm gonna knock this guy out in the first round Tuesday, I tell her, and then the next morning I'm buying you a ring.

August 10th, 1943. That's the day I go see the first judge I ever come before who wasn't there to give me trouble and heartaches. This guy married us. And you never believe who's my witnesses. Yeah, two strange detectives they pick up in the hallway. What could I tell you?

Norma and me is practically broke, but this was the biggest day in my life. She was eighteen and I was twenty-two. We spend our first night married in a flea-bag hotel on Fourteenth Street, and then we go to my house and tell my mom and pop we got married.

My pop walks out of the house with a big puss, but my mom fixes us something to eat and starts moving things around, doubling people up, so we could have one of the matchbox rooms all to ourselves. And now the little tenement is as crowded as a subway train durin the five o'clock rush.

Around this time, my managers book me a six-round semifinal fight with a goodlookin kid from Brooklyn called Steve Riggio. When I look him over I figures I hit him with one of my bombs in the first round and I save him the trouble of going the other five.

The fight goes off in August of '43. What I don't know is this kid shoulda been a track star. He coulda won the Olympics for the mile, and he could do it faster backwards than most racers could do it forwards.

I chased this fuckin guy around the ring for the whole six rounds, and I never connected with a single punch. Meanwhile, while Riggio is running backwards he flicks out an occasional jab that touches me just hard enough to chase the flies away, and they give the guy the decision. How do you like that? Shittin in his trunks, and he wins the fight. Me, I'm so embarrassed I don't show in the neighborhood for a couple of weeks. I know the whole neighborhood musta bet on me. I put this aside in my head for awhile and I go about my business of chopping down most of the fighters I'm booked against.

The money gets better but it ain't never enough, and my Norma and me are living with my folks, and because I'm always running off with my buddies we had our share of fights, just like everybody else. I gotta give her credit. She could take it, and she was never ascared of me. She just stuck her little Jewish nose under mine and gave it back, toe to toe. I guess I was spending more and more time with fight-mob characters instead of with her. I try to tell her I need them for build-ups and to get me good matches which brung good, big gates, but she don't want to know nuttin.

Something about, like I always gotta be with the boys that talk my language, like the buddies in the neighborhood, from my young running wild days. They were still my buddies when they out of the can and they ain't shaking time someplace.

During those days, I still see some of my buddies who ain't in the fight game, like Nunzi, Foongi, Mongo and The Rake, and all the other guys I useta run with. They come up the gym with me all the time, and we talk over old times, and we end up goin for coffee when we leave the gym, always making with a lotta laughs. Like I says before, the hardest thing in the world is trying to explain to your wife how a guy needs this. They don't wanna know nuttin about nuttin. Still, when my Norma tells me she's going out with the girls, I'm the happiest guy in the world for her, hoping she has a great time.

All Norma could think of then was gettin me out of the old neighborhood, away from my family an friends, an moving us out to Brooklyn near her folks. It wasn't that she didn't like 'em. It was just that she figured I'd spend more time with her if she got me away from them.

By now, her stepfather, Georgie Levine, and me become good friends, and I find out he's some kind of a wise guy an a big fight fan too. He's coming up pretty good hisself, and he's supposed to own a big piece of a race track in Cuba called Oriente Park. In fact, later he becomes a partner in a big gambling casino there and who they got in with them but my old idol, George Raft of the silver screen.

I hated to leave the East Side because it was still the whole world to me, even though I begun to branch uptown a little bit, with what Jack Healy called the smart money. The East Side, with the poolroom, the candy store, the clubhouse, my grandma's house, my mom, the roof hangouts with my buddies' pigeons, the crap games. It was all there. Taking me away from the East Side was like taking away all my clothes and putting me out, all alone, in a jungle someplace.

But Norma gets worse, and now she's beginning to tell me it's gotta be them or her. Make up my mind. She even complains there's ghosts in the house. She says everytime we have a fight in the bedroom she hears rapping on the walls.

The thing that finally cinched it is her telling me one day, she's gonna have a baby, and how am I gonna raise it in our matchbox room and on the slums of the East Side?

I gotta know about all the trouble I cause my mom, growing up a hoodlum, and I know no son of mine ever gonna go through it if I could help it.

So now, I tell Norma I'm ready. All of a sudden she starts talking about curtains and furniture and baby rooms and cooking, and a garden, and things like that, and she's so happy and busting that she gets me the same way.

Only, we ain't got anyplace near the kind of money we need to make any kind of a move, so I goes to see Norma's folks and I tell them, "You don't have to worry about Norma no more because I'm finally going to support her in the manner you accustom her to." And they both say, "How you gonna do that?" And I says, "We're moving in with you."

They were the kinda people I liked in those days, so I knew there's no problem there. They fix us up with a nice room, and for the first time in my life I'm warm in a house. The joint's got so much heat they could give some to my mother. Now my Norma starts becoming the housewife she always wanted to be. In fact, she's so neat with the new digs that on one of my first mornings there I get up early to take a leak and when I go back to get in bed she's already got it made.

I even start hanging out in Brooklyn, and it ain't half as bad as I thought it was gonna be.

They got Coney Island and Nathan's hot dogs, and Sheepshead Bay with all that good seafood, and they got Ebbetts' Field and the Dodgers, and a few bums like Leo Durocher, Billy Herman, Dolph Camilli, Freddie Fitzsimmons, Carl Furillo, and Peewee Reese. And through the years a lot of important people like Buddy Hackett, Barbra Streisand, Joey Adams, Lucille Ball, Sam Levenson, Gluecoe Glumcuddy, Steve Forest, Shelly Winters, and Danny Kaye, and famous Doctor Walter Nicora got his start there. And, yeah, Murder Inc. is from there too.

No matter where you go in New York, you gotta run into fight fans in those days. Boxing was then one-a the biggest sports around. And since I'm coming up pretty strong in the fight game, people's always recognizing me on those Brooklyn streets, and they come up to me all the time to talk about fightin, and the fights they see me in.

An, one of the fights they usually bring up is the one with Steve Riggio, and when am I gonna have a return and knock him dead to break us all even. I tell my managers to book Riggio, and we make another six-round semifinal for the Garden to come off in February of 1944.

Meanwhile, since my last fight with Riggio, I decisioned three guys and knocked out three. I tell myself I'm gonna clean the slate, do him a favor, and knock him dead too.

You're right. Same thing happens again. Only, this time he must've done almost all of his training on the track. Wouldja believe, the guy's running faster than before. Yeah, backwards! Again, I can't connect with a single punch out of the million I must've t'rowed. All Riggio caught was a cold from the draft my punches made. Again, because of a few light jabs the guy feathers me with, they give him the nod. After the fight, I'm back in my dressing room with my handlers, and Joe Wander, and a few other guys from my old neighborhood, and by now I'm talking to myself pretty good. The more I curse, the madder I get. All of a sudden I run out of the room with Joe Wander chasing me, and I run right to Riggio's dressing room. Joe's trying to hold me back, and I'm yellin I just gotta hit him with one punch, just one punch. Now, I'm inside Riggio's dressing room trying to get to him, and I'm yellin we gotta finish the fight right here, and all the handlers, both sides, are holding me back. I never been so frustrated my whole life. Talk about hiding, if I'da found a bus outside getting ready to leave town I'da t'rowed myself under it.

After they cool me off and we leave, Joe Wander keeps me up half the night drinking and still tryin to calm me down. Most of all now, I'm ashamed to face the neighborhood. I could just imagine how they put their jalopies, and anything else they own, in hock to raise bankrolls to bet on me.

To me, this was a real serious fight, but when I pick up the paper the next mornin I see where Dan Parker, the famous sportswriter, makes a big joke out of it. He says, "For comic relief, the Rocky Graziano–Steve

Riggio number was a side-splitting success. Rocky cut capers and flew into momentary rages that subsided as quickly as a gashouse flare-up. But in general it was very pleasant for the customers."

All I gotta say is, I'm glad somebody got a kick out of it. After this I go out to get even, using all the next fighters I get booked with. Within the next year I knock out nine guys and decision four.

All is forgiven in my old neighborhood now, and on Sundays mostly my best friends ride out to Brooklyn to my house just to call me outside to talk over old times. I still miss the East Side then, but then I look at the trees on Ocean Parkway and the fancy-dressed people I see walking around, and I remember the scrounging summer days on the hot city streets or the cold winters when I was a kid waiting for coal to fall off the trucks so I could take it home to warm up the roach trap we were forced to live in. Jesus Christ! How I remember! And I swear to God, no kid-a' mine ever gonna go through that as long as I got these two big fists.

It wasn't a son I could call Rocky Jr., like me an most Italians hope for for their first kid. It was a daughter who we named Audrey, and she was born on May 2, 1944. This was my own baby, and I don't care what it was, just so she was normal and healthy. First thing I do is jump in my jalopy and race over to the East Side just as fast as I can, just to tell everybody the good news.

The money is still scarce so I rush over to the gym an tell Irving to book a big one so I could pay my family's way outa the hospital. He gets me a fight in Washington, D.C., with a guaranteed five bills. I woulda gone anyplace, with nuttin on my mind but to knock the guy out in the first round, grab my money, and rush back to my wife an kid.

That fight was with Freddie Graham, and his bad luck was my good-luck hospital bill. I flatten the guy in three rounds, rush back to the hospital and bail out my family.

This you never believe. I paid fifty-five bucks for my broken-down Ford jalopy, but the baby carriage I sprung for put me back a hunnerd and a quarter. I knew I hadda give my baby the best buggy money could buy.

I always been a slugger, go in swingin, bell to bell, and throw so many hammers that just one needs to connect. Like I was fightin in the street like a killer, grab a guy by the throat, punch 'im in the balls, anything that put the guy away for good, what they used to call a club fighter. But now I start deciding to try to become a boxer, because even though I took on all comers managers with good boxers won't put 'em in with me because they're afraid I might ruin 'em for good with just a couple-a hammers they could get hit with by accident.

I start taking my training more serious, and my trainer Whitey Bimstein's got me doin all kinds of fancy punching. This gets me better main-event fights with more money, but Norma is always worried and scared. Specially when I come home with cuts or a few lumps. When I tell her she shoulda seen the other guy, this don't mean a ting. It's my face she gotta look at an cry over, and this hurts me more than all the punches I catch in the ring.

F I V E

Jack Healy almost never leaves my side then. He picks me up way out in Brooklyn, takes me to the gym or a fight, and then he waits and deposits me back home. Sometimes he was like the father I wanted to have as a kid, and then he was my buddy, my confidante, and my cultural adviser. I could never forget all the dreams he talked to me about when I was a kid and how so many of them rubbed off on me. I was always hoping, maybe, through me, that some of his dreams come true. Every once in awhile I think about all the Damon Runyon kind of stories he used to tell us kids about Broadway's big shots, and jazzed-up Fifty Second Street, and I remember how his whole body danced all over the corner sidewalk. You're gonna make it, Jack, just like I'm gonna make it, I'd tell him, and we both swell up with whatever it is you gotta have inside to make you get there.

After I started making it a little big, Jack Healy dresses us both up in the sharpest Broadway clothes, and when I ain't in trainin he's always taking me to top nightclubs. Jack says, all the big shots gonna be there and when I was innerduced, everybody would pass on the word and help make me popular. You shoulda seen Jack's face light up when a guy on the stage introduced me as a leadin contender for the Middleweight Championship of the World. You'd think it was him bein innerduced. Y'mean?

When Jack spotted a celebrity, he'd go over to them an bring 'em back with his arm around their shoulder, just like he knows them forever. He'd say to me, "Rocky, you gotta meet my pal Joe E. Lewis," or "my buddy Bob Hope," or "one hell-of-a-girl, Lana Turner," or "Ava Gardner," or whoever it was. This was the life Jack always dream of living, and it made me happy to be able to give it to him. He made a lot of people mad the way he argued stubborn-like and never give in. You just hadda know how to handle the guy.

There was one thing about Jack I'm glad I never caught, and that was how he was tough on waiters and waitresses. Jack was always sending things back to the kitchen, and by the time he got 'em back, I had finished all my food an all the bread 'n butter on the table. It was mostly with eggs. If the white wasn't hard an the yellow soft, back they go. Another thing was steaks, which he like rare. He'd say things to the waiter like, "Knock off the horns, wipe its ass, and send it out." He almost always sent it back saying it wasn't rare enough or it was too rare. If he thought it was too rare he'd say, "I saw cows hurt worst than that come to life again."

Anyway, his conscious musta got the better whenever he did this, because he always left a bigger tip.

Since things is always gettin better my Norma talks me into takin her and the kid to Florida for the winter season where, she says, "You could still do your trainin there for the Bill Arnold fight."

This one is supposed to be the biggest fight of my career up to then and it's scheduled for March of 1945 in New York. An this Billy Arnold is one tough son of a bitch, my manager and everyone else is tellin me. The guy racked up a string of twenty-eight knockouts. And me, they got me down for a ten-to-one underdog. So, for this one you gotta believe I'm doing a little training while I'm down there.

Now, what's gonna happen means I gotta remind you. I gotta remind you about how I still feel then, me and my little Mafia mob I grew up with down on the East Side. Y'mean? Like how we worshipped the big shot rackies like Dillinger, Dutch Schultz, Baby Face Coll, Al Capone, and guys like that.

So I'm up in Dundee's, Miami Fifth Street Gym working out, when a couple-a tough looking guys come up to me and one of them says, "The big guy wants to see you as soon as you finish training. We gotta bring you over."

I says, "Who?"

"Al Brown."

Someplace I heard this before, and since the guy lives in Miami Beach I figures it's Al Capone. Even him, he's got the Irish phony name.

What's he wanna see me for, I'm askin this guy, when Jack Healy runs over thinkin I'm in some kind of trouble. They take Jack over to the side and when he comes back, he says, "It's all right, Rocky. Big Al wants to see you, so we go." Jack don't look worried so I don't get worried neither, an besides, he's coming with me.

Afta my shower we get in this big black Cadillac, and while one-a the guys is driving nice an slow I'm thinking about the movie *Scarface,* with my biggest hero up to then, George Raft. And I'm thinking about how they knock off people with tommy guns through bouquets of roses and how they used a black hearse to shoot from or to throw a "pineapple" through somebody's store window.

I sees a sign that says "Palm Island," and then we stop in front of a wall an on it is "93 Palm Avenue." One-a the guys gets out and grabs a phone from a box in the wall and two big wooden doors open up. We drive in past a tough looking flunky, and there's this house you wouldn't believe. I never in my life see anything like this. The place is right on Biscayne Bay, with a big dock, and there's three big boats tied there. The house looks like a Spanish mansion, with lots of rooms. I count twelve royal palm trees around the house an there's this swimmin pool like you only see in the best Miami Beach hotels. The guy's even got a bathhouse with cabanas, and around all the grounds is a high stone wall.

When we get outa the car, we all start walking toward this guy who's been throwing bread into a rock pool. Before I see the goldfish I recognize Big Al Capone hisself, and I get a funny feeling in my stomach. The guy's got these steel-gray eyes that I know few guys crossed. Right away I look at the knife scar on his left cheek, an it runs right from his ear down to his jaw. His lips are fat an he's got this big bull neck, which tells me what they mean when they put in the papers that in the old days he useta go to work on enemies with a ball bat. No matta what they put in the papers, the guy still became a folk hero.

To a lotta people of his time, Al Capone was like a governor, or even the President. If you woulda asked people then who was the Mayor of Chicago, they'da told you Big Al. I could see by lookin at him that if anybody ever decided to fuck with him an somethin coulda stopped them, they shoulda let it stop them.

Capone grabs my hand, shakin it, puts an arm aroun my shoulder, and says, "Eh, Rocky! So you're the little paisano who's been knocking everybody dead with one punch."

I could see the guy's happy, and he don't let me go even when he shakes hands with Jack Healy. I could see in Jack's face that, even him, he's looking at the guy like Capone's a big hero.

All kinds of big-shot wise guys come out of the house and from the boats, and they come over to slap my back and toss big names around. I catch only two of the names of guys there, Charlie an Rocco Fischetti, who the guys call Fisher. I know the names because I see them in the papers, something to do with running the action in Chicago.

Al Capone puts his arm around my shoulder again an walks me toward the house, and he says, "You and Jack are eating with us today.'

That's okay with me, I tell the guy, because, even though the guy ain't coming on strong, I like to see somebody refuse.

Capone gets me to thinking about my old uncle Danny Bob, who was hisself a big racketeer but he got knocked off. I wondered if Danny Bob was like Capone and I wonder if Danny Bob dumped a lotta people too. In my old neighborhood, a lotta guys got bumped off, and at the funerals relatives cry up a storm and friends talk about how some *malandrine* was one-a the greatest guys ever lived, and how he blew money like it was going outa style, how the guy bought drinks and food for the house, and how he kept some old lady from losin her home, or helped a bunch of orphans, and how he broke people's hands stoppin them from beatin him out of a restaurant tab, but nobody, nobody, says one word about how he coulda killed fifty guys to get where he got today.

Jack Healy's eatin it all up, talkin to the Capone guys about me, and looking around like he's in heaven. Me, I don't feel nervous no more. Everybody's laughing and talking my language, and I'm right at home, just like I was down in the poolroom on the East Side instead of a millionaire's mansion.

Capone is always smiling nice and talkin to me about the fight game of which he knows everything. He mentions names, fights, places, just like he was a manager hisself. "How you think you make out with Billy Arnold?" he wants to know.

"I'll knock him dead first or second round," I tell 'im, showing 'im my fist.

"Thatsa boy, Rocky!" and all the guys start sayin the same thing.

I still can't believe I'm in this guy's house who useta be "Public Enemy No. 1." He's smokin a big cigar an it looks like it goes out. One-a his boys springs over an lights it for him.

We go inside an the joint is fabulous. *Madonna mia!* I say, Whatta house!!

I can smell garlic and tomatoes cooking and I know I'm in an Italian house, no matta how classy it looks. All the furniture is fat, and I mean fat. Fancy wood and big puffed-up jobs. There's even all kinds of fancy marble and statues and paintins. On one wall there's a oil painting of Al Capone, which is just as big as hisself. And believe me, Capone's place ain't the kinda place where you wonder if they trust you when you don't see no silver on the table. In this guy's joint you better be straight, or else.

"I got fourteen rooms in this building and some more in the other one," Al says. "Nice little winter place." He's grinning all over because I get all excited.

"I take it off your hands when you get sick of it," I kid him.

Some women come in from another room, an they're all dressed up, with their hair done, and they got aprons on. They say hello an go back in the kitchen.

Everybody gets around in a big circle but Capone does most of the talking. "You know something, Rocky," he tells me, "I came from Brooklyn where you're living right now. And my folks were Neapolitan, just like yours."

I wonder how come he knows so much about me, but then I figure if this guy once owned the Chicago Police Department and had from the Mayor on down in his pocket, then it ain't hard for him to know about me.

I keep thinking about movies like *Little Caesar,* with Edward G. Robinson; *Public Enemy,* with James Cagney; and *Scarface,* in which Paul Muni plays Al Capone; and I'm thinking, all these movies had to do with Capone and his mob. The gifts they useta leave you could send you all to pieces . . . time bombs.

Capone says, "My people traded the slums of Naples for the slums of Brooklyn. You know Navy Street?"

Everybody knows Navy Street, I tell him.

"It useta be all Italian in those days, Rocky, but I haven't been back there for years."

It's changed, I tell him.

"Everything does," he says. "It was one-a the roughest places in the city when I was growing up there. If you didn't eat everybody up, you got eaten."

The East Side was pretty rough too, I tells him. I keep looking at this big diamond ring he's got on his pinky an I says, "That's some rock you got there."

Capone blows some breath on it, shines it on his pants an says, "You like it, huh?"

Then, he decides to tell a joke. "When my mother-in-law died, I bought a big stone," he says. He holds up the ring an looks at it. "This is it." Then he busts out laughin, more than me and all the other people who's laughing with him.

He turns away because somebody wants to tell him something, an I hear some guy sayin to Jack Healy, "A friend of mine who just happens to be a friend of yours, and I'm sure you know who I mean. This friend of mine who's also a friend of yours and I'm sure you could call him a mutual friend—" I notice they keep talkin back and forth like they both supposed to know who, but they never mention no names.

Al turns back to me and says, "A lotta big people been in this house, Rocky. Big politicians and show-biz guys like Harry Richman, Al Jolson, Joe E. Lewis, George Jessel, Eddie Cantor and a lot of others, and now I got a future middleweight champ standing right here."

Just the way he said it made my chest get big. He turns to one of his bodyguards who's standing on the side and says, "Find out when the food's gonna be ready."

Just with the smell, and all that training in the gym, I'm ready to eat a whole pot full of meatballs all by myself. I look at Jack an he's looking at Capone like he's his biggest hero.

"I like to fight in your Chicago someday," I tell Capone. "I hear it's one big swinging town, and I never been there."

"Just let me know and I see they give you the town on a plate," he says. Then he kinda looks off. "Aaaah, it ain't the same no more. I was king there in the good old days. No matter what the law said, the people that made the law wanted booze and a little gambling and I just happened to be the guy that gave it to them."

"Yeah, that's right, Al," the other guys are saying.

"Rocky, today all I'm looking for is a little peace," Capone says to me, "And this house gives it to me. When I own that Chicago, I do plenty of people big, big favors. They ended up with the gold and Chicago gave me the shaft."

Even though Capone is a very important guy then, it looks like the stretch he hadda put in at Alcatraz took a lotta his ass. It's a wonder he ain't got bars on the windows just to make him feel at home. I even remember reading that they found out he had the syph while he was doin' time. I wanted to tell Capone I was a small rackie once myself and mention guys like, Big Sal, Big Frenchie, and Louis the Wolf, but I thought maybe I better not.

"That's some piano you got," I says. There's this shawl thrown over this big grand piano, just like in the movies.

"The show-biz guys I mentioned all sang at that piano," Al says.

We're all sittin aroun a big table now an he tells a guy to bring him the pichers. The guy's got scrapbooks an albums, just like a star. I always knew he knew a lot of important people, an he's got the pichers to prove it. Not only the biggest rackies in the country going back twenty years, but also mayors an police chiefs, always with his arms around their shoulders like he did me. He's got 'em with the big National and American League baseball players, football stars and coaches, and champion horses, jockies, and fighters from Jack Sharkey on. He's even got a picher of him and my pal Georgie Raft. While we're looking at the pichers one of the guys steps up with a camera and says he wants to take a couple-a shots. Al gets up an says, "Come over here, Rocky. We take one together, just you and me." He has me pose like a boxer, with my fists up, and he faces me with his fists up, like we're about to go. Everybody's laughing and kidding around while they snap a half dozen shots with me and the people there.

"I'm gonna send these to you so you can autograph them for me," Al says.

Man! Did he make me feel like a big shot that day.

Some guy comes over an whispers dinner's ready. Again he puts his arm around my shoulder and walks me into this big dining room. I swear I never seen so much food in all my life. There's soup, ravioli, macaroni, fish, meat, salad, Italian vegetables, fruit, black coffee, nuts, celery, and all the wine and booze you could want.

Al Capone looks at me once in awhile, shaking his finger at me, and says "Kid, you're gonna be champ some day, and you're gonna do it for the Neapolitans, right?"

"I'm gonna bust my ass tryin." An you know something, for him I meant it.

Later, when Jack Healy and me are ready to leave, Al Capone's walking me back to the car where he's got a guy waiting to take us back to the hotel. He takes off his big diamond ring that's been blinding me all along an says, "Take it, and I want you to wear it for luck."

"No, no," I says. I can't believe the guy is really trying to give me his ring.

"I ran out of diamond belt buckles," Al says. "That's what I useta like to give my friends."

He grabs my finger and pushes the ring on it and it fits poifect. All I could say was, "Thanks, Mr. Capone, thanks."

"Things I own, somebody loaned me," Capone says. "The longest I could keep 'em is until I kick the bucket. When my day is over, that little thing is gonna go on because a guy like you is taking it on. Just knock out that Billy Arnold like you said, and I'll be even."

On the way back to the hotel Jack Healy is all happy, and saying, "Rocky, you got some idea what kinda score you made? That rock's worth a G-note if it's worth a penny."

"Wasn't there something written once," I says, "about a big shot in Chicago who was knocked off and he's wearing one of Capone's diamond buckles?"

"It should only happen to me," Healy says.

S I X

When I fight Billy Arnold in March of '45, I got a lotta people to win it for. All kinds-a stars and important people are sittin ringside. Not only do I come in at a ten-to-one underdog, but this baby's gotta be the turnin point of my life. Up to then, my biggest take-home purse is fifteen hundred bucks. Now, I win this one, I could go up into the big main events with the t'ousands. I also remember what I promised Al Capone, but this Arnold never got knocked out, an the son of a bitch is one tough cookie. It take me three, an I mean three, fierce fuckin rounds to knock this guy cold, and I'm hoping Capone's got a big bet on the fight so he could break even on the ring.

Everybody and his brother squeezed into the dressing room afta the fight. One guy they bring in, they introduce to me as the vice president. I shake his hand, t'rilled to know that the vice president of Madison Square Garden came in poisonally to congratulate me for winnin the fight. I didn't know Harry Truman from a keg of beer. One month later in April of '45, President Roosevelt dies and this guy Truman becomes President.

When Truman left the dressin room, I jump inta the shower and I get my first experience with what they call feminine stardom. While I'm soapin myself, Sonja Henie, who's a big star then, runs in all excited from the fight and tries to jump into the shower with all her clothes on. Like she must've seen a sign someplace, "Save Water—Take a Bath with a Friend." She's trying to grab me, getting all wet and fighting and scratching Healy at the same time, while he's trying to pull her outa the shower. It was like this from then on during my fightin career, people wanting to touch me after I just almost killed some guy in the ring.

As people begin to notice me more and more, I start spotting a lot more important-looking people coming back to my dressing room after a fight. They shake my hand, pat my back, and say, "Ey, kid, you done great!" Now I'm seein big business guys, politicians, rackies, and show-business people. They crowd into the dressing room, and I get inner-duced to people like a president of General Motors, and you name them.

One-a the guys somebody brings in one day is a skinny kid with a bow tie that makes his neck look even skinnier. This guy I know, because just recent, a big-winning fan took Norma and me up to the Astor Roof Club in the old Astor Hotel to watch him perform with the Tommy Dorsey Band. Even then the guy's got my Norma swooning all over the joint. Frankie Sinatra was like me then, just beginning to really get hot. Looking at him then I never dream how he was gonna one day be the biggest, and how he was gonna come into my life, and how I would be in show business, and one day be in a movie with him. But that I tell you later.

Like I said before, in my day there's no chance for guys like me. It's like the Puerto Ricans and the Blacks who come out of these same poor, tough neighborhoods today. Everybody dreams of becomin a rackie, a fighter, or gettin into show biz. Any guy on the street could tell you there was no other way to bust out.

The big singers when I was a kid were guys like Russ Columbo, Andy Russell, and Bing Crosby. Bing was number one. There was also a couple of other young singers who were comers like Frankie. One was Tony Martin and the other Perry Como, a barber kid from Pennsylvania, who was singin with the Ted Weems band.

Everybody looked up to these guys, especially to Bing who was already makin movies.

But, like I say, when Frankie comes aroun to see me for the first time, already everybody's talking about him. I should know, because, beside seeing him perform, me and my girl Norma are feeding a lot of nickels into neighborhood jukeboxes so we could sing or do the Lindy Hop to his band vocals. I never forgot the songs because these were what Norma and me fell in love to. One record I remember us wearing out was a song Frankie sung with Harry James called "All or Nothing at All."

The jukes had other Sinatra records like "I'll Never Smile Again," which was then number one in the country, and "There Are Such Things," which became number one after "Smile Again." Frankie made these last two with Tommy Dorsey, who he went with after separatin with Harry James.

If Sinatra came to the dressin room after a pushover fight and he could see I wasn't tired, he'd break everybody up clowning around with me, just like he was a comedian. But, I look in his blue eyes and I see the same hunger to come off the streets and become somebody big like I know is on my face, and we understand. It's just like we're tellin each other we both gonna make it right to the fuckin top. When he wrap his arms around me after a winnin fight, I hear him saying it all and without one fucking word.

These name singers were just like fighters in more ways than one. They always had entourages, and a couple of their guys always look like wise guys. I know the wise guys are hired to keep the kids from tearing off the celebrities clothes whenever they make an appearance someplace.

All Frankie's people knew other people in my dressin room, and they talk to Jack Healy and me and other guys, and I hear them all excited, tellin' each other what a job I done on my opponent. They fight the fight all over in my dressin room even telling each other how I t'row all the important punches.

I know Frankie is my friend but there's always too many guys crowding around that we never talk too much in those days. But then, as I keep moving up, we see each other more often, and he tells me how his father was a pretty good pug in his day, just like mine. I figure maybe this is why he's such a big fight fan. Sometimes I get the idea he wanted to be a fighter more than he wanted to be a singer. He even puts up his dukes kidding with me, and I could see how his pop must've taught him good. All's a guy have to do is put up his mitts in a fightin stance an without t'rowin a punch I could tell you right off if the guy could t'row one. Frankie knew how. The action in the streets he came from helped teach him how to fight, too.

The stretch between the Littly Italy in Manhattan that I come from an the Little Italy in Hoboken that Frankie come from was maybe a stone's t'row. Hoboken's tough guys not only acted like us, they even talked the same language. And when I say like us, I mean they either gotta fight their way or go find a hole to hide in. Those-a you who know Frankie today know he never looked for a hole to hide in in his life.

Through the years, I sometimes run into guys who useta know Frank as a kid in Hoboken. They tell me he was smart, tough, an had a head like a rock. They say in Italian these kind of guys are usually *Calabrese* but Frankie was Sicilian. An like me he was always fightin in the street as a kid to prove he wasn't a pushover just because he was skinny. The guy'll still fight you today, no matter how big or tough you are, if he figures you fucked with him. In fact, it wasn't long we know each other when he starts coming to the gym to work out with me in earnest. He ain't lookin to turn fighter. He just wants to keep in shape and know he could protect hisself. All us guys tease the shit out of him makin girl voices, callin out "Oh, Frankie," and then fallin on the gym floor like fainting.

When he come up to Stillman's to work out, all the newspaper guys start saying he was scouting for fighters an putting together his own stable. But it was more like Frankie was picking up the tab for fighters who needed a stake while they trying to make it boxing.

Since he's moving up the ladder pretty good during those days, he moves his whole family out to Hollywood, where he buys hisself a big house. He's already got a couple-a movies under his belt by now but he never forgets where he comes from or his old friends. He comes East a lot to make appearances, an he never misses my fights. That year I fight three of the biggest fights of my life. In January of '46 I fight my first fight with Sonny Horne in New York and get the nod in ten.

Another guy who's fighting career Frankie followed in those days, besides me, was a light heavyweight called Tami Mauriello. Tami fought the best, including a heavyweight championship with Joe Louis.

Whenever Tami fought, Frankie would drop everything just to be ringside rooting for him. But Tami, just like a lot of fighters before him, pissed everything away an ended up broke when he hung up his gloves. When Tami quit, Frankie hired his trainer, Al Silvani, to keep hisself in shape an to act like one of his bodyguards.

It was just like being born again, meeting all the important people I was meeting, and what made it even better was all those bigger purses which kept growin with every new card. An you know somethin, there ain't nothing in this world can make a guy turn honest like money in the bank. And the money in the bank buys us a champ little brick house in Brooklyn in 1946. It's nothin like Al Capone's mansion in Florida, but it's mine and Norma's and it's the first security I ever have in my life. When I buy it, I says to Norma this is *your* house, and she starts bawling like a baby, hugging and kissin me, and she makes me feel like the biggest guy in the world. I think back and I tell myself I never have to live in a trap again with thirty families arguing an fightin over the dirty hallway toilets or their piece of the hallway.

An best of all, I know now that my runnin wild days, with all those years I spent caged like an animal, are gone forever. I'm no more like a wild horse who don't know which way to run. It was like, maybe one day, somebody threw a lasso around my neck and yelled, "Whoa!" It was the honest boxer who was gonna be Champ of the World, that pulled up the rope on the crazy kid an taught him something else to do with his free hands.

And, talkin about free hands, when our anniversary comes up what do I get from Norma but something I been wanting for a long time. She give me a professional paint set with brushes, the oils, the easel, the whole bit. It brung back a lotta memories of Gehrig and those steel jail-house bars, but that don't matter no more. I sit right down an paint my Norma a picher of a bouquet of flowers, and this she tells me is the best gift I coulda ever give her.

In 1946, I hadn't learned how to play golf yet but I'm still on the Englewood Golf Course a lot. That's where I useta do my roadwork. The reason I do it there is because, if I was to do it in New York I could get shot at. If a cop was to see me sailing down a New York City street, he'd probably figure I just robbed something. Only thieves were street jogging in those days.

Anyway, I'm jogging along, and as I pass a couple-a guys one of them yells out, "Ey!" I don't want to stop and lose my stride so I keeps running. All of a sudden a caddie races to me, catches up, and while he's jogging longside-a me, he says, "Mr. Costello and Frank Erickson want you."

I never met these two gentlemen, but when I hear the names I make a fast right-turn detour, and I keep running in a big circle till I get back to where they're standing. The two of them act very happy to meet me, and I'm happy to meet them, specially after all I heard and seen in the papers about the "Big Man." When they're shakin my hand I'm remembering how I worshipped these kind of guys when I was a kid.

They ask me to meet them in the clubhouse for lunch when I get through. I go there a little later and they start innerducing me around to a lot of big shots, like I'm a king, or something. Frank Costello sits me at his big table for lunch and he says, "Rocky, anything you want, anytime you come here, just sign my name. You got you a membership here from now on." There was one guy who never had impediment of the reach.

Right away I take up the game and start playing golf. I figure, if tough guys like Costello plays it, then it can't be a sissy game.

The biggest surprise to me is right off I was a natural, an I start playing the game like I been doing it for years. I guess it was, maybe, because I already was very athletic.

I also take Costello up on somethin else, the permission to sign his name. For years, I'm never a member there. I just sign like he done, "Frank C."

I'm at a testimonial affair one night and the place is loaded with celebrities and champs from a lot of sports. Joe Louis and Willie Pep are there, and so is ball player Phil Kennedy, an Rocky Marciano, rest in peace, Billy Graham, Ray Robinson, Carmine Basilio, and who else but Frank Costello is there too with his girlfriend.

Costello comes up to me all night tellin me, "Dance with my girl."

So I dance with her, and some of the other guys dance with her too, but Costello never dances hisself. I finally ask him, "Ey, Frank, How come you don't dance with your girlfriend yourself?"

He says, "Tough guys don't dance!"

Ain't it a funny thing, how for years they want to send Costello to jail for being a bookmaker, when there's another friend of mine doing the same thing, you could say, getting a big city salary, and a chauffeured limousine. John Keenan, the guy I'm talking about, is legit, making book for the city running O.T.B. (Off Track Betting).

Like the whole world is getting more beautiful every day and I want to put the whole thing on canvas, but I ain't got the time. It's *me* in the finals now, and the sportswriters are followin me around an writing about me alla time. They say things like "Rocky Graziano is the new Stanley Ketchel." All the old-timers say Ketchel was the toughest middleweight ever lived. One writer ghee called me "the deadliest killer in the ring since Jack Dempsey." Because I put so many guys to sleep, one guy names me Rockaby, an then all the newspapers are callin me that.

By now, I'm fightin all kindsa fighters and some-a them were wacky. Some fought tooth'n nail. They bit an scratched, an some-a them blocked everything I t'rew. If somebody'd t'rown in a hat, they maybe block that too. I also fought some colorful fighters. They were yellow. And since I'm telling you about them, I might as well tell you about the clean fighters, the kind that took showers before going into the ring. One fighter told me once, he knew he lost the fight when he seen a guy sprawled over some seats in the fourth row and it turns out to be him.

I was up at Greenwood Lake trainin camp once, getting ready for a big fight, and all my gang is there, Johnny Peanuts, Mongo, Terry, Lulu, Big Gumball, an all the rest of the guys. Whenever I go away, I only feel comfortable if my mob's close around.

Irving Cohen is always on me about knockin out all my sparring partners durin the training. He says he can't hire nobody to get in the ring with me for no money. So I tell this one guy, who looks pretty careful, that I'm gonna take it easy with him, but then, when I start sparring I accidently t'row one-a my hammers, and even though the guy's got one of these big headgears on, he goes to the canvas with a slam. The guy jumps up, t'rows off the headgear with a loud shriek, jumps over the ropes, and outa the ring. He runs away yelling, "That crazy bastard wants to kill me," and nobody ever seen this guy there or in Stillman's ever again.

One bad thing happened at Greenwood Lake. My wife Norma worked a whole year knittin a sweater, which she ask me to take there so I don't get cold at night. One-a those fuckin' bums I invite out to the camp stole it, and I was afraid to go home. I knew she kill me when I showed without it. What she said that day is still singing in my ear. I could only hope the ghee who swiped my sweater heard her.

When I become a contender for the middleweight crown, Terry Young become a contender for the lightweight crown. Everybody was lookin to get their pictures took with us.

One story I always like to tell about Terry Young happen on a train on his way to Montreal for a fight with Johnny Greco, who later died in an automobile accident, rest in peace. Terry was on one end of a sleeper car sleeping in his bunk, an Ray Arcel, his trainer, was up at the other end of the car.

It was six in the morning when they crossed the Canadian border. Somebody reaches inta Terry's berth and shakes him.

"Eh, who's dair?" Terry wants to know.

"Customs," the guy says.

"Take a fuckin walk!" Terry tells the guy.

The Customs guy works the rest of the car, comes back, nudges Terry again.

"What the fuck you buggin my ass for?" Terry says, an the guy can't understand him too good, so he says again, "Customs."

Terry leans out an yells up the car, "Hey, Ray! C'mere! There's a bum up here named Customs, an if he don't stop bothering me I'm gonna punch him right in the fuckin mouth."

A short time after comin back from Montreal Terry gets convicted of an armed robbery he was out on bail for, for a long time, and they send him up to Sing Sing for a nice long stretch.

During this time my fighting luck is holding out real good, and my lovely Jewish wife, Norma, with our little Audrey, was never happier. I can't begin to tell you about the fights I have out of the ring with my Norma. Just like everybody else, only she win them all. There was times she got me so mad I wanna kill her, but, even though I go against her sometimes, I still let her call the shots. Because, well, because more than anything else I want, I want my Norma to be happy. As they say in church, she's the guiding light of my life.

I got one of the toughest fights of my career comin up, with no other than Marty Servo, the Welterweight Champ of the world. He beat Freddie Red Cochrane for the title after I flattened and ruined Cochrane in a nontitle bout. When I fight Servo, I knock him out in the second round with a busted nose and a flattened-up face in another nontitle bout.

This puts me in the big dough, so I buy myself a Cadillac. I also buy a ton-a toys for Audrey and a fur coat for my Norma. I even get a Great Dane which I name Junior. Because since I ain't got a son yet, I make him my son. That summer of '46 was the best of my life up to then. Like the whole world was opening doors. We were even taking winter vacations to Miami Beach. I'm loving everybody, but specially my Norma an the kid. I couldn't get enough of them.

When I go to Miami for the winter, I always find fighter friends there and a lotta people I know. Willie Pep, who's the featherweight champ, starts going with me, specially to the Hialeah Race Track, an we have a ton of laughs when we don't lose heavy money.

Willie, who's no bigger than the jocks, is like a frustrated jockey hisself. He knows them all and gets me to meet them, guys like Con Erico an Eddie Arcaro, and we have a ball with them.

Jockeys in the stables rib and chop each other up just like fighters do in the gym. And I wanna tell you, these little guys are strong and tough. They even hold fight contests between theirselves. I see one jockey walk up to a full-sized tough-lookin guy, and say, "Buddy, you better get your fuckin head in line or I knock you right on your ass!" and the jock wasn't kiddin either. Not only that, all these little guys were going out with six-foot show girls from the Beachcomber and Latin Quarter nightclubs.

So I go back to Brooklyn and wouldja believe my house got burglared. Now it's me that's getting robbed instead of the other guy. It was gettin so's you couldn't get a doctor to make a housecall like if your life depends on it, but that don't mean you can't get a house call. Burglars, TV repair guys, and plumbers were still showing on the scene. All my best things got swiped. I get fuckin mad you wouldn't believe when I first see this, but then when I sleep on it I figure they're trying to break even like I once did, so it don't bother me too much no more.

Along in here someplace, I get fifty Gs for a fight and they deposit it in a bank at Forty Second Street an Eighth Avenue, which was right near the old Madison Square Garden. I go to pick it up next day and I ask them to give me cash, and in one-thousand dollar bills. I play with them in my pocket and look at them when nobody's around, and I do this all the way home.

You shoulda seen Norma's face when I t'row the whole fifty grand up to the ceilin in the bedroom an the tousan' dollar bills come down scatterin' like a deck-a cards. Norma's running around picking 'em off the bed and floor fast she could, calling me all kinds-a crazy names, laughing hysteric.

I forgot to tell you, while I'm on that last trip to Miami, besides bettin on the nags, who I find out ain't taking only jockeys for a ride, I'm even making the big casinos with my buddies, and there I also lose a bundle shooting craps. I coulda told you even then that the only way to double your money is fold it an put it back in your pocket. Even guys makin mental bets lose. Those guys lose their minds.

Norma knows I'm goin for a lotta loot so she starts working on me to make her the manager of the money department. I finally turn everything over, and maybe it's the best thing I ever done. Like I always say, I been very, very lucky in my life, but I still coulda ended up in bad shape if it wasn't for my *real* manager. One thing I know for sure, Norma ain't the kind of a wife gonna leave my dirty suit in the closet an take me to the cleaners. I guess what Hitler done an her knowin this happened to her people, musta made her wanna be strong. This kid always knew, better than me, that strength was cash in the bank. In fact, my wife never cared for perfume until she started smelling money, she said it had a perfume all its own.

In September of '46 the big one finally comes along. It's now or never when I step into that ring to fight Tough Tony Zale for the Middleweight Championship of the World. That night it seems, almost for the first time in my life, my whole world crumbles down. I couldn't stop the tears when I comes to and finds out that I get knocked out for the first time in my life, an Tony Zale is still Champion of the World.

Norma is cryin too, but for days she's consoling me, reminding me that we cut up $350,000 between Zale an me. You gotta quit, she keeps telling me, we got all the money we'll ever need in our life. But how she gonna know what I really need, how that championship was gonna wipe my whole rotten slate clean, and I could get even for all the grief the early years brung me, how I could now get the respect of every guy that walks. Believe me, I love money better than anybody you know, but during those sad days it wasn't the money. What I really needed, more than anything in the world, was to get even with Zale, and win the Middleweight Championship of the World. I had that fuckin title so close I could taste it, an that taste was so rich I just had to cut it. And beside, how could I let all my friends an all my fans down?

In January of '47, Al Capone dies of syphilis, and in July of that year the date of my return fight with Tony Zale comes up, and it's being fought right in Capone's Chicago. This had to be the hottest summer night of my life, and I know this is going to be the biggest fight of my life, ever.

The Fisher brothers came to see me, and just about every important guy in the United States is gotta be there. News photographers musta snapped a million pichers of me that week. And I tell you something, even though Capone wasn't on the scene no more, they still give me the town.

When that bell rang for the first round we both charged out throwing punches like two animals trying to kill each other.

Just before the sixth round, blood all over the place, mine an Zale's, I just know it's now or never.

While I'm waitin for the bell, I look around the ringside at all the screamin faces like I expect one of them to be Al Capone. I ain't gonna let him or my family or my mob, or a million other people down again. I come out for the sixth round throwing punches like I got a lead pipe in each hand, an I don't hear nuttin, and all I see is the bloody guy I'm trying to kill. All of a sudden, Jack Healy an Irving Cohen are holdin me in a hug an yelling in my ear that I'm Middleweight Champ of the World.

The next day the press called it the most savage fight in history. They called us the butcher boys. Even though my face feels like a piece of raw meat, I know my family never have to worry about a thing again as long as I live.

That year in Capone's Chicago was the beginnin of my life and the end of his, along with the era he once bossed. Rest in peace. What could I tell you?

That winter Norma is pregnant again, an I'm wishing with all my heart it's a boy, a good playmate for Audrey an a kid who's gonna get all the breaks I never had.

Norma and I are just playing along, waiting for the kid now, and everyplace I go you'd think I'm the most popular guy in the world. Frank Sinatra is appearing at the Copa, and him we gotta always see whenever he appears in New York. It was a cold night that year when we go to the Copa with a few friends. People are standing on a crowded line outside, five abreast, waiting in the freezin cold, just to get inside to watch Frankie perform. They're stretched halfway down the block and we find out they even got confirmed reservations. On this line, whenever Frankie's appearin, you could see mayors, or even governors, so we gotta know we're pretty lucky when a boss takes us through the hotel alongside an down through a back door. Seeing Sinatra from a ringside table was, like to me, the biggest charge in the world. And ya know somethin'? There's Norma right there swooning, and I bet wetting her pants. Y'mean?

About this time Frankie had begun to feud with newspaper guys who's always looking up his ass, and they don't leave the guy alone. They put him down for fallin out with his wife Nancy, for maybe gettin in a fight he couldn't help, or even for the way he's helpin some politician he believes is right. In any case, this don't hurt his career one bit.

Newspapers are coverin me pretty good too in those days, but I'm mostly on the sport pages.

In February of '48, my second daughter is born and since we still don't have a Rocky, we make it close and call her Roxie. She was luckier than Audrey. She come home in a Cadillac instead of the junk-box Ford that Audrey go home in four years before.

Yeah, I still wanted a boy in the family, but I also know how sweet an soft and pretty a little girl could be, and I never regret my two wonderful girls, and I fall in love with my Norma all over again every day. Of course, that's when she ain't yelling at me for somethin stupid.

I sign a return fifteen-rounder with Zale for the championship, at Ruppert Stadium, Newark, New Jersey. The guarantee money is big, and for this one I train harder than I ever train in my life. While I'm in trainin for this battle, I go down to Washington, D.C. to do a benefit fight for J. Edgar Hoover. This was in April of '48, an that's when I meet him, shake hands, and take a lot of pichers. This F.B.I. leader is the kinda guy I bucked all my young life, and now I'm Middleweight Champ and I'm fighting for him for free, to help him raise money for a "Helping Out Kids Fund" that he set up. For this, I fight a guy by the name of Sonny Horne. I had figured this one for a good warm-up fight before the championship, due in two months. Only, this kid is tough an I can't knock him out, but I decision him in ten.

About this time, Terry Young gets out of Sing Sing on parole an looks me up. He goes back to the gym, gets in shape, an starts fightin in the ring again. I'm Middleweight Champ of the World, on top as high as a guy could go, but poor Terry is another story. He ain't got it no more. The can took all the zing out of his ass.

When my pop hung up his gloves, got married, an turned to luggin crates, it musta been the same as when Terry knew he was through, his punch all punched out an legs that turned rubber everytime the other guy landed a punch. All of a sudden I'm beginnin to see things a little different than I useta. Now I know inside how it gotta feel to be all washed up while a guy is still young.

Next thing I hear is that Terry is out tryin to declare his way in with the mob, bookin horses, numbers, and gamblin away his money.

SEVEN

I'm training pretty good in those days. I know my return bout is with a killer like myself, and I know what to expect from Zale in our third fight. I'm going to be ready for it, so I just make up my mind to hit Stillman's gym every day.

Now, I gotta tell you, when I was a thirteen-year-old kid in the Catholic Protectory, another name for a kids' jail no matta what they call it, we always hated fags and there was always a few around tryin to grab off the good-lookin kids.

So when I spots this young blond kid always watching me train, that's the first thing I think about. Gotta be a fag.

He looks like the kinda guy you find delivering groceries for a high-class grocery store. I punch the light bag, skip some rope, do some

71

shadow boxin and some sparring, and he's always there. I go away an come back the next day an there's this guy, maybe leaning against a post, watching me for a long time. He's got on a T-shirt, worn-out sneakers, and dungarees. He's dressed just like the kids dress today, only in those days when you dressed like that you were down 'n out . . . a bum.

I try not to pay too much attention to the kid, but then I see he's hanging around more and more, and he don't watch nobody but me. That's when I start figuring he gotta be queer.

In those days, anybody who hangs around the gym who don't train, who don't look Italian, Spanish, Jewish, or Black, or who ain't got that mean killer look could be a fag. But, this good-looking blond kid has a terrific build, nice shoulders, big arms an chest, and a small waist. Y'mean?

After a while I spot the kid dancing around in trunks trying to copy some of my moves, so now I figures he's looking to become a boxer. Then he's coming up every day and I see he's learning how to t'row punches pretty good, so I don't figure the kid for a fag no more.

Before ya know it, he's bringing me my towel when I need it, and he's asking me real nice if I teach him how to stand and t'row a few punches, and maybe spar with him a lil bit. I figure he gotta be crazy to spar with me. All I gotta do is hit 'em with one-a my hammers an he's through for good.

I say, "Eh, what's ya name?" and he says "Bud." I look at the kid kinda funny, an he says, "Lotta people call me Buddy." That sound better when I think of the song, "Buddy, Can You Spare A Dime?"

He talk a lil funny. It don't sound like New York, so I asks him, and he says he comes from Evanston, Illinois, but he was born in Omaha, Nebraska. That's two strikes ya got, I'm kidding him.

I says, "What's a nice looking guy like you doing in the gym? With a face like that you could getcha self a rich broad," and he says, "I gotta get in shape first."

So I spar with the kid once in awhile and I even send him on a few errands.

He don't show up once for about two weeks, and he comes in with his nose looking flatter and different.

"I never lay a glove on ya," I tell the guy. "What happened?"

He wants to spar with me and he says, "Go easy till it heals. I got it busted. It was an accident."

I tell 'im, you were too pretty before anyway. At least nobody gonna take you for a fag now.

He tells me he was boxin with a stagehand in the basement of the theater where he works, and the stagehand connected without meanin it and broke his nose.

"You an usher?" I asks him.

"No, I'm in a play," he tells me. He says, "You know, Rock, you could do me a big favor if you come and see me. I get you two of the best seats in the house, on the arm."

Up to then, I never seen a play in my life, so I figure, okay, where's the tickets?

"Just come back stage and I get you the seats," he says. "You won't need tickets."

"How 'm I gonna find you?" I asks him.

"Don't worry," he says. "I see you when you come in."

Like the guy's really t'rilled. "You don't know how great it is, you coming to see me," he says.

How can I turn the guy down? I go home and tell Norma we're gonna see our first play that night, and she goes along.

When we get to this Broadway Ethel Barrymore Theater, like, you know, this cop outside on the horse, he calls out, "Hey Rocky!" The doorman, people on the street, they all know me and say hello. Even the guy at the door backstage. They all know me because I'm always in the papers, with lots of pichers, from fighting all those main-event fights, and the Championship.

I don't even know the kid's right name. His name is Bud, I tell the doorman. I'm supposed to meet him here. I'm describing him to the door ghee when the kid comes running over. The kid's still wearing the same kinda clothes only his T-shirt is ripped and he looks like a real slob. He makes a big fuss with Norma, walks us out front, sits us in a couple-a good comp house seats, and says, "Come back to the dressin room after the play. We go out and catch something to eat," and he starts to take off.

"Eh," I say, "I don't wanna miss you. What act ya in?"

"All of 'em," he says.

Wonder how he got all this pull, I say to Norma afta he goes away. I figure he's got a part of a messenger or maybe a soda jerk, or somethin like that. It's still early and nobody's in the seats yet, and nobody gives us a program, so we don't know what's going on.

"Who is he?" Norma wants to know.

"I don't know, kid just trains up at the gym sometimes. Probably got a nice bit part."

After the curtain goes up an everything's happening, I get the shock of my life. This kid I been sendin on errands is the star. Jesus, that's him, that's the kid I been sparring with in the gym, I tell Norma. She keeps pullin on my arm, tryin to keep me quiet, but I get too excited and I keep sayin, that's him, that's the kid. That's really him. Y 'mean?

In two hours this twenty-three-year-old kid is the biggest star on Broadway. *Madonna!* I mean big! A big, big star! I was stunned by the brutality of this kid, who I once thought was a sissy. I din know what hit me. All of a sudden he became like the toughest guy I ever fought in the ring. When I hear him yell Stel-la from the middle of the stage, I know I ain't never gonna be the same again.

When we get up to leave, we hear people saying things like, "this kind of performance you see only once in a lifetime," "stupendous," and "the greatest show ever seen on Broadway."

The play, *A Streetcar Named Desire,* won a ton of awards, Tennessee Williams who wrote it got the Pulitzer Prize, and the play won the New York Drama Critics Award.

We go backstage and I wanna call him Stanley Kowalski but now I know his name is Marlon Brando. Buddy was his name back in Nebraska and Illinois.

The guy's all sweated up an his feet are all dirty. He sez I be with you in a minute, so I figure he's gonna take a shower and dress up. Instead, he just changes into another pair of jeans, which is all full of paint from paintin his apartment. he puts sneakers on, without socks, or washin his feet. And he puts on another T-shirt and says, let's go, just like a bad boy who never grows up.

We fall into a lil joint and I'm patting his back all night.

"How come you in this business?" I ask him, and he says, "I ain't strong enough to turn down the money." He also tells us he's only on that stage because the part got turned down by two heavy hitters, John Garfield and Burt Lancaster.

Marlon Brando and me become best friends, and now it's me going on errands. I'm just kidding about the errands, but I'm the guy gets thrilled after that. He starts taking me around, meeting all his friends and contacts, and that's one of the ways I get started in show biz myself.

I tell Marlon one day, "You know something, I just finished four years gramma school in my life, an it always bothers me how the way I talk, like I can't speak good English." And he says, "How about me, too? Didn't I get thrown outa high school? When a guy's gotta make it, he's gotta make it, because something inside forces him to go out an make it. All that school does is give a little more help for guys who need it." He says, "Didn't you ever read any Horatio Alger stories?" I gotta remind myself to get one-a those.

Marlon Brando useta come up with funny things like, one day he's looking way off someplace and he says, "You ever have a pet raccoon, Rocky?" Before I know what he talkin about, he change the subject, but then, when I go to his joint once, I see a wall which is only half painted, all zig-zagged on one end, and it's dry. There's a pail of paint on the floor, all dried up with a stiff brush stuck in it, and coiled up next to the can is his roommate, a raccoon who he introduces to me like a person. "Say hello to Russell," he says. "Russell stinks like mad sometimes and he's always fucking up, but he's my friend." He useta put the rat on his shoulder and walk all over Manhattan with it. What could I tell ya?

When I get to know him good, I understand a lotta things, but I can't understand why a good-lookin star like him, who could date the most gorgeous girls from Broadway an Hollywood, is always dating poor waitresses and homely secretaries, and chicks like that. That's where the guy's heart was, and if he's happy with these kind of people, I gotta love the guy. Y'mean?

When the Zale fight comes up, it's just like the other two. There's a lot of action an blood, and that one punch I gotta run into, outa hunnerds t'rown, lands square on my jaw in the third round, an there goes my championship. I cried right there in the ring and if my handlers hadn't grabbed me, I'da broke both my hands punchin the ring posts.

I was almost thirty years old. My title was gone, and with it a hunk of my heart, but I got somethin no money or title could buy. I still had my terrific family.

I keep myself in shape and fight an occasional fight with long layoffs in between, but my heart's no longer in it. Losing the championship after that long, hard trip to get there took a hell of a lotta heart out of me.

I did a lot of thinking during those days, wondering what I was going to do when I finally had to hang up my gloves. And, this I knew, couldn't be far off if I wanted to quit with all my marbles.

I start runnin from one place to another, always looking for new friends with some new action. And my old an new friends were always looking to take me someplace to show me off as their closest friend, Champ Rocky Graziano. I swear Norma and I got took to every big nightclub show that ever hit town and every big-shot restaurant you could think of. But you get tired of this too, you know, so we start cuttin down on the invitations and we only accept to go out with people we like and really enjoy.

One day, Marlon Brando comes around and he says, "Come on with me, Rocky. I take you someplace where you meet some good people and have a few laughs."

He puts me behind him on this beat-up motorcycle he owned in those days, and he takes me to this little apartment on West Forty Eighth Street. The place was known as Eddie Jaffe's joint, a combination apartment, hangout, and office.

When you see Eddie Jaffe in his place, he looks like the kind of a guy who's got a maid, only she ain't showed for six months, maybe even more. The way he's got paper and belongins t'rown all over the joint ya'd think a burglar just got through ransackin it.

On the way, Marlon tells me he's takin me to meet his press agent, one-a the biggest and best anyplace, and he give you the shirt off his back. Marlon says the guy works his ass off for nuttin if ya ain't makin it an travelin tap city.

I'm Rocky Graziano the prizefighter, and I don't need no agent because I ain't in show biz, but Marlon's just beginning to do good, so he need him.

We stop by this old three-story house with Zucca's Restaurant underneath, and I remember I eat spaghetti there coupla times. I find out later a lotta important people paid rent in the upstairs apartments at one time or another. People like Ed Sullivan, Walter Winchell, Jack Dempsey, Damon Runyon, Mark Hellinger, Jack Kearns, and Bugs Baer, mostly Broadway writers and show-business guys. Toots Shor, too, once owned the restaurant downstairs before it became Zucca's.

When I walk inta this top-floor apartment, there's two rooms. One room is a small bedroom. As I go by I look inside an there's a big mussed-up bed with beat-up sheets, and the bed's all spread with old newspapers, magazines, and things like that.

Just inside, there's a big room, and it's like crazy. A coupla girls who look like show girls, are pasting pichers on a midget piano. A few guys are yelling into telephones like they own New York, an two guys and a sharp looking chick are slouched on a beat-up lookin couch. It looks like one-a those couches, ya know, like they say, if it could only talk. The few chairs are filled too. In a corner is a big rock pool, an there's a giant white poodle drinkin water out of it. Y'mean?

I find out later these guys on the phones, and sittin around, are just friends who come around like Marlon and me. Another t'ing I find out later is that Billy Duffy, a front man for the mob that made Primo Carnera World Heavyweight Champ, useta train Carnera right in this apartment when Duffy had the joint. But like they tell it, the shit didn't hit the fan till this guy, Eddie Jaffe, takes the pad.

There's a big round table in the room with a coupla phones on it, and it's also stacked with shit like papers, beer cans, and a pizza box with a coupla clammy pieces of pizza, topped with scraps, cigarette butts and ashes.

Eddie Jaffe's got a big smile behind a pair of glasses. He's a small wiry guy with wiry hair, but he don't look like no fighter.

Without a lotta hullabaloo, he just says, "Hey Rock, come in, come in." He takes my hand an gives me a nice shake. All the other guys are sayin things like, "Eh, Rock! What-a-ya say, Rocky!"

Eddie looks at Brando kind-a funny an says to me, "What's a nice guy like you doing with this bum," an he means Brando. Then he turns to Marlon and says, "Where the fuck you come off takin my clean socks outa the drawer an leavin your dirty ones there. Ya got some fuckin nerve!"

Marlon and the other people in the joint are just grinning an Jaffe's still yellin, "I didn't say nothin when ya always borrowing my clean shirts, but shitting in my drawer is another thing."

"Aaah, I get you a dozen pair," Marlon tells him.

"Don't matter," says Eddie. "Ya done it."

Marlon leaves me with everybody talkin to me about my fightin and he goes into the bedroom, flops on the bed, and starts readin a magazine.

I ain't kiddin when I tell ya I'm surprised with all the cursing. I always figure people in show business talk real high class like Katharine Hepburn and Cary Grant. I begin to find out that stars, men and wimmin both, all say fuck and things like that when they get mad, just like anybody else, and a lotta times they say it just joking.

Eddie says, "Have a seat," but I don't see no place to sit, so I says, "Where?"

He t'rows a guy off the couch and says, "There."

I sits down, and the guy who gets t'rown off sits on the arm next to me.

Eddie then yells to the guys with the phones growing outta their ears, "You fuckin guys tryin to break me? Jesus Christ! Ain'tcha never heard of coin phones?"

All the time he smiles, shakes his head, and talks to everybody at the same time about show-biz things, just like these guys are wound up like this all the time.

Eddie Jaffe looks inside the bedroom an yells at Marlon, "Get your fuckin shoes off my sheets," even though the sheets are already full of footprints. What could I tell you?

Marlon comes back in the big room, eats something outa the refrigerator, then sits at the piano and starts yellin, "Hold it, hold it!" He insists everybody listen while he plays a one-finger solo on the piano. "Just wrote it myself, today," he says to the chick next to him.

"Want me to sing it?" she says.

"I got no words yet, but if Sammy Cahn and Julie Stein could work out a whole musical on Jaffe's piano so can I."

"Why don'tcha go home an finish painting your flat," Eddie tells 'im.

Another guy yells, "Hey, Marlon! Tell Rocky about the time ya filled Melvin's violin with horseshit."

"You tell him."

The man roars. He says, "Marlon put back in it what came out."

"Ey, Eddie, the phone on the shelf's ringing," another guy says.

"Answer it. Gotta be for one of you guys anyway."

"She's a movie star," the guy next to me says as the girl on the couch goes to the kitchen sink, which is stacked high with dirty dishes.

"Whereya get all the dirty dishes?" she asks Eddie, as she starts washin them.

"Dirty dishes is the only kind we got," he tells her, while he starts scatterin papers on the table. "Where the fuck did it go?" he says as he heaves the pizza box an the empty beer cans into this three-foot-high garbage can he's got in the middle of the floor. "Where the fuck did that fuckin page go?" he keeps sayin. "Couldn't walk away. Just wrote a first page for a story and it's gone. Where the fuck did it go?" All the time he's talkin to himself. "Well, I came over here with it."

"Come on, Eddie, where ya hide it?" one guy kids him.

Eddie's cleaning off the table, throwing things into the big garbage pail, and Marlon says, "That's one way of seein what kinda finish that table's got."

"Fuck you! . . . Okay, who's got that page . . . Maybe it's here . . . No, it ain't here.

I'm beginning to think this a real nut factory Marlon brung me to, but I'm gettin a lot of laughs. Everybody's clowning and cracking up like this pad's a big hangout for bedbugs and out-a-funds people.

"Goddam it!" Eddie screams. "This is a fuckin business office! Where the fuck you guys think you are?" And then he looks at me with this big grin on his puss, turns to Marlon, pointing at him, and says, "You got a sad face and it'll probably make you millions, so why don't you stop being such a fuckup and act a little sad."

Marlon just whacks away at the piano and don't pay no attention.

Another guy says, "Ey, Eddie, when ya gonna put the goldfish in the pool?"

"I'm afraid one of you bums'll come up hungry someday and fry 'em when nobody's looking," Then he turns to me an says, "How ya doing, Rocky baby?"

One of the girls wants to know why he always takes care of some broad's poodle but won't babysit for hers.

"One's enough," Eddie says, "and besides, I break even."

"How?"

"He's a good licker so I let 'im lick all the stamps." Eddie's face lights up an he says, "Hey you guys, we gotta do something for Rocky. We gotta get him in show business."

Wait a minute, I start to tell 'im, but the next thing ya know he's on the phone yelling, "I got Rocky Graziano right here in my office. He'd be great for an appearance on your show. Yeah, great little actor. Nothing but personality."

Like these guys are excited like this all the time. While somebody's holding Eddie on the phone, he says things like, "Rocky, you were the greatest fuckin fighter ever lived." Then he turns to one-a the guys and says, "Run down the hall and see if Nat Hiken is in."

I like the fast crazy way the guy moves, and I can see everybody loves the guy. There ain't one phony streak in him. A spade's a spade.

A young guy by the name of Jackie Mason tells a joke, and Eddie says, "You got a horrible Jewish accent. Why don'tcha stick to learning how to be a rabbi."

I guess the biggest compliment you could give a comedian is say he made you laugh, but this Eddie knocks 'em right and left an they still love the guy.

All this time people are goin out and new people coming in, just like Grand Central. One new guest even breaks into a tap dance to show the girls his new routine, and he don't stop till he's outa bret.

This guy Nat Hiken comes in and I t'ink he's gonna get sick when he spots me. "Rocky! Rocky Graziano!" he keeps saying. The guy starts talking about the fight game, an Eddie can't get a word in. The guy's an out-an-out fight fan.

Eddie introduces him, big writer, producer, wrote for an directed some of the biggest acts in show business.

Eddie Jaffe's on the phone back an forth, telling people he's got me in his office, and he keeps turning to me to break in with "whataya think about this or that?"

Even though I been getting shots on T.V. sport shows as a guest, I ain't too serious about show business. But I like the action at Eddie's place, so, afta I leave that day, I starts going back once in a while.

They never t'row too many last names around so it's always hard to figure who's some of the people I meet there, except the ones I recognize like Phil Silvers and Milton Berle.

Some of the people I meet there the newspapers call glamorous celebrities, but when they come to Jaffe's they sometimes got hair in coilers and wearing loose, sloppy sweaters, and stuff like that.

Some of the comedians I meet there are just coming up in their racket and the things they pop out with make me piss my pants and roar.

Most of the girls are knockouts no matta how they dress up. Dolls like Julie Newmar, Gwen Verdon, and Margie Hart, the high-class strippa who once made seven thousand bucks a week.

Jockeys like my buddies Eddie Arcaro and Con Erico make the scene too, and Jackie Gleason, who Eddie sues over his fee. I even spot some of the Marx Brothers there, and singer Dorothy Dandridge. Ya never seen so many celebrities in your life. A lot of broken-down Broadway actors make his gaff, but he's even got John Wayne coming ta see him.

They pass each other in an out of Jaffe's doorway twenty-four hours a day. You name 'em, tap dancers, jockeys, headwaiters, acrobats, pan-handlers, cops, con men, artists, musicians, show girls, strippers, and even hookers for who Eddie was a sometime "John." All these characters made Eddie's joint a sort of restin place. His door wasn't locked to nobody. I even find out Marlon slept all over the building as a free guest when he first hit town broke an trying to make it in show business.

Wally Cox, a kid neighbor of Marlon Brando from Illinois, is up there when I go one day. Marlon also brung him there first time Wally hit Jaffe's joint.

Wally does a comedy act for Eddie Jaffe. He's trying to work it up and he wants Jaffe to tell 'im it's great. Y'mean?

"You know somethin," Eddie tells 'im. "That'd be a tough act to follow. Whatever you do, don't quit your job as jeweler's helper," which is what Wally was workin at for a livin. Rest in peace.

Some people come there with problems and they always got Eddie's ear an a lotta sympathy. One time I come in an find a couple neckin pretty strong on the broken-spring couch, and another time, I find some broad on the couch cryin hysteric while Jaffe's trying to calm her down. The guy's got the warmest heart anywhere. I woulda swore he musta been drinking canned heat.

Another time I come in an there's only one guy in the joint, stretched out asleep on the couch. Nobody cared who slept where. I come back, and even with people there the guy's still stretched sleepin on the couch. They tell me it's Ed Tryczinski and he wrote *Stalag 17,* which later won William Holden the Academy Award. He been sleepin there because his apartment burned down.

Ya never seen nuttin like it. Most of the time they fill up his small joint, and even where he sleeps, and he sometimes yells, "Ain't you fuckin characters got a home?" But then, as soon as somebody gets up to leave, he yells, "Where the hell ya going? Hang around awhile!"

My fightin days are just about over so I start listenin to people who keep coming up with all kinds of deals, you know, like puttin me up in nightclub business, fronting for something, or working up some kind of a show-biz act. I ain't worried too much about the loot department, because my wife Norma hid most of the gelt from my big fight purses. So I starts listenin to Eddie Jaffe even more. He tells me tings like, "If Tony Canzoneri did it, so can you. And how about Slapsie Maxie Rosenbloom and Max Baer? Didn't they make a bundle in show biz. I know it, Rocky. I know it, Rocky," he says. "I can feel it. You could be the biggest star that ever left the ring for the bright lights."

I tell the guy, "Look how I talk. I'm a mumbler. People say I got marbles in my mouth. The only people who never ask me to repeat nuttin was my East Side mob an the guys in the gym.'

"The guys that wantcha to repeat do it for laughs," Eddie tells me. "They wantcha to make them laugh. In show biz you could make the whole world laugh and rake in a bigger bundle than you ever made in the ring, without getting hit. What you talk is pure Graziano. Listen to me, you dope."

I gotta tell you, I listened, but I figure then I never do it. Eddie's the kindest guy ever lived, and ya never seen such imagination. Never wantin nuttin from nobody. Ain't a guy in the world could knock this ghee. Always moved like a fuckin bank.

Eddie calls for the landlord once an tells him he's gotta do somethin about the roaches and rats. But the landlord's been looking to throw Jaffe out because of all the commotion in Jaffe's pad. The landlord looks at the couch and says, "There's what's bringing a lot of 'em, that sow's bed over there."

Thanks to Eddie, I like to know how many important people, like Marlon Brando and others, got up offn that sow's bed and went out and made it.

Eddie is right about the bundle I make some day, which got my Norma still stashing the loot. Through Eddie's connections I got other connections, an which I still got today.

In case ya wanna know, so you can t'row some action his way, the guy is alive and kickin, making with the same bit at a new stand at 140 West 55th Street, in New York City.

EIGHT

In April of 1952 I lose my last big-one to Ray Robinson, and now I know for sure the message is loud and clear. A few more like that Robinson fight and I wouldn't be able to pick out my own wife in a room fulla Chinamen.

I fight one more after that with a college kid, Chuck Davey, who I can't get near enough to lay a hammer on, and so he gets the decision. If this don't tell me, nothin can, because to go on means I gotta become a punchin bag again, like I was for my brother Joe when I was a kid.

I go home and tell my Jewish banker, manager, my love, that I hung 'em up and I'm through. You never seen a happier lady in all your life. She reminds me she salted away plenty of loot, and we ain't got nothin to worry about, not that she had to remind me but she always did.

I'm thinkin then, about going into the bar business, maybe in Miami, Florida, my favorite city outside of New York. I'm thinking this way because, well, because I'm a well-liked guy down there, and I figure I could make it with anything.

You gotta know how tough it is, coming outa all that excitement, thousans of people cheerin in your ears, hunnerds of friends, an all of a sudden you get scared thinking you gonna be all alone.

Like I say, I think about Miami, but I can't make up my mind. All kinds of guys come up to me with all kinds of deals, an they still come to me with these deals today, like pushing something or manufacturing something you could sell anyplace—in Brooklyn, a men's toilet, a grocery store, in gas stations, on street corners, in a spaghetti house, on a pushcart in Naples, in garages, your own house, in your uncle's house, and even on the moon. Guys come to me with one item, or a thousan items, which they claim could be sold anyplace by the millions, and all they need on it is my handle. I ain't even figured out what it is they want me to push. And letters, they even keep coming today telling about the big important deal that nobody in the world got but them. These letters are sometimes up to six pages and the whole bullshit, including the signature, is mimeographed.

The time's slippin by, and here I am near the end of '52. I'm thirty-one years old, and I'm hangin around the gym more an more because it's the only place I'm comfortable. I even take a crack at managing a fighter, the first and last guy I ever manage. The kid's name was Lenny Mangiapano, a good-lookin Italian kid. Wouldn'tcha know, the kid's last name means "eat bread" in Italian, and this kid was workin in an Italian bakery.

Lenny was a tough, hard puncher and he have the makins of a good fighter, but I could see he had nothing but pussy on the brain, and his heart wasn't in fighting like it shoulda been. The kid was always showin up at the gym with a couple-a wild-lookin broads, and sometimes he just wanna hang around and skip training for that day. I tell Lenny there's a lotta dough in the fight game, but the only dough he ever gonna make is the kind he's rolling in his bakery cellar. He took my word and quit.

But the guy I gotta worry about is me. Since I always know how a lotta good top fighters turned out, I knew I could end up a dart board or a

jackass that somebody look to pin a tail on. I gotta find a good anchor
soon or maybe go crazy. It was like I was standing on some corner tryin
to make up my mind which way to walk.

When I quit fightin I was still makin a few appearances, but these
were all favors. I do one charity bit down in Washington D.C. and I get to
meet Truman again. This time the guy's the president of the whole
country. He remembers me good and comes on like a comedian. Truman
put his hands up like a fighter, and says, "Whataya say, Rock? You
wanna go a few rounds with me?"

The guy was in terrific shape. He told me, every mornin, real early, he
walked the ass off his Secret Service guys, making them follow after him
with a fast, steady walking pace for five to eight miles. The guy play a
pretty good piano, too. I tell him he could come home and play mine and
have it all to hisself. The guy hadda been a frustrated entertainer when
he was young.

Another guy I'm with on this same trip was J. Edgar Hoover, for
who's charity I once do a fight for.

Talking about fights, I never missed a good one after I hung up my
gloves. When I show up and get innerduced in the ring, and the fans
almost bring the house down with their cheers, it's the sweetest sound I
ever hear, and it's still like that today. I gave 'em everything when I was
in the ring. No guy ever left an arena where I fought where he didn't get
his money's worth.

I also make a few sports appearances on radio and TV, and one of
these favors I do on the arm is for Nick Kenny's TV show. Kenny is also a
"gentleman of the press," who I find out a long time ago is not a
Brooklyn tailor. In all the years I was fightin and getting into trouble, the
guy never rapped me once. Always a sweetheart. Y'mean?

At one of those sports affairs I was always getting invited to, I run into
a sports writer, Rowland Barber, who I know a few years. He come up to
me to say hello and outa nowhere he says he been thinking a long time of
writing a book about my fight career. I tells the guy he's crazy. How's he
gonna get a book outa me? The guy says there ain't a boxer in history
went through what I did to become Champ of the World. Make a long
story short, we make a deal and right away he goes to work on the book.

One day when we working on remembering things he says, "You know, Rocky, nobody ever fought the way you did to make it to the top, and nobody ever had so many obstacles thrown in the path."

I says, yeah, I guess somebody up there likes me. The guy jumps up like I just stuck him with a needle and he's yelling, "That's it, Rocky. That's it!"

That's it what? I want to know, and he says, "You just give me the title for the book—Somebody Up There Likes Me."

Writing that book was one-a the toughest things in my life, even tougher than the woist fights I had in the ring, because here he makes me dig down through all the tears that broke my heart while I was fightin my way up outa the cellar.

While we're workin on the book I don't do nothin else, just go up the gym a lot and hang around bullshitting with all my buddies. A guy's up in the gym lookin for me one day and somebody steers him to my ex-manager, Irving Cohen, who's there too. He tells Irving he's lookin for me because he like to give me a shot on a television show. He says he seen me on the Nick Kenny Show, and he thinks I might be just right for something he wants to use me in.

When I walk up to them I recognize the guy, and I says, "Ey! Don't I know you from someplace?"

"Sure, Rocky. I'm Nat Hiken. We met at Eddie Jaffe's place. You remember, I got an office in the same building." His eyes is all lit up.

Irving says, "How much money Rocky get?"

While Irving's asking I'm remembering what a great fight fan this guy is, but I know right off he ain't like the ghees who come up the gym all the time, you know, rough like. He's not too tall an not too heavy. The guy's got a round face, sandy hair, and he wears these thin-rim glasses that make him look like a school teacher. I could tell by how soft an slow the guy talked that he's a right guy. You could see he likes people.

The guy is sayin to Irving he don't make the prices. So Irving says, "When ya make the prices, come back."

Irving don't know nothing about show business, let alone me, or anybody else in that gym. The guy talks to me about fights for a little, he watches a few workouts, and then takes off.

The guy comes back, day or two later, and talk to me again. You know I ain't training an I'm ready to listen to anybody. I'm only hanging out in the gym because where else am I gonna go?

I didn't drink too much in those days, and I didn't smoke. I went there just to be with my cronies. I was always innerested in people, and I was very obsoiving with people, an that's why I am where the hell I am today.

Now the guy starts talking about the Martha Raye Show, and he's offering me a one-shot spot as Martha's boyfriend.

I say okay, I do it for five hundred. And he says, I'm just the producer and writer of the show. The agency pays you." I listen to a little bullshit, and then I says, okay but what should I do?

He says, I had to go to his office to look at the script. I went with him, but when he hands me the work what I din realize was I got lines on about fifteen pages which I gotta memorize.

Now, first time in my life I'm scared. I don't read good, and besides I never hadda memorize anything in my life before, school or anyplace else. I get up off the chair, drop the script on the guy's desk and go for the door saying "I'm sorry, I can't do it." I says, "I never even remember one line."

Nat Hiken stops me saying, "But Rocky, there's nothing to it. You're a natural. You'll be rehearsing them with Martha and everybody for a week. Give it a try. What can you lose?

But me, I'm thinkin I got a lot ta lose because you know I was Champ of the World and a very popular guy. For me to make goofy mistakes this time of my life could make me look like a fuckin jerk-off.

"That's the whole thing," Nat's saying, "You got a lot of charm, and people like you. They like you just as you are, and that's all you need in this business."

"Yeah," I tell 'im, "but you got me here like a comedian. I ain't funny, and besides, everytime I fight outa town, everybody useta think I was talkin in some kinda code."

"That's just it," he says. "It's the way you say things. It's the guy that delivers the lines that makes them funny. All humor comes from your own character. All you got to be is yourself."

I always thought a guy hadda go to school to be an actor, I tell 'im. "You sure you got the right guy?

"If a guy like you were to go to school," he says, "you throw everything in the garbage can. The public doesn't want to buy what somebody could change you to. They buy you like you are, and they're going to love you."

I tell you, this guy was a good salesman. He takes me and the script over to his lawyer, Arthur Hershkowitz's office, and the lawyer turns out to be another fight fan. Right off, he starts kidding me. He says to Hiken, "How you going to hold this guy still long enough to sign a contract?"

And I give 'em both a laugh, telling Hershkowitz there was lots a times I coulda used him along with a good alibi. And I wanna know if he's the kind of lawyer who fight your case down to your last nickel.

Nat Hiken wants to know why I wear this gold horn I got on a chain aroun my neck. I tell him it's Italian, and it keep the evil eye away. I had enough horns put on me when I was a kid, and that devil never get inside me again long as I wear my horn. Believe me, I ain't superstitious, but it's nice to believe the horn works. What I got to lose?

The guy was right about holding me still. In those days I really had ants in my pants and I run around like crazy, but I never go anyplace. Some people say I'm still like that today. So, one lil bad move from these guys and I chuck everything and go right out the door. Y'mean?

We all laugh over a few little stories, and Hiken's telling Hershkowitz how he meets me at Eddie Jaffe's place, and the crazy things that go on there, and how Marlon Brando sleeps all over the building and Hiken's place too.

Then Nat Hiken tells me he's people like me, except that he come from Chicago and his father wasn't a big shot either. His old man ran a shoe-repair supply business and took care of all the Italian shoemakers in Chicago.

I quick show him Capone's ring and tell him the story.

Nat an his lawyer can't get over Capone givin me the ring. Then Nat's telling me he was so broke when he started in show biz, got five bucks a week, that he has to hire all relatives who don't want no money. And he started this way with people who could play theirselves.

And I say, "Didn't somebody put down you should never hire relatives or friends?"

"Whataya do with your back up against the wall?" Nat wants to know.

They're changing the subject back an forth, show business to the fight game, and Hershkowitz asks if I know judo and karate?

Where they come from? I wanna know. They laugh it up, and all of a sudden, like outa nowhere, they shoot this paper in fronta me, saying I got this one-shot deal for five bills, and I sign it. And I gotta tell you my hand never shook when I signed big purse fight contracts but it's shaking now because I'm scared. But, Jesus Christ! I wanna make it again. And they're giving me a chance to make it in something I love since I was a little kid. Show business! Like it's everybody's dream who comes from nothin. But me, it's even more. I could maybe make it three times in my life. Once out of the slums, once Champ of the World, and once to the stars. If I could only tell you how excited this makes me.

When I was a kid, maybe seven, eight, I useta go to the Nickelodeon on Fourteenth Street to see guys like Douglas Fairbanks swingin across castle towers or from chandeliers with a sword between his teeth, or Charlie Chaplin and Harold Lloyd, or cowboy'n Indian movies. In the cowboy movies they had stars like Tom Mix, William S. Hart, Hoot Gibson, Buck Jones, and Hopalong Cassidy who was Bill Boyd.

I useta get so excited I never went to pee when I hadda, because I was afraid I might miss something. I piss against the seat in front of me, and see the picher two, three times.

It wasn't that I was stagestruck or anything like that. It was like some kind of magic was making all these things real for me. I think now, I spent all that time in the Nickelodeon because I didn't wanna leave the *real* world in the show house for the one outside, which I figure to be phony.

The vaudeville even grabbed me more than the movies sometimes. Vaudeville was an extra special, like the dishes they give your mom on Tuesday night.

Like I say, I never once thought I could be apart a this world but while I'm in that movie house, there was no other world. My eyes musta been like two baseballs, glued on the magician, or the comedian and his partner, who could also be his girl shill who sang, or a jugglin act, guys with trained dogs, monkeys, or seals, tap dancers, one-man bands, a bicycle or tightrope act, and all the greasepaint odd-balls who dodged the rotten vegetables that the bigger wise guys t'rew at 'em.

How'm I gonna tell you now how I feel when I left the movie house and went back outside blinkin my eyes, with the sunlight reminding me who I really was, a fuckin poor-slob kid who hadda steal almost everything he ever got in those days? But then, I grow up an become Champ-a-the-World, an the big money's rolling in, and everybody's noticing me, and I got that magic world once more in my pocked, but this time it's real.

And then, one day, boom! The championship goes, and with it a nice piece of that world.

You know, I wasn't about to wait till the marbles in my mouth move up to the top of my skull, and I wasn't about to stay in the fight game until I hear boidies choipin when there ain't no boidies there, so I gotta make this move no matter how scared I am.

I take the script home and I study it best I could, and I figure I got it down. Then I gotta go to a hall every day where we all rehearse. I always remember the first time I meet Martha Raye. She called me "Goombah," which means godfather and she talk to me with a smile on her face that stretch her mouth from one ear to the other. Caeser Romero is gonna be on the show too, and the both of them tell me, don't worry if you make a mistake. Nobody's gonna know about it except us. They say, don't stop. Just continue on, say anything and we take you right out. They say, even Nat Hiken won't know. He'll think he wrote the lines like he's hearing.

I never in my life believe these great people could treat me like a king. Me, a poor fuckin ex-hood from Tenth Street and First Avenue.

I hear somebody discussing Martha, and somebody calls her one of the greatest clowns ever lived. It brings back one of the greatest thrills of my life, going into the ring in Madison Square Garden for the first time. Whatcha can't know is what I was rememberin that night. First thing I done when I climb through the ropes, was look up, and in my mind I see a lotta white-dressed trapeze artists swinging, an flying, right above me. You better believe, that old place on Eighth Avenue and Fiftieth Street was a magic place for me years before I fight there.

Just like it was yesterday, when Father Mangoni took me and three other little hoodlum buddies of mine to the Garden to see the circus. The good father musta got the same feelin somebody gets when they pick up a stray beatup mutt and gives it a home. Taking us to the circus was the way Father Mangoni done it.

It musta been some kind of a special kid's day when he took us there, because when Father Mangoni walked us into this big sawdust-filled arena it was packed with thousan's of wild, screaming kids, and this made us start yelling too.

He buy us each a box of popcorn, and warned us, don't nobody get out of his sight. He knew, anyone of us get a chance we slip off an rob anything that wasn't nailed down. He didn't have nothing to worry about because the action going on all over the place got us bug-eyed. Y'mean?

The thing grabs me the most is the clowns warming the audience before the big action. I'm jumpin up and down, laughing so much I spill half my popcorn over the kid in front of me. One clown gets exploded out of a big crate. Then I see a midget robber clown with a mask get shot by a sheriff clown, and a extra head on top of the robber's costume get shot off his shoulders, like it's his real head. The clowns are doin all kindsa funny tricks, drivin little firetrucks and police cars, getting hit over the head with rubber sledgehammers, and one guy t'rows a bucket-a water right at us, but it turns out to be confetti, which is all over our clothes.

I always figure this is what a clown is, a guy with baggy patched pants, big funny coat, and faces all painted up like Halloween, a guy who makes kids laugh till they pee right through their clothes.

Then I grow up and find out there's other kinds of clowns and some are women. An I hear songs like "Pagliaccio," an "Laugh, Clown, Laugh," and I hear Frank Sinatra sing, "Where Are the Clowns?" and just the other day I hear Anthony Newley do a song he wrote, "The Man That Made You Laugh," and these kinda songs always bring those little-kid days back, and sometimes it's sad. But, you know something, we all gotta grow up, and some of us lucky, or unlucky enough, get to become parta that, just like it was lucky for me when Nat Hiken come along and team me up with Martha Raye, the greatest lady clown of 'em all. When I'm in my first rehearsal and I hear somebody call her a clown, first thing I wanna yell is, where's the popcorn?

N I N E

Now, all of a sudden it looks like it's gonna be more fun than work. And I find out that Martha was with this action all her life, right back to the baby carriage. Her Irish mom an pop, Pete and Peggy, were in vaudeville before she was born. They had Martha in their act even before she learn how to walk.

Martha appeared with the biggest, in movies like *The Big Broadcast, Give Me a Sailor, Double or Nothing, Tropic Holiday,* and *Monsieur Verdoux,* with Charlie Chaplin. Radio give her some good shots too, with guys like Al Jolson, Eddie Cantor, Bob Hope, Rudy Vallee, and Edgar Bergen and Charlie McCarthy, so you see I was in big company.

During the second World War, nobody put out more than this chick, traveling all over the world entertaining servicemen in an outa hospitals. Martha still makes these scenes today.

She ain't a big girl, but she got more pepper in her ass than any ten women t'rown together. When she opens her gapper you could see Brooklyn and hear her all the way back in Butte, Montana, where she was born, but the voice is pure gold.

Took a lotta guts to get before a mike, with rehoised lines, when the real day came. It scared me like no guy ever did in the ring.

In fact, I gotta wear a top hat an a monkey suit, something I didn't even wear at me brudder's weddin.

The show was called "The Comedy Hour," and I was scripted in as Martha Raye's boyfriend.

In that first show I can't keep a straight face. Caesar Romero comes to date Martha and when he finds me there he get's tough. He wants to know who the hell I am. I say Rocky, Rocky Graziano. Caesar does a double take, and runs and hides behind the couch.

Martha could never call me anything but Goombah, and now that's the name in the script. She breaks everybody up yellin it all over the place, and even though that was like better than twenty-five years ago some people still call me Goombah when they see me anyplace.

One-a the people on this first show I'm in is a opera star, Rise Stevens. I don't know nuttin about opera so I call her "Rise" the way I read it, an everybody breaks up. They tell me you pronounce it "Reesa." But Nat Hiken hears me and runs over to say, "That was very funny, Rocky. Don't change it. Keep calling her the way you did when we're on the air."

Another goof I make durin rehearsal, I'm supposed to mix this real salad in a big salad bowl. Hiken says when Miss Stevens says on cue, "Toss the salad," you start tossin it. I says, where, an Hiken says, right there, where it is. So when Rise says, "Rocky, would you please toss the salad," I pick up the bowl an fling the whole bowl and salad way across the stage against the wall. Took a good ten minutes to stop everybody from laughin. They all pissin in their pants. How'm I supposed to know that toss means to mix it?

When Hiken gets through laughin he says, "We're leaving that in, just the way Rocky did it." And that becomes one of the funniest things in my first show.

Sure, I make flubs, not that bad, but people think it's part of the act. I musta done a good job because everybody in the audience is laughin hysteric the way I done my lines, I was so nervous it looked like funny. After the show, everybody is congratulatin me, tellin me how terrific I was. Martha grabs me in a hug, yellin in my ear, "You done great!" I thought she was never gonna let me go. I know right then, I never have to get in the ring and fight again. I never seen so many nice eggs in my life like the ones running the show. When I come in, everybody says, "Hello, Mr. Graziano. How are you today?" And then Martha sees me, she makes a bigger fuss. I know she's trying to put me comfortable, make me feel like I belong there. I tell everybody, call me Rocky, but some still call me Mr. Graziano.

Man, is it different back in the gym, specially with those guys with even dispositions, always mean. They'd say, "Ey, you bum! Let's go! Work in there, work! Get the fuckin lead outa your ass!"

When Martha and her people say "You done great," they meant it.

Back in the dressin room after the fight you also hear, "You done great!" but I like to have a nickel for every guy who left and once outside call you a lousy bum. I like to see who's gonna tell me this acting bit ain't got it all over fighting for a living. Nobody's bangin you around, and besides, you wind up with a bigger piece of the purse. My show-biz manager is only getting ten percent, but my fights had toirty-tree an a toid cut outa them.

Before the Martha Raye Show I never go out for lunch in my life. When a guy useta say, "Eh, what's for lunch?" it meant what's in the olive oil and garlic saturated hero you got in your paper bag?

Nat Hiken, the boss, swells my chest bigga than anybody when he tells me I was a smash, and one-a the easiest guys to direct. Being I was a fighter and hadda listen to the trainer, it was easy to listen to the director.

Next day I read in the newspaper, things like, "Nat Hiken startles show business world by successfully using Champ Rocky Graziano as Martha Raye's foil." Hiken said, "Nature and Zale made Rocky's face a thing of endless interest to all. People love him on sight. Rocky Graziano acquired the complete Actors Studio technique soon after he began to walk. He was born mumbling." I start thinking maybe I oughta take speech lessons to loin to talk more stupid.

Now Hiken wants me on every show, an he even comes up with more money.

I'm the happiest guy in the world. Before long I'm right in the groove, playin with the biggest stars in show business, and the way Hiken moved me around on stage and the woids he put in my mouth made me realize the guy was an absolute genius. The guy made me a comedian, Italian style. I never seen a quicker mind. Brilliant. The guy was shy, but when he took command he was tough. People useta say he was the deadliest wit around, anyplace. Sometimes he useta script me long words I couldn't pronounce. I ask him to shorten them, and he does.

Martha Raye is like the whole show, so, the big guys decide to change the name to "The Martha Raye Show." There are some days I gotta pinch myself to make me believe I'm on the same show with superstar Martha Raye. And how you like that, nobody's layin a glove on me. When Nat Hiken first ask me, I thought it was gonna be one of those things, I go on, say "Hello Martha, hello everybody," they pay me, and I go home. Now, I'm getting like almost a star myself and everybody's breaking up and rolling on the floor, and I start getting confidence. When I goof lines, Martha says, "What didja say, Goombah?" and the way she makes with her eyes, I know I fucked up. I do the line again. And besides, she's always breaking me up with lines that ain't on the script.

Martha gotta be one of the greatest there ever was. Maybe it was the way she got broke in. But I gotta tell you, the way she taught me is still the way I go today. I just play me an let the chips fall anyplace they want. Martha spent a lotta her free time, sometimes with a drink over a bar, givin me tips and talking to me about her business. She says you could have the greatest reviews in the world an word of mouth could kill you. I could see she love me, but not like a sweetheart. More like a big sister who hadda put her kid brudder straight.

I also figure, maybe I should start hangin around with comedians who come on the show. People always call Henny Youngman a walkin joke book and the poor man's Bob Hope. Maybe guys like him teach me some jokes that ain't dirty.

One day I go to Martha very serious, and I say, suppose I go out and take some acting and diction lessons?

She says, "You do that an you'll be out of a good job. If those marbles fall out of your mouth, you're in trouble."

When I useta go to the gym after I started this acting bit, everybody's kiddin me like I'm a fairy. They make their voices like girls and say things like, "How are you, darlin?" and "Did you have a nice day?" They talk with these high voices, and make these girl signs because they think acting is for sissies. But then, when I start telling them I meet Caesar Romero and Edward G. Robinson, and the pay is good, and you don't have to take any punches, then they all lower their voice and start begging me to get them shots on the air. They even make up an entourage, and come to the rehearsal hall to watch me, and I know every fuckin one-a them is looking to get discovered.

I play all kinds of parts—porter, janitor, laborer, pushover, anything they t'row at me. An old burlesque guy tells me I was a "second banana." He tells me that in his day, the second banana never got any funny lines of his own, and the pay was real bad. The "top banana" got the funny lines, and most of the money. For me it was different; not only was the money good—all I hadda do was open my mouth and act natural, and I could see everybody splitting their sides.

I even play a ballet dancer on one show and I gotta dazzle 'em all over again with my footwork. For this I hadda take a few ballet lessons. I remember how we make fun of Jack Palance, when he show us a few ballet steps in the gym once. We made like Jack was big fag, just like the guys did me now. I warn all the guys coming to watch me rehearse, I catch anyone making fun-a me, I flatten 'em right where they stand. Even though I warn 'em, while I'm making like a woiling doivish, doing my *pas de chats* an my *entrechatty*'s in my tights, I catch 'em all snickerin with their hands over their mouth. I wanna t'row them all outa the joint, but as long as the teach says I done great, I don't care no more.

Most of the rehearsals were even funnier than the show. I'm rehearsin a funny dance once, where I'm supposed to t'row Martha in the air. The way I squeeze her, lifting her off the floor makes her let out one-a the loudest farts you ever hear. It take everybody a full fifteen minutes to stop laughing. Martha laugh so much herself, tears come down her face, specially when I tell her she coulda beat the Nazis single-handed with the gas she exploded.

One-a the funnier skits on the show happens with a steam room. Me, Caesar Romero, Jack Healy, and Tony Corrado are supposed to be naked in this steam room. We're just talking funny and all of a sudden the steam starts to clear an who's in there with us, supposed to be by accident, Martha Raye. You shoulda seen the way that audience break up when they see her face. Hiken knew how to bring out the best in me, Martha, and everybody else. And that Martha had the patience of a saint with me. She was always saying, "You did great, Rocky," even though I knew I made a trillion goofs. I could always see why some newspaper guys was calling her things like the "Clown Princess of Comedy."

One of the shows we do has Errol Flynn on it, and this guy was always my man. Rest in peace. He always reminded me of Douglas Fairbanks with the pirates, the swords, and all that shit. I can't tell you how excited I get. When he smiled and grinned at something I say, I got so confused I shadow-boxed the scripts.

I met so many celebrities on the show, I had 'em coming outa my ears. Some of the important ones I appear with were John Barrymore, Edward G. Robinson, Humphrey Bogart, Margaret Truman, Tyrone Power, Irene Dunne, Paul Lynde, Ezio Pinza, Faye Emerson, my Sicilian friend Robert Preston, Jimmy Durante, Tallulah Bankhead, Jerry Lewis, Hedda Hopper, Milton Berle, Jayne Mansfield, Phil Silvers, Johnny Ray, Cary Grant, Zsa Zsa Gabor, an a lotta other stars I forget. Maybe you think I'm name-droppin, but I don't how'm I gonna letcha know how happy I was to be makin it big again an with such good people.

Some of the stars, specially the girls, like Tallulah Bankhead, and some of the others, were what they call tempramental. When they start popping off I just look at Frankie Gio or one-a the other fighters and say, that kid's had too many fights.

We got our share of accidents too. I wasn't in on this one but I gets called in to help make the peace. After one-a the shows, some of my pug friends, who come around, wind up in a bar outside that Robert Preston is also in. An Preston, I gotta tell you, is one-a the nicest guys I ever know. There's some kinda misunderstanding with Preston and the poor guy winds up gettin three teet knocked outa his kisser. If they'd-a known he was a Sicilian, it woulda never happened. Anyway, Preston hadda go to Doctor Walter Nicora and buy three new teet. I can't tell you how mad and how bad I feel when I hear about this skirmish, but they straighten it out, apologies and all. But tell me, where's a guy gonna go to get his own pickets back?

One thing I get a kick outa is some of the hipsters and jazzed-up musicians I meet in show business. A million funny cracks, and some of these guys make the Boston Tea Party look like a sewin circle at a old ladies' home. They'd even go into Central Park and tear up lawns when they run out of weed. A four-foot musician got so high on grass, he went outside during a break and tried to step over the theater. Lucky for him that the windows was closed while he was inside or he'da tried to fly away.

On my first show with Martha, I get five bills, but after just a few shows under my belt they get me up to twenty-five hundred a show. All I gotta say is that's pretty damn good for just memorizing a few lines an having a lotta fun. Here I am, makin thousans, just talking stupid like I do all my life. Making it in a new career all over again was like I come down a small hill on a bike, start up a bigger hill, pumping the hell outa myself to the top, and then, like now, I come off the pedals and just let her sail down the other side with all that beautiful breeze hittin me in the face.

I useta get all kinds of laughs out of Martha. The girl's fanfuckintastic! Everything she does and says is funny. Just like she's on stage all the time. We're out on Broadway once, and she walks me into a drugstore. A chick behind a counter starts trying to hustle her some special perfume while Martha's looking the stuff over. The counter chick is sayin things like, "It's irresistable. It'll work all kinda wonders," and all that bullshit.

Martha tells the broad, "If it can do everything you say, how come you still working here?"

When I get to know Nat Hiken real good, I ask him to put my friends on the show, and he says, "Wasn't it you who said you should never work with relatives or friends?"

So I gives him a big grin and says, "What could I tell you?"

Jack Healy, who's the first guy I make Nat put on the show, is a real natural, since he already useta be in show business as a hoofer. The lucky stiff gets on almost every show.

Jack and I come a long way from the candy store down on Tenth Street and First Avenue but we always go back to visit. I felt I had to go back to my beginnins every once and a while. It was just like a magnet was pullin me back, an the first thing I do is go looking around for all the ghosts outa my past. I could never tell you how my head and my heart swelled up happy with the memories, even though a dog shouldn't hafta go through what I did.

I also tell Nat what happen to fighters when they hang up their gloves and they're through for good, and could he give them a break once in awhile. You never seen a guy love fighters the way Nat Hiken does. He give a break to every broken-down pug I suggest. I become, like a guy says in the papers, an unofficial casting director. Among the guys who I got on the shows was, Walter Cartier, Frankie Gio, Billy Graham, Willie Pep, Paddy De Marco, Lou Nova, Vic Delacorti, Joey Giardello, Barney Ross, Joey Scarlotta, Petey Scalso, Tony Zale, Jimmy Herring, Tony Janiro, Maxie Shapiro, and a lot of other fighters I forget. All Nat Hiken wanted to know was, could they talk? A newspaper critic once give the Martha Raye Show four cauliflowers.

One guy I get on the show is my old jail-house buddy, Hammerhead Jake La Motta, the Raging Bull, who also get to be Middleweight Champ after me. One of the reasons I feel sorry for the guy is his wife just dump him for clashing with the drapes.

When I told Jake I'm getting him on the show, he says he can't act, and I gotta remind him I saw him fighting.

I get him on the third show I do with Martha. I shouldn'ta done it for him, because I'm still mad at the guy for the time he talks me into going partners with him at Green Acres Gambling Casino in Miami Beach. We both have a bundle then. He asks me to go partners with him shootin' craps, and I go with him. Jake decides he's gonna do all the rolling, and gamblng for both of us. I find out too late, not only was this guy jinxed with his women, he ain't got no luck, no how, with shootin crap either. He lose all our cash and starts signing markers. Every other marker he makes me sign. When he t'rew in the towel, I know no towel ever be able to wipe the bath we took. We owe the house ten grand each. And this I have to pay, because the guys running this casino were "The Boys." An besides, not honoring a marker is like spitting on the floor in church. You don't do that neither. Almost anybody'll tell you, the greatest points on interest are seven and eleven. For us they was points of disaster.

Like I say, even to today, I don't forgive the bum for losing my moolah. You gotta remember, this guy could lose money in a gumball machine. Things got so bad for him somebody even stole his garbage, an with his luck the cops found it an brought it back. Still, like I tole you, I get the guy a shot and for this bit Nat Hiken writes in a fight scene. Even though we were both middleweights, fightin at the same time, we never fought each other in the ring and we once turn down a hunnerd grand for a match. Now we end up doing it for laughs. Y'mean?

But Jake takes this acting thing serious. He gets hold of a Shakespeare script someplace and he walks around like a t'espian, emoting stuff like, "What light tru yonda winda breaks?"

When Jake 'n I did the fight for the TV cameras, we wound up beltin each other for real, and we had the bruises to prove it. Martha told the newspapers later that it was one-a the best shows they ever put on the air. She didn't know that Jake 'n me decided to go for real for awhile, just to give her and Nat a good show.

In fact, I even got Jake's brother, Joey La Motta, on a show. Joe was a pretty fair pro boxer hisself, but he quit when he seen you could get turned inta a dummy.

The show Joey's on is got Margaret Truman, the President's daughter, as a guest. She's a nice kid and she's pretty good, but when she sung that opera stuff, I gotta tell you, I not only hide, but I hide with my ears covered. While she's on the show, even doing repeat jobs, her pop, Truman, was running the country with an iron hand, and that's the way he played the piano.

Another ex-pug who turned comedian was Slapsie Maxie Rosenbloom. He come up to rehearsing hall to see me once, an right in front of everybody, he starts yelling I'm stealing his act, and he says, "What's more, you stink doing it." Professional jealousy, right?

Only one time I goofed as a talent scout. We're in a scene, buncha guys are supposed ta sing. They all get handed a music sheet for the words. I'm watchin them rehearse and I notice one fighter, he's just standing there. Hey! I tell 'im. You gotta sing wit them. I figure maybe he's ashamed he can't sing good. The poor guy looks at me dumb-like an says, "Geez, Rocky, I can't—I don't know how ta read."

Another fighter, Maxie Shapiro, the only Jewish fighter I bring in, makes Hiken very happy because he's Jewish too. It makes Hiken very proud when Maxie comes on like a very intelligent guy. But what he don't know is Maxie gets a little crazy sometimes. He starts seeing this, and Maxie's action with everybody, the bullshit, nutty things and all, and I could see Hiken's now wondering if Maxie's out of his fuckin mind. All Hiken keeps saying to me is, "Rocky, are you sure he's all right?"

Another guy I get on the show is an older guy, a friend I treat like my father. His name is Tony Corrado. Tony been following me since my early four-round fights. And I even dedicated my first book, *Somebody Up There Likes Me,* to Tony. The guy never approve some of the crazy things I did in those early days but he loved me an took me an my wife with him to nightclubs and best restaurants, and he's happiest when grabbing the biggest tabs you could imagin.

Fact, I gotta tell you here about the first time Tony took me to this real high-class place and I see a waiter go by with shishkeabob, the meat flamin on a sword. I didn't know what it was then so I calls out, "Eh! what's that?" an the waiter says, "A customer who only left a dollar tip."

Tony never let me or anybody else come up with penny one. To this guy, mixed greens was a bundle of fifties an hunnerds.

Tony Corrado was the last guy to need a job as extra with the twenty-five a day they pay him on the show. He was the executive-owner of a few-million-dollar business, distributing cables, and the guy's still active in it today. He just loved the show business action and to be with me. I said to Tony one day on the show, how come you always jump an say, yes sir, whenever they push you around? You're a millionaire! I tell 'im.

"Rocky," he says, "there's one important lesson in life. You've got to always learn first who the boss is. In my place, I'm the boss and everybody knows it. Here these people are the boss, and I respect it."

Even though Tony gonna need a Brinks truck to haul his money behind the hearse to the cemetery, he never act like he had a nickel. One night after rehearsal, he had the word passed around that he was taking the whole cast to dinner. The guy was fantastic! Tony Corrado picked up a tab that would stagger Vesco. Nat Hiken went up to Tony to apologize for havin been rough on him while he was directing. Tony says, "No sir, Mr. Hiken. When you're on that stage *you're* the boss!"

One time Nat Hiken tells me he's going out to eat with Zsa Zsa Gabor, who's got a shot on the show, and he's takin me with him. He wants to know where we could go to get some good Italian food. So, I take 'em to the Grotto Azura, a restaurant down in a cellar in Little Italy. Here we are with a broad that's been wined and dined by some of the biggest and richest lovers in the world, guys like Rubirosa, George Sanders, Conrad Hilton, and you name 'em. And like they say, this chick has played and danced with the royalty of the woild, got homes she ain't even lived in, and eaten in restaurants that only cater to the highest-class society. An where do I take this chick? To a cellar off Mulberry Street.

I order my favrit, spaghetti with clam sauce, and I tell the waiter I want it *al dente.*

When Hiken asks me what kinda food *al dente* is I could see he don't know nothing about Italian food. I tell him *al dente* means not too hard and not too soft. He laughs like he's thinkin somethin dirty. He wants to know how the cook knows when its *al dente.* I tell him they t'row it up against the wall. If it don't stick, it's *al dente.* The guy believes me.

There useta a lot of *malandrines* go to the Grotto Azura in those days. Everybody knew it was the eating hangout of the good people, "the Boys." So now, Zsa Zsa is smackin her chops on that good Italian food, eating up a storm, and she's got diamond rings like potatoes, and jools all over her. They say she give back a lotta engagement rings but she always keep the stones. This broad don't even go out to empty the garbarge can without a trillion dollars' worth of ice on her frame, and when she takes a bath she leaves 14-karat rings. Believe me, about the only things you could give this broad that she ain't got is a can of Draino.

So, at the Grotto Azura, she's looking around and she spots some of these wise guys gunnin her from other tables. She gets this scared look on her face, and says, "Dahling, Rocky, those men look like the people on The Untouchables.' "

You gotta know this broad acts a little wacky sometimes, so I say, don't worry, Zsa Zsa, you wit' me. But this broad don't understand me too good no matta what I say, so I say it again. You ain't got a t'ing to worry about cause you wit me. In other woids I'm tryin to tell her, maybe with somebody else she get robbed right off, but since she's wit' me nobody gonna lay a glove on her. She still don't look too happy, so I tell her, dincha ever hear of respect? What could I tell you?

I says to her, when these guys is your friends you never got nothin to worry about.

And Zsa Zsa says, "How do you know if they're your friends?"

So I tell her what Al Capone once says to me. Capone says all you gotta do to find out who's your friends is do what he useta do. He buy a melon, put it in a shoppin bag all wrapped up, and take it to somebody's house. He say to the person, I just killed Luigi, or whoever, and I got his head in this bag. What should I do?"

If the people run him off they wasn't his friends. If somebody says, don't worry, Al. Bring it in an we bury it in the cellar, then that's your friend.

Zsa Zsa look at me like I'm crazy and says, "Oh, Rocky dahlin! You certainly like to pull my leg!"

Funny part of it is, Zsa Zsa thinks I'm a great actor and all this is part of the act. She thought it was great I could talk the way I do. She don't believe I really talk the way she hears me. She wants to know how I learn to talk like that and how I become a comedian.

I tells her, when I quit fighting I bought a rocking chair and it busted from under me once. When I sees I'm off my rocker, I become a comedian.

Here's this broad tellin me how I talk, and when she goes on the show her Hungarian gets her so twisted her line comes out, "Dahlin, it's a business to do pleasure with you." I look her over pretty good, and I say to myself, who she kidding? This broad knows every move she make.

Rocky in training

Trainer Whitey
Bimstein putting Rocky
through his paces

With Lou Stillman
outside Stillman's
Gym

Jack Healey, left,
introduced Rocky to
George Raft, a man
Rocky had
worshipped
throughout his
youth.

Tony Zale takes a hard right from Rocky in a championship bout.

Rocky teaches Paul Newman the finer points of playing Rocky in the movie *Somebody Up There Likes Me*.

Martha Raye always called Rocky "Goombah." He played her television boyfriend regularly on "The Martha Raye Show."

With Frank Sinatra. They've been devoted friends for many, many years.

On cover of *Esquire* with Jack Palance and Raquel Welch

At dinner with Rocky in Little Italy once, Zsa Zsa Gabor mistook real gangsters for actors playing characters in "The Untouchables."

"Little Caesar," Edward G. Robinson, once asked Rocky to take him to meet some genuine gangsters.

Rocky being made-up for a female role in *Miami Undercover*

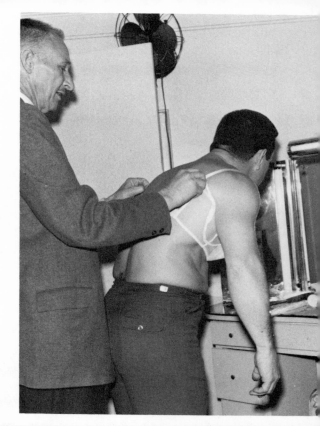

Rocky, Martha Raye, and *The Raging Bull*, Jake La Motta

Rocky in costume for
Miami Undercover

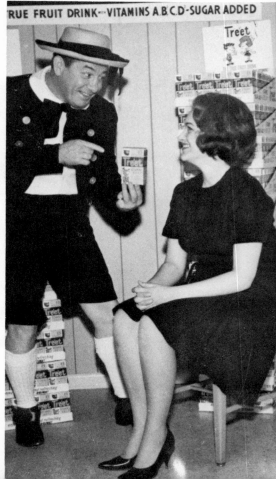

Making a fruit juice
commercial

With Lisa Minelli

With another champ, Sugar Ray Robinson

Rocky and wife Norma.
She once locked him,
naked, on the terrace
outside their
apartment.

Making a pizza
commercial.

Waiting to make a commerci[al]
for an auto transmission
repair chain

With New York's Terence
Cardinal Cooke

Rocky the painter and some of
his creations. He has had
one-man shows at important
New York galleries.

Rocky and New York's Governor Carey were once neighbors.

When Rocky worked in films years ago with an actor named Ronald Reagan, he was "promised" that he would be named Secretary of Education should Ronnie ever become president. Rocky campaigned hard for him in the 1980 election.

MARTY LYONS

Reagan Bush

CHUCK RAMSEY

ROCKY GRAZIANO

TERRY BRADSHAW

T
E
N

As the Martha Raye Show goes on week after week, Nat Hiken starts hanging around me more an more. He calls me his good-luck piece, and I'm finding out that in show business Hiken's considered one-a the greatest writers there is. Before the Martha Raye Show, he wrote for Fred Allen for seven years, wrote three years for Milton Berle, wrote for Bert Lahr, wrote an directed Broadway reviews, and Nat wrote and produced the Johnny Carson Show. The guy had the greatest sense of humor anyplace, and one of the kindest, gentlest men you ever wanna meet.

He starts taking me and my wife Norma along all the time, when he takes out the celebrities doing guest shots on the show. Even though the celebrities are some of the biggest entertainers in the business, Hiken knows I can make them laugh. Hiken hisself could write the greatest gags you ever heard, but he couldn't tell them too good. He needed guys like Phil Silvers and Milton Berle to deliver them for him.

I remember breaking everybody up once when Hiken takes us to the first Japanese restaurant I ever been in. We all gotta take off our shoes and leave 'em in the hall. I says, "Is this so we don't hurt the waiter too much if we get mad and gotta kick his ass?"

Nat an me knew each other for years, and we played a lot of golf together. One time he says he like to go to the Westchester Country Club sometime. Me, I hit every club around New York and New Jersey since I started playing in '46 or '47. I play in all of them, and I never belong to one. At the time Nat ask me, the Westchester Country Club was still kinda restricted, you know, they don't allow Jews but like on the QT. Nat don't know this. Me, I don't give a shit. Nat Hiken's my friend, and if he wants to play there we go.

We park the car at the club and I take Nat right to the first hole, carryin our clubs. I don't talk to nobody. A boss comes up to ask what we doin there. "Say there!" he starts, and then he makes me out and says excited like, "Hey, Rocky Graziano!"

This boss hadda know I wasn't a member, so I says, "Mind if I play the course?"

"Not at all," the guy says. "Go right ahead. Come back anytime you like."

This makes Nat very impressed and he gets all kinds of kicks watching me buffalo my way through all kinds of clubs while he's wit me. I says, "Tell me Nat, how they gonna keep a celebrity like me out?"

I'm playing a pretty good game today, but I remember when I got started. I never hit a boidie but I hit cows, horses, dogs, an even other players.

If there was a guy loved life more than Nat, it hadda be me. We hit Lindy's an all the best places, rode motorboats in the summer, seen baseball games together, and went to see all the fights. The guy was even a big horseman. Nat owned three of his own race horses, and we make the track as often as we could.

We're both out at the Belmont Race Track one time when a guy comes up to me and says, "Mr. Graziano, the president would like to meet you. Could you come for a few minutes?" What could I tell you? Sure I go.

Again, I think like once before, when I make the same mistake with Truman, like this guy they want me to meet now is the head of Belmont Race Track, but then I hear rumors that Eisenhower is in the clubhouse, where I am too, so I know this guy's gotta be Secret Service, and besides, there's another waspy-lookin guy in a business suit standing right alongside him.

The two Secret Service guys take me to where the President is and they say, "President Eisenhower, this is Mr. Graziano." The guy also says something about Mrs. Eisenhower, who's with him, but I don't hear. The President takes my hand, and he's calling me Rocky, and telling me what a great fighter I was while hunnerds of people are coming around, stretching their necks, trying to get close so they could see what's going on.

Funny part of it is, as I'm meeting more'n more famous people, I'm beginning to see they're no different than anybody else. Whatever personality a guy's got, he's got, no matter how much money is in his pocket. A guy is either a regular guy or he ain't, no matter where you know him from. It's just that people like me are used to seeing a guy different, accordin to where you run into him. Take for instance, you see a well-known character stumbling around drunk in a fancy joint like J.B. Tiptons over on Second near Fiftieth. Everybody'll call the guy a charmin playboy. You see the same character in Clancy's Saloon on Third Avenue and there everybody calls him a fuckin drunk.

It's like that with Eisenhower. He just look like another horseplayer making a few bets, but you still better believe I'm thrilled. In fact, we talk a little about this an that, and for a minute I even forget the races. My mind is spinning back to Tenth Street, and the political pin buttons we once get paid to pass out, and all the wood crates and old furniture we burn up on those election fires.

Mamie Eisenhower brings me out of my thoughts when she asks, "Have you got a horse for me in this one, Rocky?"

Bet on "Sheer Luck," I tells her. This horse gotta go. Mamie give the runner two dollars and says, "Bet it to win." The horse went off at sixty to one. I knew this hadda be my lucky day, so I bet it sixty across the board. The nag won the race and you shoulda seen Mamie's face when the runner counted out a hundred twenty buckeroos. The President never even made a bet, but he was happier than her.

Like I said, it did toin out to be my lucky day all around. On the way home I thought, I wonder if the President ever walked down First Avenue past Lanza's Restaurant and past Tenth Street, and what might happen if he walked there with his arm around my shoulder and stand with me lookin inta that big 'lection' fire. Wow!

Since I'm talking about the track I gotta tell you about some of the funny things I see happen at the track that a guy never see anyplace else. Guys come up to tout you on a nag and they even go as far as saying they were, just that morning, eating out of the same feedbag with the horse, and the horse tole him . . . One time, we're standin behind a guy yellin like mad, sweet-pleadin while the bang-tails are off and running. The guys saying, "C'mon, baby! C'mon sweetheart! Hang in there. You're doing great. I love ya, baby, Keep coming. Great, baby, great. Weeee! Looka my baby go! Just looka that sweetheart go!" And then, right at the finish another horse beats him across the wire. All of a sudden the guy's sweet tones change to, "You dirty no-good fuckin sonofabitch! You dirty no-good bastard! I'm comin back to the stables and break every one of your fuckin legs with a baseball bat!"

Another time when the last race is over and everybody is racing to get out of the parkin lot, every and which way, a car runs right into the side of another car, and as we pulling alongside, I call out the winda to the guy who did the accident, "Eh, howja do today?" and he yells back, pointing to his banged-up car, "Just blew another five bills, got no insurance, no car, no nothing now."

Rowland Barber's book, *Somebody Up There Likes Me*, which covers my fight-game years, comes out and makes a big hit seller soon as it hits the book stores.

Norma is in there now, moving with celebrities like she lived it all her life. She takes up tennis, horseback riding, and things like that, and we get invited to all kinds of big-shot parties and events, and you never seen a happier family. Norma's making with the beauty parlor, glamorous clothes, furs, you'd never know today that this was my little Norma Unger from Brooklyn. Y'mean?

One day she tells me she sold the house and we moving to a penthouse in New York. And, I wanna know, who gave her permission to sell the house, and she says, "You wanna hear your exact words when you bought it? You took me to it, and you says, 'Norma, this is *your* house.' " Anyway, I finally traded the fire escape I had as a kid for a big terrace in Sutton Place.

One day, during one of our Martha Raye appearances, Jack Healy come to me very serious and says he just got outa the hospital where he been for a month. They cut him open and find him full of cancer. They tell him like a spade's a spade, sew him up, and that's it. Jack says his insides gotta look like a egg that somebody t'rew and splashed up against a wall. He even laugh when he tell me about it.

Jack starts takin those x-ray treatments, and he's always saying how he's gonna be the first guy to beat the big "C." He argues like the old days, stubborn as fuckin hell.

He starts smokin grass, and he's smokin it all the time, everyplace he goes, pockets full of joints. In those days it was a much worse rap than today, and chances were you could go to the can, even without a record, for as much as three years for just one joint. So we all worried about him when he gets pinched for possession one day.

The lawyer tells the judge that Jack Healy got eighteen months to live, and they got letters from three doctors to prove it.

The judge can't close his eyes altogether, so he gives Jack a one-year suspended sentence.

Another time on the Martha Raye Show Edward G. Robinson comes on as a guest and the guy is acting more thrilled to meet me than me with him.

It was years before that I seen him in *Little Caesar* and I came out of that movie house ten times tougher than when I went in.

After we talk awhile I starts imitatin the way the guy talked in *Little*

Caesar and broke everybody up. There was a couple-a lines I never forget right up to this day. "You do that better than me," he says when I come out with, "Mother of Mercy, is this the end of Rico?"

Not too long before this, I see him in a picture *House of Strangers,* with Richard Conte and Luther Adler playing his sons. The picture was about an Italian family, and you never believe the job these guys done. In the early days, Edward G. Robinson played characters who come up off the streets and made it big, mostly as gangsters.

And whataya think he asks me? He says, "Rocky, I want you to do me a favor an take me to meet some real gangsters." I think first he's kidding with me, but then I see he's dead serious. I tell him, you don't want to go meet these kind of guys. They rob you in a minute, and even make sure you ain't breathing when they leave you, because they know a guy what's breathing could have you arrested.

The guy just laughs and keeps insisting, "Come on, be a sport and take me to meet some gangsters."

I keep tellin him, he needs to run into these kinda guys like he needs a hole in his skull, but then, I figures, why don't I take him down to the Lower East Side, show him off, and innerduce him to some-a the hoods I useta run with. After all, some-a them did grow up tough guys, even though they made their rep on being pinched. But who's gonna know the most serious pinch some-a them took was for knockin over tombstones or mopin on the corner? Anyway, most-a them were so crooked they could hide behind corkscrews. To him they still be gangsters.

One afternoon I take him, and on the way downtown I tells him, if my old gang could-a rode horses they'da made Jessie James look like a priest. An I give him a rundown on some-a the guys. I says, take "The Rake" for instance. He got t'rown offna bus once for sneakin on without payin and he gets so mad he tries to blow up the bus.

"What happened then?" Ed wants to know.

I tell him nothin happen to the bus, but The Rake burned his lips on the exhaust pipe.

When we get down on the East Side I take him driving up an down the streets looking for some of "The Boys," but I don't find nobody. I'm looking specially for Big Gumball, Calabash, Nunzi, Foongi, Mongo, and the Rake, anyone-a them. I ain't been here for a long time, so I don't even know if these guys are out on the bricks or not. I can't wait to see their faces when they see me with famous Edward G. Robinson.

Everyplace I go ask, they tell me mosta the guys are vacationing in Sing Sing and like resorts. I find out Mongo's in prison for robbin his kid brother's bank. I want to know how they could send a guy to the Big House for just busting a piggy bank. The guy says, I probably don't remember his kid brother went to college, the whole bit. The kid brother was working at the First National Bank.

One guy I run into tells me Nunzi is shaping up on the docks for a day's pay. An, if he ain't there, he's either at the unemployment office waitin in line for a check or he's out casing a job someplace. When we drive by the Peter Stuyvesant monument in a small old cemetery, I tell him how me and my gang stole some shovels out of the coalman's cellar when we was kids and we went and dug up the monument because we heard there was buried treasure there. All we found was rocks an blisters.

We run into one guy, tells me he jus seen Big Gumball selling watermelons offn a truck on St. Mark's Place. We drive over, and there's Big Gumball yelling, "Watermelons!" and he sound like one of those boat horns when there's a fog. I ain't seen him for a long time, and he looks even fatter, like he pick up another hunnerd pounds.

"Ey, Big Gumball!" I yells, and when he pokes his big head in the car window and sees who I'm wit', I thought he was gonna pick up the car and hug it.

We have a lot of laughs right there in the street, and Big Gumball even offered to go out and stage a holdup in Robinson's honor. I assure youse, he was ready. In fact, when we start to leave, Big Gumball wants to take off with us, leaving the truck with all the melons right there in the street in front of the poolroom.

Since I can't find Robinson no genuine gangsters I figure I take him up to Stillman's to see who's out of the can that's back training there.

When the guys at the gym spots me and Robinson they all quit trainin and come around us, all talking, and tryin to put their two cents in at the same time. They're laughing, and joking, and asking Ed to make like a tough guy. So he says, just like he done in the picture, "See here you guys. No one fools with Little Caesar. See! See!"

After that, whenever somebody brings up Robinson, or he appear on a show with me, I use that same line imitatin him. I think I get more miles out of that line than anything I ever say about him. Rest in peace.

Time goes by, and I'm becoming like a veteran. Shots start coming my way besides the Martha Raye Show. My manager even books me into a weekend spot in a small club where they got a strippa called Foxwell. I gotta tell you some of the spots I got in those days I wouldn'ta given a dry cleaner. But I learn fast the best place to go do a show is for the boys doing time. There the audience can't walk out on you. My manager even booked me commercials, and this was great. You didn't have to go for a lotta action, and the bread was better than some of the show purses.

One of the shows I do outa town is with Vaughan Monroe, in Youngstown, Ohio, where my old adversary and now friend, Tony Janiro, come from. In this town I do my first shot at a personal appearance on a stage in a theater. I got booked for three days and three nights, an I'm supposed to improvise a little singing and dancing, and tell a few stories. First thing I come out doin is a imitation of Vaughan Monroe singin, "Racing with the Moon."

After I get over being nervous, I like the way everything is bringing back memories of vaudeville when I was a kid, only now it's me the hecklers are heckling, and I stop to remind the wise guys that I useta be a pretty good bouncer too.

I find out with being a comedian I gotta flatten hecklers with lines instead of my fists. I tell 'em things like, I'm formin a attachment for you. I'm comin out there to personally fit it over your mouth. But, I tell you something, I never have any trouble. Guys looking to give me any grief knew they better have bodyguards with guns if they fuck with me serious.

A guy could pick up a lotta lines, and some good clean jokes from waiters, bartenders, and cab drivers. Soon as they see you're somebody they quick wanna crack you up. Like just the other day a bartender says,

"You know what they put on the old maid's tombstone'?" and just like I'm supposed to, I say, "What?" And the guys says, "Who said you can't take it with you?" I gotta remember to use that one.

Some of the little funny bits I tell is like I go into a bar and I asks the bartender for somethin cold and full of vodka, and he says, "You just ordered my wife."

And the guy at the next table who yells at the waiter, "Ey! What I gotta do around here to get some water?" And the waiter says, "Set yourself on fire."

And things like, first time Santa Claus came down our chimney my pop lit the fire.

I also find out fast, there's only one place they hold you over when you're bad, and that's in the can.

While I'm away from home doin these shows, local people ask me to go talk to kids in hospitals an orphan homes, an things like that, and all I gotta do is remember when I was a kid and I break my ass to get to these places, just to be able to look in their faces when I make 'em laugh.

I never in all my own kid days ever believe all this good luck could happen to me.

While I'm out in Youngstown doing this show, just as I'm winding it up, I get a call from New York and that's how I find out my father died. Now it's me who needs the song, "Laugh, Clown, Laugh." I keep getting sadder all the time on the way back home. I don't know why, except I think maybe it's for my mom. But then the more I think about him I start to cry. I think about what a mean bastard he was, but by now I could understand a lot, specially how my pop musta felt when he had to quit boxing, the only real action he ever knew in his life, to go out and try to scratch out a fuckin' living lugging crates. I wanted to talk to him, tell him how sorry I was for causing him and mom all that grief with the cops mosta my life.

I never told my pop how I felt about a lotta things. Up to the day he died I could never talk to him about anything serious. Only when he was in his casket could I tell him how sorry I was for the life he had to live, and me making it worse. I looked at the box right up to when they t'rew the dirt on top of it. And wouldn't you know, it was raining. The last thing I told him, even though he couldn't hear me, was, "Ya gotta forgive me, pop."

I loved him and I hated him, and sometimes I hated that broken-down bum enough to wanna kill 'im. But you know something? Every once in a while I think about the old guy and I miss him.

As for my brother Joey he never went no place, but when we grow up we unnerstand how things was and we love each other like brothers should. Joe never wanted to be the champ of anything. He just wanted to be Joe, a nice neighborhood guy. When he scored a little he open up a poolroom on St. Mark's Place, down in our old neighborhood, and the guy was happy just racking balls an cutting up with the neighborhood wise guys.

An as for my pop, Nick Bob, with the tools God give 'im he done the best he could.

E L E V E N

I'm watching TV one day and this show comes on about a boxer, and there's Marlon Brando in it making all my moves, acting just like me. And then, another time I go to see his new picture, Budd Schulberg's *On the Waterfront,* and there's Marlon again, and I gotta laugh watching him making just like me again. So now I know all that time we was running around together he was studying me real good. So now I know I pay him back a little for bringing me around an innerducing me to all those big people in show business.

There's a scene in *On the Waterfront* where Rod Steiger, who plays Brando's racketeer brother, is in a cab with him and Brando says, "Oh, Charlie, Charlie, you don't understand. I coulda had class . . . I coulda been somebody instead of a broken-down bum—which is what I am . . . I coulda been a contender."

You know, I cried when I see this scene. I saw the picher twice.

And so my heart swelled up real big when I see him walk up on this big stage to accept the Academy Award for the job he done in *On the Waterfront*. Elia Kazan, another friend, and a big writer today, won the Oscar for best director for his work directing the picher.

The picher won awards all over the world, and Marlon Brando was the youngest actor who ever got an Academy Award.

Marlon was never what the big shots call a conformer, but the guy was always for somebody who needed a break, and he always gave it. He helped *me* to meet some big people, and you know, like the Indian bit, or the Blacks. For these people he's right there without them asking.

Near the end of the Martha Raye Show run I get approached by M.G.M. and I sign a couple-a hunner-t'ousan-dollar deal with M.G.M. to turn my book into a movie.

After that I'm getting called all kinds of nice things in the newspaper. Like one guy said, "One of the most successful cases of rehabilitation ever known," whatever that means. All's I know is, the biggest fight of my life wasn't in the ring. It was with me, an I hadda win it or else. After I sign that deal with M.G.M., I know for sure that nobody gonna ever have to t'row a benefit for Rocky Graziano.

I was Martha Raye's boyfriend "Goombah" for over three years, an these was some of the happiest years of my life.

Nat Hiken, who became one of my best friends, is different from me like day and night, but for some reason we both like the same things and we go on makin a lot of scenes together.

It's gettin so I can't get on the street anymore without people stoppin me to say hello, and I give them all a few words and a big smile. How could I ever forget where I come from? I get so much show offers I gotta start turnin most of them down. When I'm on a show like "The Dunninger Mentalist Show," I think I have more fun than the audience. Only, I can't figure out how this guy Dunninger knows what's in my head.

A guy I learn a lot from is Henny Youngman, who they call king of the one-liners. Him and me do a show for A.B.C. after the fights on Friday

nights. You know, one-a those chitchat deals where we talk about fights
and joke with each other. Henny says, "How does a guy really feel if he's
in the can shaking time and he's gotta be separated from his girl or wife?
Guy must go crazy jealous thinking she's making it with even his best
friends."

And I says, I knew a guy in the can who had the wildest chick in the
world and he could bet a million dollars, if he had it, that she wasn't
fooling around with another guy.

"Why?" says Henry.

"She was doing time, too."

Two shots I do, different times, on Allen Funt's "Candid Camera," was
also a hell of a lot of fun. In one they use a real beauty parlor with
customers coming in. I got on one-a those white wraparound apron jobs,
and I'm supposed to be an Italian hairdresser. They hadda wait till a lady
comes in who don't recognize me. Then they tell this lady, "Wouldja
please try our new beautician? He just arrive from one-a the highest-
class places in Rome."

The customer was recommended to the place, and since she got
nobody in mind she takes me on. I talk to her in Little Italy gutter Italian,
mixed with a few words of broken English, and I'm pulling on her hair a
lil and patting it with my hands. All of a sudden she starts gettin a scared
look. I go into a drawer and I'm looking for a tool and I'm making like I
don't know what the hell I'm doing, banging everything around, and
believe me, I don't know what I'm doing. She's getting off the chair and
trying to undo the bib I put on her, and when I try to stop her she starts
like she's gonna scream, and that's when Allen Funt comes out. You
know the rest. Y'mean?

On the other deal with Funt, I gotta walk into a lunch counter, sit next
to some little guy and make sure he don't recognize me.

The puny guy I sat next to had ordered ham'n eggs. Soon as the waiter
put 'em in front of him, I grab the plate, slide it over, and start eating the
guy's eggs.

"Hey, waiter," the guy calls out. "Isn't them my eggs?"

"Yeah, what'cha let him take 'em for?"

The guy makes some of those double-take faces, which is saying what's with this bedbug next to me, but I know the way he's lookin me over he figures he better pass trouble up. So, he calls out, "Say waiter, could you fix me another order?'

"Shit, no," the waiter tells him. "Those are your eggs and you gotta pay for them."

The poor guy's about to fall off his counter chair, with looks you can't believe, when Allen walks in an says, "Smile, you're on Candid Camera."

What I like about these shows is, not only am I havin more fun than I ever have in my life but I'm also getting paid better and better as time passes by.

Now, when I'm in the street, and everyplace I go, everybody's asking me for my autograph. Cops who useta be my biggest enemy when I was a kid are now my friends. A few of my best friends, like Ralph the Gun, Nick Corsalini, and Sonny Grasso, are ex-detectives.

These cops don't tell me no more, "Ey, kid, you ain't singing the right tune. Move your fuckin Guinea chops, or you gonna get your ass worked over good!" And I don't have to spit out things like, yeah, over my fuckin dead body, and hear them tell me I ain't worth spit!

In fact, you know something? Even after all that grief they give me, I think maybe next life I come back as a cop. I could see today that there's more excitement chasing than being chased. It's a long time ago I give up thinking a square working guy with a blue shirt was some kind of a creep.

And let me tell you something else. When you hear a guy cryin that he's a loser, and he ain't never gonna be nothing but a loser all his life, just point at me. I popped out of the sack with three strikes and I never even went to bat. The horns were on me all my growin-up days, and without looking like they was ever gonna leave me. But you know something, I never give up. I hadda know it was possible to find a new life without kicking the bucket, or disappearing to someplace new. And today, here I am, Rocky Graziano! And I found my new life right in the place I wanted to be most, my New York City.

I don't care where I am, when I hear the songs "New York's My Town," or "New York, New York," I want to bust right out happy singing.

I have a lotta fun in Miami Beach too in those days, but this is still the place I gotta always come back to.

Ain't that something, after knockin myself out half my life, I come to find out some of the nicest things in the world is to respect the other guy and to always say please, thank you, and excuse me, and a guy don't have to yell or start t'rowin punches to make people notice him.

Not too many years before this, almost all my friends was guys with broken beaks and cauliflower ears. They still my friends, but now I got friends who are actors and some who are millionaires. I begin to know guys who are so rich they lend finance companies money. An I can't begin to tell ya how good that makes me feel. Just being around them makes me know how great everything is when I'm honest with me and everybody else. And another thing started happening to me, hanging around with these big shots is, I catch myself using bigger words and learning to talk better. But then, I quick realize it's the deez, dems, and doze that's making me rich, so I throw the dictionary into the garbage can and I stick with the street what I growed up in. Only thing is, whenever I run into guys from my old neighborhood, first thing they say is, "Ey, Rocky, where didja park the truck? You know, big as you got, you never change." And this makes me feel better than anything else they could tell me, because with these kinda guys it's still the most comfortable I ever feel.

And a lotta people, including some of my buddies, really believed I was Martha Raye's boyfriend. I got all kindsa cracks thrown at me everyplace I go. Sometimes I be driving along with my wife an kids in the car and if I stop at a red light, somebody was always yellin in the window, "Ey, Rocky, where's Martha?" They can't understand how she ain't in my car.

One time, my friend Perry Moss takes me and my wife Norma out on his boat, and it gets real foggy. He could barely see a fishing boat about fifty feet away, and Perry yells out, "Ey, which way is Port Jefferson?" And this fishing guy with a big hat and beard spots me right through the fog and yells out, "Hey, Rocky, how's ya girl Martha." It's good my wife understand.

But I gotta tell ya, that Martha is one hell of a woman. Many times I saw her passin out money, or askin her ex-husband Nick Condos, who was also her manager, to make out a check for fifty or a hunnerd for some broken-down actor or actress who was down on their heels.

You gotta know that even the greatest car in the world's gonna wear out, but not this broad. She just goes on and on. Her funny faces and her big voice make her reign for years as the funniest woman in the world. A windstorm, with a big mouth like rubber, but still one-a the most beautiful broads ya ever seen.

For one thing, *I* sure learn a lot from Martha, and her and Hiken sure prove it to me every day that a guy needs a lotta faith, an you don't need a college or even a high-school education to make it big in our beautiful America. I find this out a long time ago, when I see that there's a lotta guys with big school educations, working for people who never have no education at all. And you'll even find guys with college degrees stretched out in doorways on the Bowery today. Go look for yourself.

Goes to show you when they say, one guy's loss is another guy's gain. Because for me, and ya can bet your sweet fuckin life on it, success in this business was my answer to everything.

And as for Nat Hiken and the way he masterminded that Martha Raye Show for three years, what else could a guy call him but a wizard? During the run of the show, newspapers useta estimate that any one audience could be thirty million people.

It's now 1955 and people still mobbing me on the street and now I'm gettin more popular than even when I was champ. In the ring it was fight fans, but during the Martha Raye show, *everybody* becomes my fan. Something ya can't help is that a lotta wrongoes sidle up to you too, but I blow soon as I feel the draft.

Now I start making loads of commercials, and I belong to all the actors' associations, and I got an actor manager, and I get deals for shows on my own, while Nat Hiken makes hisself a million dollar deal with C.B.S.

A guy once told me, there's that one time in your life when you happen to be in the right place at the right time, and if you goof it, it never comes again. That guy hadda be up there, because for me it came twice. Once when I become Middleweight Champ of the World, and the second time when an angel by the name of Nat Hiken come up to Stillman's lookin for me. I remember how he first look at me then, like I was a little bad boy you gotta be nice to, or else. An there was times he make me remember a little kid running home to his mom crying because of something that happen. My mom would wash my face and comb my hair and then fix a piece of bread with olive oil an vinegar on it, and it was the greatest thing I ever eat in my whole life. That's the way I sometimes feel about Nat Hiken. He washed my face and combed my hair and gave me a piece of oil-an-vinegar bread.

T W E L V E

Kid by the name of Jimmy Dean, looks me up one day an tells me he's been picked to play me in the movie. There's not too much out about the kid yet. Maybe a year before, he won a Donaldson and a Perry award for the part of an Arab servant that he played on Broadway in *The Immoralist*. But just the past April, Elia Kazan's movie called *East of Eden* was released, and everybody who saw Dean in his first starring role just flipped over the kid.

The newspapers started writing about him being a rebel, copyin my friend Marlon Brando, being a crazy young beat, and things like that, but they rave about his acting.

I like the kid right off, and I could see it's true that he acts and talks like Brando. He tells me he just finished making a picher called *Giant* for

Warner Brothers, and there's another picher in the can about to be released called *Rebel Without a Cause.*

Dean asks if he could hang around, and maybe I show him how to t'row some punches. The kid also tells me he's rehearsin for another part as a fighter in Ernest Hemingway's "The Battler," a special show they makin for TV.

I figure we gonna have some fun palling around together, and then he's gotta go back to California on some kind of business.

On October 1st 1955, I pick up a newspaper and get smacked with a headline, "James Dean Dies in Fiery Crash Death."

The paper goes on to say how he always like to speed his German Porscht at a hunnerd twenty miles an hour on the California highways, and how the troopers had grabbed him for speeding a few times. I don't guess they was surprised when he missed a curve. It sure scare the shit outa me. I watched my driving for a long time afta that.

Jimmy Dean had just turned twenty-four, and aftawards, when his other two pichers come out, he gets more famous than any live star around, but what good's it gonna do him?

Right away they gotta come up with a guy to do this "Battler" TV thing, which is about a forty-year-old punchy panhandler. For this, they pick on another up'n coming actor, Paul Newman.

Robert Wise, the director signed to do my picture, *Somebody Up There Likes Me,* spots this kid doing a terrific job on the TV show an signs him to take Dean's place in my story too.

The studio arranges for me to meet Paul Newman and he shows up for the meeting wearin beat up slacks and a T-shirt. We click it off right away, when he grins at me like he's known me all my life.

"Whataya say, Rock!" he says. "I read your book, and I saw you fight. It's amazing to see you are a man of letters."

He makes everybody laugh, and even though he kids me I could see right off there ain't one thing phony about this guy. Maybe there was. He was too good lookin. In fact, the guy is pretty. That didn't matter because I knew they could fix up an flatten his nose for the part, an if they couldn't I do it for them. I could see in the guy's eyes that he was a fighter. He's got bright blue eyes, but when you look in 'em you see a hard look dancing around inside. Only one other guy I ever see these same eyes on an that was another friend of mine, Frank Sinatra. When their blue eyes spot a wise guy, the eyes say, "Don't fuck with me, man!"

At that time, Newman was about twenty-nine or thirty, maybe three, four years younger than me, and his weight, around a hunnerd and sixty, was what I weighed during my best fighting days.

I find out the guy's an all-round athlete. Tennis, skis, swims like a fish, great ballplayer. The guy not only does 'em all, he does 'em good, and now I'm gonna teach him how to fight in the ring. When you see this guy with his clothes on, he's a fooler. I find out fast in the gym that Paul is a lot stronger than he looks.

To get back to that first meet in the office, he says to me when we're leaving, "Rock, what do you say, we go out and bust up a few cans of beer?"

I got nothing snapping at my ass, so I go along with the program. This guy wasn't kiddin about the beer. He drank up four cans of beer an ate two bags of popcorn while I was still working on my first can. I never seen a guy pop popcorn the way he shot 'em into his mouth one-a the time. Not one kernel hit the deck.

Then he wants to shoot some pool, and here I figure I got a chump and maybe I take 'im for a few bets. I practically lived in the poolroom when I was a wise guy, an I know I shoot a pretty good stick, but this rube ain't a rube. He's a fuckin whiz. If I didn't know for sure he's an actor, I'da swore the guy's a pool hustler.

I start taking him up to Stillman's, an hardly nobody pays him much attention because he ain't that big yet. I got 'im working out every day and I can see the guy is straight. All we gotta do is make a meet an he's right on the minute, a hunnerd percent honest and a woid like a bond.

I ask him once if he wanna play some golf, which is then my favorite sport. He tells me he never plays golf. Too rich for his blood. But we hop in the car and go out to the course. Even though I play a pretty good game of golf, in the seventies, this guy starts beatin me right off. He's like a champ. Ey! I ask him, how come you bullshit me you don't play golf? An he says, he don't, but drive balls, yes. He useta work on a golf drivin range and drove and putt a million balls, but never played the game.

I never seen such a natural athlete in all my life.

Paul also told me he's worked on a farm in the summer as a laborer, and this explains the muscles. He was born in Shaker Heights, suburb of Cleveland, Ohio. His father ran a sporting good store in Cleveland, and I guess all this equipment hanging around made Paul go the way he did with athletics. Paul also work in his father's store as a clerk.

Paul Newman ain't an East Side sort of a kid, but while he's hanging around me, more an more, I see him getting to be like all the guys I always know. We go down to my old neighborhood, Tenth Street, and he hangs around like he's been there all his life. We shoot some pool, and go to the club to play cards, and he talks to the boys just like he's always been there. I tell him the only difference coming from where he did and coming from here like me was, if we ever got wiped out by a fire, total loss would have been about eighteen cents.

I know how I walk an I know it's my own fighter's walk, and now I see he's walking just like me, with what a newspaper guy called a "shoulder-shruggin shuffle." An when I catch him copying the way I talk, I gotta remind him," Ey! Din I hear ya say to somebody that ya had a Bachelor Degree in English?"

Up in Stillman's he get better and better. When he punches the light or heavy bag, he does it better than a lotta pros, and when I spar with him he t'rows some pretty good punches. I was a pro fighter over ten years and never got hoit, and now I'm gonna get kilt by an actor.

I tell Paul he's ready, an ask him one day, serious, if he wants me to book him a four-rounder. You never hoid a guy so adamant when he says, "No, sir! Not on your fucking life!"

I know the guy is beginning to feel like a brother when he starts borrowing my Cadillac. I like the guy, so I give 'im my heap so he can ride in a classy car. What could I tell you?

I remember how Paul was always trying to pump me about my family. One time, Bob Wise and Paul try to get me drunk to make me open up. While we drinking, to try to get me started they both tell me their life histories.

While they're trying ta get *me* bombed, they both get so smashed they're on the floor and they're trying to hold on. They didn't know it was a habit with bartenders saying, "Rocky, have a few rounds on me." I hadda pour both in seprit cabs at four-thirty in the mornin.

When they see me again, they laugh up a storm saying how they tried to get me drunk so's I'd talk, and all they wound up with was hangovers that the slamming shut of an asprin box lid could have toined inta nervous breakdowns. They shoulda only known how some-a the toughest cops on the lower East Side useta try to get me to open up when I was growin up there. And they never wound up with any hangover. They wound up daffy.

The place M.G.M. set up to do the indoor filming, where they needed sets, is a New York place called the "West Coast Studios," and it's right here on Fifty Seventh Street. They did all the filming here, either on the streets or in this place.

When they bring all their equipment down to the East Side, you shoulda hoid the people cheering, like it was one-a the biggest celebrations ya ever seen.

Sal Mineo, who played the part of one of my klepto pals, says to me one day, "Ya know something, Rocky, this is one picha I don't have to act in. Down here on the East Side is just like the Italian neighborhood I came from up in the Bronx. We useta do all these things up there too."

The guys playing my gang are doing all kinds of crooked things, and instead of these citizens looking to kill 'em, they're cheering. The gang strips a car, wheels, radio, and all, while the camera guys are filming. Then the cameras follow them around while they running away from cops or going into their hangouts. In one scene the miniature Mafiosos highjack a bunch of furs from a truck in broad daylight, and then run off down the street, yelling and holding the furs in the air like they was trophies and they expect the people watching to cheer. And ya know something, if my people down there saw you swipin something from a rich guy, they did cheer.

When I remember these things I gotta be honest and admit it was big ball then, no matta how tough it got sometimes.

I watch them filming Paul Newman sellin the swag to fences, and the guy does a hell of a job on playin me. He plays me so good I think he's my brudda. In fact, it scares me a little thinking how I coulda spent my whole life in the can for what I useta think were kicks.

They also got in some pretty good shots of the neighborhood. Lanza's Restaurant, the candy store, the poolroom, and the club.

Paul looks at me with a grin once, and he says, "Tell me, Rocky, did you ever have one fuckin dull day in your whole life?"

Still there's one part of the movie I see them filming one day and I squawk like a sonofabitch, telling all the big shots they gotta change it. I even almost punch some guys in the mouth because they telling me it's too late to change, and it would cost a fortune, they'd have to hold up production, and all that shit.

The thing I don't like is the apartment they made out to be where I lived as a kid. Sure, the tenement house was a broken-down rat and roach trap, but inside the apartment we lived in was always clean. In the movie they made it out a scurvy, dirty hole that wasn't fit for animals. I gotta say, that even though my mom was sick a lot, and they never had any good furniture because we were so poor, she still kept the house always neat 'n clean, an the curtains an sheets, torn an sewed I don't know how many times, were still always washed 'n ironed. To the day my mom died, she loved her family and did all the family washing on a scrubboard in the kitchen washtub. And she useta get down on the linoleum floors and scrub 'em with a brush, on her hands an knees.

Another thing they do in the movie, I tell them I don't like, is how brutal and dirty they make my old man. They never once even show him with a fresh shave, and always in a torn beat-up dirty undershirt.

Don't get me wrong, my old man was no saint, but he was no pig either. Just like I says, when he come home, he beat the shit outa me, scare my mom, and make me fight with Joey, but this was when he was outa work, comin home drunk and mean, and figuring the world give him one big fuckin swift kick in the ass. The guy had a lot to be bitter about. Whenever he come home sober from looking for work, which he couldn't find, he sit at the window an when I look at him sometime, I'd hear him callin somebody all kinds of son of a bitches, and there was nobody there. Then he rub his eyes and look like he was gonna cry. If he catch me watchin him, he quick yell, "Get the fuck outa my sight," and I dash out the house before I catch a beating, I know my father today better than anybody in this world, but in those days I didn't know how to tell those movie people about him. I could tell you this, my pop was mean and belligerent, but only because he had reasons in his head. He was never a slob.

They make one scene in the movie exactly the way it was. That's the time I come back from Chicago as Middleweight Champion of the World. The old neighborhood got this motorcade waiting for me, an they put me sitting high on the back of this big open car, with my wife Norma and my closest people, and they parade me around the neighborhood, blowing car horns outa ya mind. The whole avenue is decorated with signs with my name on 'em, and banners, and all kinds of ribbons, and they make me feel like some kind of a king.

That hadda be one-a the most beautiful days of my life.

Now, when I watch Paul Newman and Pier Angeli doing it for the cameras, ya know something, I hadda sneak out my handkerchief, and wipe a couple tears outa my eyes.

To do the part of Tony Zale, the producers decide, since he don't have to do any lines, they get Zale hisself. They brought him inta town and paid him good money, like about fifteen hunnerd a week, and it looks like they got 'im scheduled for about six, eight weeks. They put him and his family up in a big hotel, and give 'em a chauffeured limousine at their beck and call.

Now they start filming his shots. They school Zale on what he gotta do. Easy as pie, no grief, no sweat. All he gotta do is fight natural but pull his punches.

Paul is in top shape and he learnt how to t'row a pretty good punch hisself, but he ain't no match for an ex-middleweight champ, let alone any pro. When one of us guys hit ya, even long after a fighter's washed up, if you ain't conditioned you'll think you stopped a train.

They tell Zale to let Newman get in punches, that Newman's gonna pull the head punches but not the body punches. But then, if you know Zale, anything Newman can t'row is gonna feel like powderpuffs against "The Man of Steel," as the sports writers call Zale.

They warm up in the ring, doing some footwork and shadow boxing, gettin useta each other being there, and the camera crew goes to work. The real ring gong goes off and they're in there t'rowin punches, and it look pretty real to me. All of a sudden, Newman grabs his side, doubles up a little, and yells, "Whoa, man! You trying to fucking kill me?"

I jump up in the ring and grab the Polack. "Ey!" I yell at 'im. "What the fuck ya doin?

"I din mean it, Rock," he apologizes, but what's the difference when the guy is hoit.

I could see Newman's afraid now. He's finding out a few things he didn't know. In show business it's like I always say, "Ya done great" and people saying, "Good luck," before a scene. But here in the ring, a guy better have that luck. Usually, they got a stunt man ready to take the falls but this guy, Paul, is what they call a perfectionist, and he's gotta do it all hisself. Now he's seeing ya could get your mouth busted up and all yer teet knocked out. If he don't know before he stepped in the ring, he knows now, ain't nuttin like yer healt'.

When Zale's in there swinging, all he's gotta do is hear a bell an he don't know no more that it ain't for real. To him the gong means go, just like the green signal light on the corner. Those three fights he have with me, that a news guy called the most savage in history, had to leave him a lil whacky.

Now everybody's up on the ring apron, having a big conversation about how Zale gotta pull his punches, this ain't for real, and if he ain't careful he could hurt the star bad. Zale is nodding his head serious, mumbling he's sorry and don't worry, while he's punching his gloves together.

Newman looks a little pale when the gong rings and they start t'rowing punches again. Afta a few seconds I look at Zale's face and I could see by that, and the way he's t'rowing punches, that he's slipping into his "for real" stance again. He shakes up Newman with a coupla light hooks to the head, and then comes in with a right to the stomach and Newman is down on the deck gasping for air.

I jump in the ring and start massaging Newman, and now he's

moaning pretty good. Zale's got a dumb look on his face, sayin, "Wha' happen? What'd I do?"

Took Newman a good five minutes to get all his breath back. First thing he says, when he could talk, was, "That's it!" He throw up his hands, goes through the ropes, and yell to somebody, "Take off these fucking gloves." That was it for that day. Newman wasn't about to get kilt doing this picher or any other.

Tony Zale blew the whole bit because he was like the whore who don't know the customer comes first. They pay Tony off for what he done so far, and go looking for a guy to take his place, while Newman's recouping from his banged-up ribs which, I gotta tell you, were sore for a month.

One of the M.G.M. guys is in a bar one day, and he can't get over how much the bartender looks like Zale, broken nose an all. He tells the guy, "Ey, you know you look just like Tony Zale," and the guy says, "I hear that all the time."

"You know how to box?"

"Howja think I got to look like Zale?" The bartender tells this guy he was on the college boxing team, and he was an amateur champ.

In no time they sign the surprised guy up with some pretty good paydays, and he puts in about four to six weeks. This guy's real good in the ring, and when he's in there swinging he looks just like Zale. It also give this bartender a big break, because now he's an actor and different studios want him for all kinds of fight scenes.

When they stage the championship fight, with the announcer, crowds, and all, you'd swear it was the real thing.

They put all my writer friends at ringside playing their own selves reporting the fight. They had Jesse Abramson of the *Tribune,* Caswell Adams of the *Journal-American,* Jim Boyach of the *Pittsburgh Courier,* Lester Bromberg of the *Telegram,* Al Buck of the *Post,* Jim Jennings of the *Mirror,* Joe Nichols of the *Times,* Murray Rose of the *Associated Press,* Sam Taub of the *Sports Bulletin,* Gene Ward of the *Daily News,* and Harry Wismer, The Mutual Network sports broadcaster. These guys were all great friends. When I was comin up in the fight game, they covered all my fights and never rap me once.

I hope they all make a few good paydays.

While Newman continues on with the film he gets inta the part so good, he must be beginnin to believe he's me. One night, when he's pretty good beer-stoned, he's drivin outa a restaurant lot in Queens where he's living, he drives right across the lawn, rippin up shrubbery on the way to the street. Before jumpin off the curb, he tries to soccer the johnny pump across to the other side of the road with his car. The water from the broken fire hydrant starts shootin all over, and a patrol car cop sees it and Newman speedin away. They chase him down, cut 'im off, an when he gets out of his banged-up car he says he's Rocky Graziano.

The cop says, "My name is Rocky too, and you're under arrest!"

The way I read it in the papers, Paul starts to t'row a punch, tellin the cop, "Put up yer dukes!" He's still got Stillman's gym on his ass, but it don't work with these cops. They grab him, t'row handcuffs on 'im, and take 'im in for a night in the growler. That's watcha call getting into the part right from the horse's mouth.

When he comes up before the judge, he got a nice husky fine, and hadda pay for all the damages. And the name of the arresting officer was really Rocky. Rocco "Rocky" Caggiano.

When the picher *Somebody Up There Likes Me* comes out, it fast become a big smash, and also gets nominated for a load of awards. Paul Newman tells me the picher did more for his career than anything he done. One thing I could say, he got plenty of schoolin on tough guys, and he enjoyed every minute. The picture was definitely the bullet that shot 'im to the stars, and nothing was gonna stand in this blue-eyed wonder's way no more.

I can't begin to tell ya the kick I got poisonally, reading all those great reviews by the columnists like Sidney Skolsky, Peter Maas, an Archer Winston, and the things they say about me, Newman, and the picher.

To interview Paul Newman is another thing. When writer guys wanna talk to Newman they gotta meet the guy in a place like Downey's on Eighth Avenue, because the guy don't dress up for nobody if he don't want to. An ya know he ain't gonna get into the "21" Club or Sardi's wearin his regular uniform, which you know is jeans an T-shirt. All the newspaper guys was sayin the same about him as they said about Jimmy

Dean, that he was copyin Brando, but me for one, I knew, whatcha saw was whatcha got. If ya ask me, I say all three of them, Brando, Dean, and Newman were copyin me.

Newman tole a newspaper guy, "If there's any moral to be drawn, don't try followin in Rocky's path. You couldn't possibly be tough enough to survive to write your life story and have a movie made about you."

Paul also tole a reporter, "I had no trouble getting into the part. Rocky was very helpful, a lot of fun, and a joy to be with. I didn't, as reported, try to imitate him; rather, I tried to find a balance between him and me. I tried to play a Graziano, not the Graziano. He never once took offense at my jives, or my mumbling, and shuffling. He'd just grin and say things like, 'Ey, you know you do that better than me.' The part I played still had to be brutal, or it wouldn't make sense. Rocky's whole early life had been the business of survival."

The picture was released in 1956, an Paul showed up for the premier carryin a six-pack of beer. The only reason he didn't bring his own popcorn, he knew he'd find that inside.

My story helped make Newman the hottest property in Hollywood, but it also did a lot for me.

THIRTEEN

After the movie was released I can't begin to tell you how my mailbox starts jamming up with checks and invitations for everything under the sun. As long as a one-shot appearance is for an honest charity—kids, do-good organizations, straight politicians, or maybe just a friend who wants me to show up in some restaurant to help the joint with me just being there, then I don't mind doing it. But now I begin to see that there's a lot of characters looking to use me. Things like some executive looking to impress a business connection or close a big deal with me an Norma along, getting paid off with a high-priced steak dinner. I gotta tell you, it don't take me long to shrewd up on these kinds of users. Also, the big business affairs, sales meetings, manufacturers' conventions, things like that, where they want me to show up on a stage, say a half-million words, an get paid off with some kinda phony brass-plate award. Yeah, I learned pretty good. I don't turn them down anymore but I make them come up with top bucks if they want me to show.

I ain't looking to hold anybody up, y'mean? But there's still times when I figure I got the best part of my young life to get even for. And I know money alone don't do it, but it sure as hell helps.

With everybody looking to me for appearances I know I gotta now try to select. One of the first TV shows I do after the movie come out was a Sunday spectacula called "Atlantic City Holiday." Besides me, it's got Polly Bergen, Jack Carter, Bill Haley, Jonathan Winters, and Pat Boone. All the shows got top stars and it look like the fun I have doing them is never gonna end. I also do a show with Buster Keaton. Rest in peace. Another, I'm in "The Steve Allen Show," which was the biggest thing on the tube. A show I'm a regular on, during that year, was called "Can Do" with MC Robert Alda. In this the audience participated for prizes. On the show with me are people like Dave Garroway, Sal Mineo, Gypsy Rose Lee, an Polly Bergen. All these people I mention were some-a the hottest TV people around.

The only show I'm on that year where people are asleep is a radio show, "The Morning Star," which I hosted for one week, as a sub for Ernie Kovacs, rest in peace. The reason they was asleep is because I come on at 6:30 A.M. It ended at 9:00 A.M. To take a lil of the strain off I got friends like Phil Rizzuto, Toni Arden, Yogi Berra, and Allen Dale to come in and give me a hand.

Norma and me were still seein a lot of Paul Newman during those days, and we even go to Grossinger's, a resort up in the Catskills, where we spend nice weekends getting kicks outa the top comics in the country, who always play what they call the "borscht circuit." Norma loves to go horseback ridin with Paul Newman. And me, I play him a lot of golf in which he still beats the ass off me, and like I tole ya, I play a pretty good game.

It's now 1957, and every day I wake up breathing I gotta pinch myself to know the guy I'm lookin at in the mirror is really me. It makes me wonder if that guy upstairs, and all those guys down here, didn't pick me out just to show it could be easy long as you could fight your way outa a paper bag.

This same year I'm getting some shots at the hottest things around, like repeats on "The Steve Allen Show," and I also make two movies. I gotta go to Hollywood to do one of these which stars me and my ole spaghetti buddy, Zsa Zsa Gabor. It was called *Country Music Holiday,* and it was produced by Ralph Serpi for Paramount. In it I play a song-business executive.

Going to the coast makes me get together with Frankie Sinatra and Dean Martin, and all their other pals, and these, like I always say, were the best times-a my life. And since Frankie is now a big song exec too, he gives me a lotta pointers on how to play this part.

The other movie I do was called *Mr. Rock 'n Roll,* and I do this one with Teddy Randazzo and Allen Freed.

As for Frankie and Dean, far as I'm concerned there ain't two other guys in the whole world like 'em. We all know Frankie had a couple of bad downs, wife problems, career, things like that, and me being close, I'm one of the happiest guys in the world, seeing him punch his way to the top even stronger than ever. And this makes his old columnist enemies like Dorothy Kilgallen and Lee Mortimer start sharpshootin again, and Sheila Graham writes that Frank has a God complex.

Me, for one, could tell you that Frank never preach to anybody on how to treat him, or look to him. He never even acted like he *wanted* people to fall all over him like they do. People worship the guy because *they* wanted to, and only his talent make them do it.

Anyway, Frank's too strong to get hurt with this shit anymore, but it still makes him mad enough to call 'em all kindsa names which other people print. But, for every knock they give him in a newspaper there's ten guys gotta be honest and tell it like it is.

One of my old trainers, Al Silvani, was then with Frankie, too. Frank hired the guy like a bodyguard and trainer to keep him in shape. He also got Al lots of small parts in movies. When I go to Hollywood, I see Al too, and we talk about the old days at Stillman's gym and Al's biggest fighter, Tami Mauriello. Sure is nice to run into a guy who takes me back to my roots once in awhile.

You know, I also gotta have a few more crap-shooting stories under my coiffure. Here I want to tell you a few things I know about a guy called Dino Crocetti, then you'll know why I love the guy, and I'm sure he gotta love me a little too. Yeah, this guy t'rew out a pair of dice and the roll took him right to the stars. Maybe it don't happen right away, but what's the difference if that's where the ghee wound up? When I say he t'rew out a set of dice, I mean just that. Not too many people know that Dino used to be a stickman and card dealer in a Steubenville, Ohio, gamblin joint before he makes it big in show business. The guy had poor immigrant folks from Abruzzi, Italy, the whole bit.

Dean even try boxing for a living before he got discovered as a talented singer. After he made it he got his fighter's nose straightened out, but you could still see some of the cuts over his eyebrows and a cut on the lip. One time when he's telling me why he quit fighting I tell him the cuts make him better looking.

All us Italian kids was in the same boat in those days. The only thing different about the boat today is the color of the kids that's in it.

When I'm with them, same like with Frank, I love these guys because they're me. They just talk to ya a little better, but we all came up from those same rough beginnins and that makes us all brothers. Dean's a lot like me in a lotta ways, like he's always gotta be with the guys too. An this the women can never understand. Dino likes playin rough, boxing with the boys, and like me he could play golf all day long, and talk rough like a truck driver when he wants to.

Dean Martin made a lotta big money in show biz, first teamed up with Jerry Lewis and then on his own as a singer. All the great movies he made helped too, but this guy never changed.

I can never get tired of telling you what guys like Dean do to me. Once in a while, when I'm in their company, I think about me being out in the winter trying to steal some coal to keep our ass warm, and now, with these guys, I swell up so much inside I think I'm gonna bust. All you kids today who don't think you got a chance because you come from the asshole side-a the tracks just take a good look at guys like us and say to yourself, if a skinny pipe-job like that Frankie, a dice hustler like Dino, and a bum like Rocky could make it, so can I.

Dean once tole me he started singing because it hurt less than gettin punched in the mouth and it pay better than moppin windshields. He says to me, why don't I become a singer like he did after he quit boxing, so I does an empersonation of him singing, "Everybody Loves Somebody Sometime," and the gang broke up an roll on the floor. I thought I was good.

You know somethin? Maybe I don't like to wear a tie and maybe I was born to be a bum, but I know why they laugh, and I know I never be a bum no more, no matter how I talk. Even though I still can't stand people putting makeup on me, I don't think actors are sissies anymore. I find out a long time ago that fuckin with some of them is like fuckin with some of the toughest guys ever lived. I remember when I useta say, if I had any real guts I'd be out sticking up a liquor store like a real man. Lucky for me that thinking about jail bars and about nightsticks bouncing off my skull kept me straight when I needed to. And now I know, what really takes guts is gettin up before a crowda people to make 'em laugh, cry, or whatever.

While Dean keeps on makin one good move after another, I'm makin a lot of good moves myself. Maybe not on their scale, but for a guy like me, who got thrown out of the sixth grade, it wasn't bad. Besides making that movie with Zsa Zsa in Hollywood for Ralph Serpi, I even become a self-appointed expert on juvenile crime. And believe me, when I go out talking to kids in schools, clubs, an homes for bad boys, I give it to them right from the horse's mouth. A lotta people say it's their folks make a lotta them go screwy. I don't know. When a kid comes into the house today wearin one of them black plastic jackets with names on the back like "The Skulls" or "The Undertakers," I think they even bulldoze their old man. With some-a these kindsa kids, if I was their folks, I'd wait till they was out of the house, pack up the furniture, call a movin van, and take off without leaving no forwarding address.

All their pops say is things like, "When you go in your room, don't play your TV too loud." What happened to those raps in the mouth like I useta get when I was a kid?

How'd I get off on that kick?

Anyway, when I come back from Hollywood, I got another nice shot waiting, and that was going on Jerry Lester's "Open House," with Dagmar. Never seen a girl with a chest like that in my life. Filled the whole TV tube with just her tits.

Durin that part of my life, I never had it sweeter. I'm on the Gary Moore show, and even the Tony Franscioso show.

FOURTEEN

Everybody you have something to do with changes your life. Anyway, that's what a guy told me once, and that's what this book's about, but here I gotta tell you about a guy who goes around telling everybody I changed *his* life.

In September of 1957, I'm out in the street in front of the Stage Delicatessen, looking to flag an empty cab to go to the Yankee Stadium to see the Carmine Basilio–Ray Robinson fight for the middleweight championship. Cab stops, and this guy who looks like a Brooklyn round-face apple-cheek character while I'm gettin in he yells, "Ey! Rocky Graziano! Jesus Christ, it's you!"

Right away the cabbie starts telling me he seen almost all my New York fights. He knows so much about my fight record that I know the

guy's gotta be a genuine fight fan. I could see on the card with the picture
that his name is Bernie, so I start callin him that.

Then, while we're goin uptown, the guy is tellin me his story, about
how he was the sickest kind of a gambler, came from the Bronx, had a big
successful restaurant there for ten years, and he blew it an all his savins
on a big gambling spree.

The guy ain't tellin me the story crying. He's telling it so funny that he
got me pissin in my pants. He says nobody would even talk to him no
more, and everybody even stopped sending him Christmas cards.

He stops at a light and I says, hold it. I get out an go sit in the front seat
with him, so I could hear him better. I tell him I useta be a pretty fair crap
shooter and horse player myself. What could I tell you?

Bernie tells me he gotta stop at a gas station because I got him so
excited it's affectin his kidneys. When he comes back from the toilet, he
says, "You know something, Champ, you got me so rattled, when I went
to that john and see the sign, 'Clean Restrooms,' I started to clean them."

Then he goes on from where he left off and says, "I listen to every
fuckin body, and anybody and their uncle, and cousins and brothers, and
any sonofabitch who says they could get me even. I borrow money from
every shylock in town and run outa them too. I promise them the moon,
kill their mother-in-law, anything, to break them even. Last shy I plead
with for a new bankroll, I promise, I pay tomorrow, even though ain't a
chance in the world I pay him back ever. When I promise him tomorrow,
he says, 'I could be dead tomorrow.' Whatta ya worried about, I tell the
guy, I swear on my mother I put it in your coffin. I was like a drowning
guy grabbin the straw. Even though I'm sharp enough to know all the
gimmicks, I got sucked in by everybody. To show you how stupid I was, I
even got sucked in by those touts who buy two-dollar tickets on every
horse in the race an then keep comin up to you showing you only the
winners, and telling you how they're in with the jocks, or they got this
unbeatable system, but they betting small because they're temporarily
suffering from the shorts.

"What else they gotta lose but your money?"

Bernie don't ever come up for air, but he's funny so I listen. He goes on
telling me, "If a horseshoe is supposed to be lucky what good did the

four do the horses I bet on? Most of them came in last and next to last."

I keep telling the guy he shoulda been a comedian. He says, he once had a little shot. One place where he hustled as a waiter he doubled as MC for the two-bit acts they useta have there. He says, if he had any sense the thing he shoulda done was hang hisself a long time ago. Bernie says, "Here I am, completely broke, blew my whole life away, thousans, and now I gotta push this fuckin cab around New York for a lousy eighteen bucks a night, very down an disgusted, just so's I could go on feeding my wife and kids. One thing I gotta tell you. Losing all my money brought our family closer-together. We hadda move to a smaller place." I'm easing the character along but you can't help but break up, the way he's telling me his tale of woe.

"You know, Rocky?" he says. "One time I'm leavin the track after the last race, beat out of all my foldin stuff. You know how you do. I start shaking down all my pockets and whatta ya know? Don't you think I come up with a ten-dollar bill from a pocket where I forgot I stashed it. I'm so fucking mad about the bundle I lose that I eat the sawbuck yelling like a crazy man that they wasn't gonna get that too!"

Another story Bernie tells me, he's getting ready to leave his bar hangout for the track with a thousan–buck bankroll one day when the bartender asks him to buy a couple of raffle tickets on a box of cheer.

"The box was filled with good liquor," Bernie says, "So I buy two fifty-cent chances and take off for the track. I come back to the bar after the races, stone broke, blew the whole fuckin bundle! Soon as I walk in the door, the bartender yells out excited, here's the big winner, and he puts the box of cheer on the bar, saying 'It's yours, Bernie, you won it.' Here I am, looking for eight new shylocks or a pushover bank to rob, and I win a fuckin box of liquor. I pick up the box with the twelve bottles and with a A-One yell, I t'row the whole fuckin box of cheer over my head an across the room. If you don't think I was a candidate for a white coat, you better believe it."

About this time, I'm wondering if this Bernie might get the idea to use his cab for some kind of a bullet, and with me in it.

Bernie says, "I useta be ready to bet on anything. I woulda even bet a guy I could lean outa a window further than him. This woulda been one of the few bets I'da won, even though I wouldn't have been around no more to collect it. In those days if a guy shook my arm, my eyes woulda spun like the cherries on a slot machine.'

"I gotta tell you this one, Rocky," he says. "One night I dream the number five. Without an alarm clock I woke up at exactly five o'clock. It was the fifth day of the week, on the fifth of May, which just happen to be the fifth month. I know this gotta be the one luckiest day of my life that God put there for a reason. I drive out to the track and gets parked in section five in a space which is number five. I go up to buy my admission ticket and the guy who sells it to me has the number five on a badge on his hat. I wait for the fifth race, go to window five, and I'm the fifth guy in line. I bet five bucks on number five, the longest, biggest odds in the race. My horse come in fifth. One of these nights I'm gonna aim this junk-box cab out of New York and run away from home. Tell me, you think it's better I drive off a dock with me in the cab?"

While we driving across the bridge over the Harlem River, Bernie says, "You got two cents?"

I says, "What for?"

An he says, "For two cents, I let you out here an drive right through that railing."

You know somethin? I was afraid to give him the two cents, but kiddin, I say, you do that, how you gonna collect this fare?

"Don't worry. You can send it with the undertaker."

Then he tells me, "You know, Rocky, one day I'm leaving the track, broke, except for a few coins in my jacket pocket. Next to me is another kookoo loser, Tony Lip, who I go to the track with. In the parking lot I yell out, mother-fuckin sonsabitches, an I heave the pocket change as far as I could. I'm still cursing the nags, the jocks, the starters, the track, and everybody else's brother, while I'm driving out the parkin lot. I spot a pole up ahead an I say to The Lip for two cents I run my car right into that pole. This jerk was more stupid than me. He takes out two cents an gives it to me, figurin I'm kiddin. 'Hold on!' I yells, an crash! Right into the pole. I took one look, radiator driven into the motor, bumper wrapped aroun the pole, an water runnin out on the ground. I say to Tony Lip, let's go! If he didn't have the subway fare, I'da hadda walk all the way back to the Bronx."

I'm glad I din' give you the two cents, I told him. Even though I could see the guy's a little wacky, he's so funny I keep telling him he should be a comedian and tell these stories to an audience, just like he's telling me.

"I love comedy," he says, "but who the fuck wants to hear my problems? The only guys you can tell them to are guys like you who ain't got no problems. How many guys like you, you gonna find? And, like I didn't have enough problems today, I hadda go pick up a fare that makes me see myself better. Now I know I gotta go hang myself."

This guy Bernie is doin everything to make me laugh harder, because it's making him happy to look at hisself that way. But now we getting to the Stadium and he starts getting sad, acting like he's gonna lose the best friend he ever had. I reach over with a five-dollar bill, and as he takes it he says, "Gee, Rocky," and almost like he wants to cry, "I hope I see you again."

I tell him "Quick, pull into that parkin lot." His reflex turn the cab right in. "Get out," I says. "You're goin inside to see the fight with me."

"You gotta be kiddin," he says, while he takes the ticket from the parkin ghee.

Bernie ain't too tall but he's got husky arms, one of which I grab an rush him along, while he's looking back at the cab, shakin his head like he can't believe his eyes.

I just happen to have an extra ticket, I tell him. The guy's face is lit up now like you never seen a face lit. I whips him right up to first row ringside. Perry Como an Joe Louis got the seats either side of us. I introduce Bernie to them as my best friend, and when he shakes their hand I know just what's going on inside the guy. He whispers to me, "Jesus Christ! Perry Como and Joe Louis!" He's shaking his head. "I can't believe it," he keeps whispering. "Wasn't I drivin' a cab half hour ago?" He says, "Our seats are so close to the ring, we gonna have to defend ourselves when they start fighting."

The guy give me and Perry Como and Joe Louis and everybody around us a million laughs, screaming toward the ring and making cracks while the fights is on. I really got to like the guy.

The fight was one of the greatest, with Basilio beating Robinson for the championship, with a fifteen-round decision.

Everybody's running to get out and I got Bernie by the arm, going fast by all the fans looking to stop me. We run right out the gate and into a cab. I swear the guy's in another world.

As we pull away from the curb, Bernie remembers he's a cab driver, and he yells out, "Eh, Rocky! What about my own cab?"

I says, fuck it. Leave it there. The grin he put on his face you could never believe unless you seen it, and then he busts out with one of those cowboy yodelin yells. I tells the driver, take us downtown to the Absinthe House, and I tell Bernie, you're coming downtown with me, and I'm gonna innerduce you to people who could maybe help you get in show business.

"You really mean it?" he keeps tellin me. "You really think I could do it?"

About that time I was doing a show with Robert Alda called, "Can Do," and we were hanging out at the Absinthe House, where a lot of other show-biz people came. When we get there, we run into Martha Raye, her ex-husband and then manager, Nick Condos, and Martha's new husband, a guy who just quit the cops to marry her, Bob O'Shay.

I innerduce Bernie again as my best friend, and he moves right in. I could see the guy is so happy, and this makes me feel real warm inside. Once in a while I kind of eaves drops, and see he's got Martha's ear, and she's very happy talking to him. Very humble like, Bernie is tellin her some of the things he tells me, and then once, when my ear goes to them, they got a big conversation on about clowns.

Martha loves clowns, an she got a collection of doll clowns like nobody else in the world. She got them made outa glass, porcelain, stuffed, shaped like pillows, outa wood, little dolls, big dolls, you name 'em, but nothin but clowns.

I see the guy's all right so I tells him I gotta go home, and to meet me at the Absinthe, 12 o'clock noon tomorrow.

"I'll be here, Rocky," he says. "Just tell me what you want me to do. If you want me to jump off the Empire State Buildin, just give the word and I go there right now."

When I walk in the Absinthe House next day, I never expect he's gonna be there, but there's the guy, sitting on a stool in front of a beer, and on his lap, he's holding one of the biggest dolls you ever seen. The doll is Emmett Kelly the clown, and he's got a big red bulb for a nose. Bernie laughs happy as he presses a button on the doll and the nose lights up.

"Where you going with that?" I asks him, and he says, Martha told him she was gonna be there too, because she was doing a guest shot on the show with me that day, so he brung it for her.

Right away, Bernie starts tellin me what happen after I went home the night before, and he's got me in stitches again, specially sitting there holding this clown on his knee like he was a ventriloquist. Once in a while he look at the doll an say, "Ain't that right, Emmett?" He looks me in the eye and says, "You know, Champ, all last night I was saying to myself, I gotta be nuts. When I got up this mornin, I took a cab to go get my cab at the Stadium. What'm I doing? I kept asking myself. You was the second fare I had last night, and all's was on the clock was three bucks an change. When the dispatcher sees me drive in this morning, he got frantic. 'Where the fuck were you?' he yells. 'What happened? We got cops out looking for the wreck.' I tell the dispatcher I was in Roosevelt Hospital. I tell him I had heat stroke. Guy fires me right on the spot. He says, give me the night's take. I hand him the three an change, and he gives me back seventy cents."

Just then, Martha comes into the bar with some people, and Bernie jumps off his stool, runs to her, puts the clown in her arms, and says, "Have a clown on me."

You never in your life seen anybody get so excited like Martha got. I thought she was gonna cry. Back an forth, she's hugging and kissing the clown and Bernie, who, I'm sure, to her was another sad clown.

I can't tell you how it hit me to watch this. I hear Martha invitin Bernie to bring his wife and kids to her home for dinner, and she's writing her address on a piece of paper.

Well, just to show you how things got a way of turning. It was months later, Bernie come lookin for me, like he's always done since, and he give me the sweetest news I ever hear about a guy who never had nothin but bad breaks. He and his family become very friendly with Martha and her husband, and they make Bernie the vice-president of a detective agency she open for her husband Bob O'Shay, who's the president.

I can't begin to tell you how happy I was for this guy. He give us all numbers, saying, I'm number one and Martha's number two. He says, "Here I was, I come from zero, and God put you in my path. I coulda still been pushing that fuckin cab. And then, through you, God put Martha into my life. Here we was, me an my wife, jus as broke as could be, and she took us into her home, knowing this, an she treated us like the king and queen of a foreign country."

FIFTEEN

By 1960 I'm still climbin up the show-business ladder. I'm doing all kindsa shows, one after another, and a few agencies keep calling for me to do commercials for them all over the country. It was about this time that Frankie's pals had become such a group of close friends that the newspapers and magazines started affectionately calling them the "Rat Pack."

All this pack wanted to do was have a ball twenty-four hours a day. If any of them were appearin in Vegas they all go there to kibitz, heckle, and jump on the stage and join the act. They cut up like a bunch of talented kids an the customers got ten times their money's worth. Members of Frank's clan included guys like Dean Martin, Sammy Davis Jr., Joey Bishop, Tony Curtis, Paul Anka, Peter Lawford, Jilly Rizzo, Pat

Henry, Richard "Nicky" Conte, Sammy Kahn, and Jimmy Van Heusen, who wrote material for Frank an Dean. An they even had two chicks, Judy Garland an Shirley MacLaine in the pack. They were always on, lookin for new kicks, an they did anything they wanted for laughs. Sometimes they jump in Frank's plane an fly half way around the world just to visit somebody or have a good time. I can't begin to tell you what these guys do to my feelins, like they giving me the best glow of my life, even when they making me the dummy for a lotta their jokes. During those years I wanna be with those guys like you wouldn't believe, like I wanna be with them even a hunnerd times more than I wanna be with my Norma.

By 1961, I been making more good moves too. The newspapers are calling me former Middleweight Champ of the World, t'espian, author, commentator, art patron, crap shooter, horse player, and the luckiest guy alive. I ain't nowhere's near Sinatra's class, but in my own little way I'm getting a share of a lot more than I got coming to me.

I'm down in Miami once during that time and I'm working on "Miami Undercover." This is a series on which I put in nine beautiful months. The star is Lee Bowman, who plays a private eye, and me, I play a Miami Beach bar owner who's his right-hand man.

We also got a *cowboy* on it called Ronald Reagan. If he wasn't already married I woulda got worried when I see the guy kissing his horse. I shoulda only known, right? All this guy Ronnie does, when he ain't on, is follow me around, laughing up a storm, askin me to repeat things. He hires me out for a few beers a day to give him diction and elocution lessons, and I get the guy mumbling pretty good. Now, I tell this actor he does it better than me, and maybe with my speech lessons he could go out someday and become a big politician. And Ronnie tells me, "I ever get to be President, I make you Secretary of Education." Gee, thanks! How you like those apples for a guy which got thrown outa the fourth grade?

During this time, I also break in a new TV show with me and Bobby Ridell, the singer, who was just nineteen then.

Another deal comes my way, is a starring part in a movie called *Teenage Millionaire,* for which I have to go back to Hollywood. I play the millionaire's bodyguard, and it's a comedy which also stars Zasu Pitts and Sterling Holloway.

I let Frank know I'm coming to California and he insists I stay at his pad. I tell Frank I go to a hotel because I gotta work on the picture awhile, and he says, "If you don't come out to my digs, I'll get you fired." I know he's kidding about the fire job, but I also know he's going to be one offended guy if I don't go.

William B. Williams once give Frank a moniker that stuck, "Chairman of the Board." So, how's a guy going to turn down the Chairman?

Incidentally, when I see Willie B., and I mention this, he says he was misquoted. What he actually said was, "Chairman of the Broads."

When I get to Los Angeles, I go right to Frank's place in Beverly Hills. The whole gang's hanging around, and there's some beautiful dolls, look like show girls, hanging around there too. It makes me remember the movie *The Tender Trap,* but this pad is out of this world compared to the one in the movie.

When Dean Martin says, "Welcome to the Vatican, Rocky," I know just what he means. His Eminence the Pope lives there and I see a lot of Jack Daniels hanging around to quench the Pope's thirst.

The whole clan is there, kibitzin with me, making a lot of noise, interrupting, trying to be the guy who's on, and laughing till your sides bust. People come and go, and the house is always filled with some of the biggest names in show business, specially the comics. They shoot lines trying to top each other like it's a big game. And Frank is always kidding around with me, doing things to make me feel comfortable.

One Saturday afternoon its kinda quiet in the house for a change, so I figure I stay in my room, watch some TV an relax. I fell asleep for a while, wake up, and decide to get myself some beer. I put on my fightin robe, which has "Champ" in big letters across the back, and I go downstairs to the kitchen. I could hear a few voices talkin in the next room, but I don't pay no attention. I take a couple-a cans of beer out of the refrigerator and turn to go back upstairs when I hear a familiar Boston voice near the doorway, "Hey, Rock! Is that you?"

I walk to the doorway and who's there lookin at me but President

Kennedy hisself. Frankie an a couple other people are smiling, and when I try to say something I stutter like a stupid kid.

"Come in for awhile," he says, and then he shakes my hand like he's gonna shake it off, and he starts kidding around with me and I get one-a the biggest thrills of my life. All of a sudden I realize I'm standing there in my robe, holding two cans of beer under my arm, so I excuse myself.

I meet Truman an Eisenhower before that, but *this* is the president I always wanted to meet, and what better place than in my Sicilian Hoboken Frankie's digs. Yeah, Frankie, you an me both, right off those streets to the top of the world.

It took me a lot of years to figure why millionaire guys jumped outa windows during and right after the stock market crash of 1929. A lot of those guys were born with millions, so, when they lost and were down to maybe their last million, they didn't know how to cope, so they flew outa the window.

Guys like Frankie and me know what it is not to have, and we know what the bottom feels like better than anybody, so if we go down we just start from scratch as many times as you need to. That's why I say, here's Frankie, down one day, and now who's he got, but the President of the United States coming right to his own house to see him.

During this trip, I also play golf with Frank an Dean and the rest of his pals, who's also my pals, and run with all them wherever they go. As far as I'm concerned, I've never met another guy like Frank, an ace in fuckin spades.

After I go back to New York, I get a call one day from Henry Gene, one of Frank's Eastern reps, an the guy says, he's gotta deliver something for Frankie. It turns out to be a beautiful white-leather golf bag, fully equipped with expensive clubs that the guy hadda spring at least five bills for. My name, Rocky, is spelled out on the bag in big red-leather letters. How do ya show a guy like this how you love him? An love is the *only* thing you could give him. Frankie is the one guy in my whole life I could truthfully say is fanfuckintastic!

Through the years, a lotta other singers try to take Frank's place, but nobody could ever budge the King.

The only guy who ever made it close was Frank's best friend Dino Crocetti, alias Dean Martin, and the great Mario Lanza, rest in peace. Guys like Steve Lawrence, Andy Williams, Bobby Darin, Jerry Vale, Vic Damone, Frankie Laine, Tony Bennett, Jimmy Roselli, Jack Jones, and a few others was also big ballad singers in their own right. There was also other guys who started when Frank did, who went on singin into their sixties an up to today, guys like Tony Martin an Perry Como, who did almost everything that Frank did. Still, there's only one King.

An you know, people's always kidding Dean about tipping glasses, but Dean told me he only gets drunk when he's drinking. While other shows are havin reruns, his is havin refills. He's the only guy who can't see anything wrong about the Tower of Pisa. On one of those Dean Martin roasts I tell the audience once that Dean's wife never knew he was drunk until he came home sober one day.

Me, for one, could tell you everybody should be able to hold the sauce like this guy. And he ain't drinking that heavy either. When he pours hisself a scotch, he drowns it with so much water there's no color left in the glass. Drunk or sober, Dean's the sweetest guy you ever seen. Here's some lines me an his other buddies kid him with. "Dean quit A.A. an joined the A.A.A. so he could get towed home when he got stoned."

"I told Dean, force yourself to take a little drink before goin to bed. Make you sleep better."

Joey Adams says, "Dean's so relaxed he never spills a word." Another guy says, "Phil Harris taught Dean every drink he knows." Or, "He could build a two-family igloo with the ice cubes he uses in a week." "The only reason Dean got home half-smashed, he ran out of money."

Belive me, money is the one thing Dean ain't running outa again. He spread it out across some pretty good investments.

Dean once ask me why I didn't get my nose fixed too. I tell him the same thing I told Edward R. Murrow when I was a guest on his "Person to Person" show, which was done right in my home. My busted nose was my badge that got me into all these great things that happen to me with show biz.

That Murrow show, I remember good, August 1963. It was one of the biggest shows on the tube. Murrow wants to know why I don't do nothing to correct the way I talk. I tell him, what wouldja say if I told you I *useta* have a speech problem.

I gotta keep reminding myself, I'm a very, very lucky bum. I had a hunnerd-nine fights, amateur an pro. I didn't know nothing about boxing and become Champ-a-the-World. I know less about acting and become a high-priced actor. Murrow says I was deceptively boyish-looking despite all my ring wars. Was that good?

Come to think of it, a lot of other things come my way in '63 that I don't think I mention before. I was also a steady weekly on the Keefe Brazzelle show, that was a summer sub for Gary Moore, whose show I also went on. On Keefe's show I was his second banana.

That was also the year Frank's son got kidnapped, an also the year when everybody's heart broke. In November of that year we all got the news, over the air, that our great happy friend and everybody's good President of the United States, John Kennedy, got killed by a nut in Dallas, Texas.

It took Frank and me, and a hell of a lotta people, a long, long time to get over this one.

As time passes and we stop mourning our President, I think back on things past, like dancing in the aisle at the Paramount Theater on Broadway, while Frankie was on the stage singing with the Tommy Dorsey band. Norma, too, still brings it up when we talk about Frank.

I sure hated to see that joint closed. I walk down Times Square by the Paramount once in 1964, an it's closed tighter than a clam's ass. There's chains an locks through the brass door handles. I go to read the sign on the door, an it says they gonna tear the place down an put stores and offices there. I think to myself, twenty-two years go by since me and Norma do the Lindy in that aisle.

I'm standing there trying to look through the glass door when a lady with fat legs come over and does the same thing at another door. She look to be about forty, forty-five, with one-a those Brooklyn bouffant hairdos and loud makeup. She turns to pose for a gray-haired guy, an the guy's taking her picture. Then she recognizes me from my shows or something, and she says, "Hey, Rocky, you remember Frankie appearing here?" She talks to me a little, then she asks me to pose with her while her bo snaps the button. I let 'im take the picture, thinking, what they don't know is, Frankie is a part of my life.

I walk off a little sad, knowin' this place was parta my youth, and when it goes, a piece of me's going with it.

One day I gets a call from Frank from Hollywood, an he tells me him an his gang are goin to Miami to do a picture called *Tony Rome,* and he's got a part in the film for me, and he wants me and Norma to shoot down to Miami. You never seen two people pack so fast, drive ninety miles an hour to get there.

On the way into the hotel I says to Norma, "Let's act like we been married a long time. You carry the suitcases." Guy at the desk says, "You want a room overlooking the ocean?" and I say, "How about a room overlooking the rent?"

Miami is some town. It's full of young girls looking for husbands an husbands looking for young girls.

Soon as I check in, I start calling the guys, and it's like ole home week again. I find out the picher is like another James Bond, only they got a lot of meatballs and garlic mixed in with guys like me. I gotta play a real guy, Kingfish Levinsky, who used to be a former heavyweight contender. The Kingfish is in Miami Beach for years, since he retired from the ring, and the guy is selling ties outa a box he carries under his arm. Everybody knows the guy. He goes around to hotel pools, restaurants, and night-clubs, and he makes a nice buck hustling his ties. I wouldn't be surprised he makes more 'n he made in the ring.

My lines in the movie are easy. All I gotta say is, "Ey, ya bum! Why dincha buy a tie?" I play me, with my own voice, but they make me rehearse that line for two weeks. You gotta know Frank is Tony Rome.

Everybody stayed at the Fountainebleau, and just Frank being there made everybody go crazy. When the gang wasn't working they mostly partied. Shecky Greene, who plays the part of a cripple hood called Cat Leg, is gotta be one-a the craziest characters you ever seen, specially when he got two, three bottles of Don Perignon under his belt. Everything he does or says, he puts me in stitches.

He'd come into a room an yell out, "Ey! Where's Frank?" When everybody just shrug, he says, "How come nobody bow their head when I mention the Pope?"

They film all day, and on the days we don't work, we go to the track or the golf course. At night Frank appears in the La Ronde room at the hotel, an Shecky is the comic who warms up the audience. You never seen such laughs in all your life. I bust my sides so much that tears come down my face. Even when they ain't on, it's the same thing. The whole gang, includin Frank, is just one bad influence after another. They play rough like a bunch of grown-up kids. A guy could just walk in and only say something like, "So, what's new?" and the way he says it everybody breaks up. Or there could be a playful fight, even with somebody gettin mad and furniture getting busted up and everybody wrestling all over the joint, and then, next day, everybody breaks up talkin about how Shecky Greene, or somebody, got knocked on his ass, and they're all friends again, and most of all they never stop loving the King.

Wherever Frank goes, word gets around and people follow him. The same happens in Jimmy Weston's Club or Jillie's West Side Bar in New York an anyplace else in the country he goes.

If Frank leaves the La Ronde club room after his show, and wanders next door into an empty Gigi Room, in five minutes it's packed to the hilt, everybody's eyes glued on his table. Before he can even say his favorite, "Bring me some gasoline," pop! a bottle of Jack Daniel's is on his table.

Brassy-looking broads in their forties or fifties are always fighting to get near him with, "Frankie, Frankie, remember me? I metcha with —" I heard one lady telling somebody, "I been sending Frankie a birthday card and Christmas card every year since he sang in Dorsey's band. He'll always be my special doll." Frank didn't even know her. "I'm sure he'll remember," she tells this person, but she still keeps a distance from his table.

One night we're all in the club, big dinner for the gang, and I spot some *malandrines* sitting at a table, and I could see they there to give Frank trouble. Even though Frank don't take no shit from nobody it's pretty hard to buck these kinda guys. No matter how many friends Frank's got, he's bound to pick up an enemy here and there, and it could be just because some guy feels offended. These guys at the table are wise guys, and I know that even Frankie's bodyguards ain't gonna fuck with them.

I go over to the table, and they know me good, and I know them. They say, "Ey, Champ! Have a seat." I pull up a chair for a minute and they tell me they're insulted and why don't I take a walk cause they gotta get even. I talk to them, then I say, come on wit' me, I straighten everything out. I take them back to Frank's table and before ya know it everybody's shaking hands an making with laughs, and this magic Frank's got is making "the Boys" act like little kids who just got their lollipops back.

Our whole gang is up the suite one day, about fifteen of us, when Frank calls up a jeweler he knows an asks the guy to bring over a few trays of watches. I hear him tell the jeweler on the phone, "It don't matter." Anyway the guy shows up with about four trays of watches, an we all think Frank wants to buy a watch. The jeweler is sayin, "You said it don't matter, so I brought up all prices, from seventy-five bucks to five-hunnerd." All Frank says is, "Just spread them out on that table." Then he says, "Okay, everybody, go pick youself out a watch."

Whatta ya do with a guy like this? Some of those guys he didn't even know good. I just like to know what kind of bundle he go for on those tickers he give away. I never in my life see anybody like to play Santa Claus more than Frank.

I'm driving my Cadillac back to New York from Miami after workin on *Tony Rome*. I'm going up Route 301 and I musta been pissin along pretty good. I gets stopped in Georgia for speeding eighty-five miles an hour. This sheriff in cover-alls says, "Hey boy! You goin to a fire?"

I tell him I'm racin to get to a motel before it get dark, so's I don't have an accident.

All of a sudden, in the middle of this lecture, he's giving me while he's haulin out his book, he says, "Say boy, ain't you that fighter Rocky Marciano?"

People was always mixin up our names so I figure no point in explaining, so I tell him, yeah.

Without looking at my license he says, "Hey boy, I ain't gonna give you a ticket but I want you to do me a favor. I wantcha to come down the road a piece and meet Joe Algora. It still up the pike and not out of your way one foot. He owns a restaurant on Main Street up in town, got your picture on the wall, an he says you're God as far as he's concerned."

So while this ghee's slapping his leg, snapping his suspenders, an slamming his hat against his knee, I says, let's go. When we get to this restaurant I figure the sheriff just got my name screwed up, which I didn't correct, but when I get in the place I see it's really Rocky Marciano whose picher is on the wall.

All they keep saying, this Algora guy and the sheriff, "Boy, you sure changed a lot." I never did tell 'em I was *Graziano*! Everybody always tell me they a little behind in some places in the South so I'm afraid they never hear about Graziano and I get the ticket after all. I drove outta Georgia very careful like.

Here I gotta tell you a little more about Shecky Greene, who became a pretty good friend of mine while we was workin on *Tony Rome*. If you could catch this guy's nightclub act in Vegas, or for that matter any other club around the country, it gotta be the biggest treat of your life and you'll never forget it. When you see Shecky on TV, what you get is bits and pieces of an act that could run till Tuesday next week. In Vegas, you get it all. Also, in Las Vegas you gotta fight for a seat for his show, because every entertainer in town, who's in between shows, is in his room beatin you out of a seat to his act. They dig him more than the outa town money does. Vegas is the best place anywhere to test a funny man in action. You ever try to make a loser laugh? Shecky don't only make 'em laugh, he gives them hysterics. An if Shecky's drinking he's twice as funny. One time there, when I'm with the guy and he's a little high, he makes a running dash toward a crap table in the casino. "Look out!" he yells, and like Moses parting water, Shecky swan dives out over and onto the crap table, scattering slow players, dice, and all the bets. With the chips flying all over the place, he yells out, "Bet my life on the hard four!"

Another time, smashed, the guy drove right into Caesar's Palace fountain. When the fuzz showed, Shecky says he drove in for a car wash and please no spray wax. He'll tell you hisself how he destroyed more bars and hotel rooms than you can imagine, while he was under the influence. Shecky's always had something in his skull that I had to get rid of too. And that's a thing to do with brass buttons, braids, and uniforms. Can't stand authority. Even a doorman shakes him up. With a general, he could go kookoo. Shecky says this comes from when we was kids, how we was kids, and where we grew up.

On Shecky's first date with Lilani, the beautiful Las Vegas show girl he married, he scared the shit out of her by racing down the wrong side of the Vegas strip. The guy thinks he's in England, driving the wrong side of the street. After he drops her off for the night he gets stopped for speeding, drunk drivin, and they hustle him off to jail where they ask him to walk a straight line. Shecky says, "Not without a net."

He love to tell the story about the gambler who loses 25,000 bucks shootin craps. The pit boss says to the loser, why don'tcha go in an see Shecky's show. Relax awhile. An the player says, "Yeah, my bus don't leave for another hour." The pit boss asks, "You takin a bus home?" "No, I'm gonna lie under it when it leaves."

One bit Shecky does is a funny imitation of me, a long boxing bit, and it's the funniest I ever seen anywhere. Too complicated to tell you here. You gotta go see it. Make you piss in your pants. From me, nobody would believe it. In fact they tell Shecky he looks just like me doing it. There's never a dull moment when Shecky's on the scene. While we was doing that *Tony Rome,* Shecky's got everybody in Miami breaking up an flippin all over the joint. But then there was also times when Frank and the rest of the gang is looking to kill him.

Shecky tells this story about Frank Sinatra savin his life during that Miami bit. Five guys are beatin the shit outa Shecky in front of the Fountainebleau Hotel and Frank says, "Okay, boys. That's enough." Shecky even tells a story about me. He says I'm in the hotel lobby and I got R. G. on big cuff links, R. G. on my shirt, R. G. on my jacket coat of arms, R. G. on my pant's pockets, and who's gonna forget my face? He says, he hears a guy call out, "Ey, Rock!" and I say, "Shhhh, I don't want nobody ta know I'm here."

SIXTEEN

In 1965, when Frank introduced, "It Was a Very Good Year," he hadda be singin a theme song, not only for hisself, but for all the rest of us friends too.

There's one thing that bugs Dean and Frank and me, and all my Italian buddies in and out of show business, and that's putting Italians down, or making cracks about us being part of the Mafia because we got some money and a Italian name. I swear, I see Dean getting pretty hot under the collar only once with a writer guy for a magazine, or something. The guy was asking him what he knows about the Mafia, and you could see the writer was asking with bad thoughts.

Dean says, "Why don't you ask me about guys like Christopher

Columbus, Michelangelo, Marconi, Toscanini, Fermi, Leonardo da Vinci, or a barber by the name of Gaetano, or about Frank's old man? How about writing a little something about them?"

Just before this, Dean sponsored a talk-a-thon for a favorite charity, "The City of Hope." After a nineteen-and-a-half-hour countdown, Dean raised eight hunnerd, four thousan smackers. Go write about that when you wanna know which people are the first to show, and for free, whenever help is needed for something.

Between Dean and his pals, they sometimes call each other dago, but they do it with affection. Let some outsider call them that and guaranteed you see the sparks fly.

For instance, one battle I know about happen on Dean's birthday. Frank and him are celebrating at the Polo Lounge with more of the gang, and they a little loud, like the boys always get when they're celebrating. When the party's breakin up, and Dean and Frank are gettin ready to go out the door, they hear a big guy telling another guy at a table, "About time those fuckin two loud-mouthed dagos took off."

Frank and Dean got to the table just as these two guys stood up to do battle. Frank took one outa the picture and Dean dropped the other. These guys hadda learn the hard way that happiness was minding your own fuckin business. Dean says he never calls nobody Nigger, Chink, Polack, or Jew, or nothing like that, so forget about him standing still for somebody calling him a dago, wop, or guinea.

We all owe those kinda creeps something, when they go around taggin people with these kinda names. What we owe them is black eyes, broken jaws, cancer, ulcers, and heart attacks.

When the cops showed for Dean's birthday celebration, nobody saw nuttin. Things like this fight in the Polo Lounge happen, but Dean still moves pretty fucking good. He says you could always avoid the bad write-ups you sure to get in the papers after these fights. All you gotta do was say nothin, do nothin, an be nothin. He says making fun of Italians, no matter who they are, is no different than making fun of his pop Gaetano and his mom, because they don't speak English too good.

About this time is when I meet President Lyndon Johnson down in the White House. He put his arm around my shoulder and ask *me* to do him a favor. He says, I hadda help by joining his Physical Fitness Council. I'da held my breath under water for two hours if he ask me, just the way he make a hoodlum like me, from the lower East Side, feel when he hold me like that. I went all around the country speaking with others about physical fitness and when I come to Texas to see L.B.J. again, he gimme the biggest handshake you ever seen and put a Texas ten-gallon hat on my head, which I still got today.

That same year, 1965, Dean breaks in a new weekly show called "The Dean Martin Show" and right away it's at the top of the charts, and the show had the longest run you ever seen. Dean gives all his buddies, including me, shots on his show. Two of his regulars I don't mention before are Dom De Louise, and Nipsey Russell.

I useta love the part where Dean sings songs and kibitzes with his conductor, Ken Lane, or when he opens a door on the stage and behind it is always a surprise celebrity.

Everybody have anything to do with Dean says he's one of the most dependable guys around. The guy's never late for anything.

And Dean says he always knows his lines. They could be wrong lines but he knows them even if he forget the others and make these up hisself.

Frank sings one way, and Dean sings another. I betcha there ain't a guy around who could copy Dean's style today, specially when he sings songs like, "When You're Smiling," "Lady Is a Tramp," "Where or When," "What Did I Do," and "Volare," and I gotta tell you what my favorite is. Every once in a while, Dean pulls it out of the barrel and does it again, "Return to Me." It was written in English and Italian by a friend of mine from Morris Avenue in the Bronx, Danny Di Minno. He wrote it specially for Dean, who recorded it, and it become one of Dean's big hit records.

Danny is another Italian who come up the hard way and ended up writing all kindsa hits for United Artists. Believe it or not, the guy even wrote a song called, "KO Graziano." To show you how stupid I was, I ask Danny once what he wrote first, the lyrics or the words, and I couldn't figure out why he bust out laughing.

I gets a call poisonally from Dean one day not too long after I finished working for Frank on *Tony Rome* in Miami. Dean wants me to fly out to Hollywood for a spot on his show.

Soon as Norma hears this she says, "Let's leave a week early. I'm coming with you this time."

"I thought you were afraid to fly," I tell her. An she says, "We're not flying. We're taking the train." I try to talk her out of it. I tell her the only risk is in the cab ride to the airport, but she says, her religion won't let her fly. She's a devout coward. That's my solid brick-wall Norma.

Right! I'm on this sooty train for three days, and I give you one guess, there's first class, tourist, and prisoner. I wanna kill her. I don't talk to my wife for the whole time. All I do is scratch in my seat and give her killing dirty looks for the whole three days. I coulda flown, sang a couple-a choruses of "Everybody Loves Somebody Sometime," and been there in a few hours. Instead, I'm boxed in like jail for three whole days *an nights.* Still today, Norma ain't getting on no plane, no time, and for nobody.

After I get there, the weight drops off and everything is like gold again, and once I'm in with the clan I get all relaxed.

Norma is having such a ball she keeps saying, "You're not going without me anymore," and I keep telling her she better go out 'n buy a pair of wings and learn how to fly.

Nothing bothers her, even when she knows I'm mad. She's in heaven, specially when Frank is with us. Yeah, right! Swooning all over the place.

I could see what Dean an Frank hadda go through when they're in restaurants. People that knows us vaguely, sometimes a friend of a friend of a friend, are always coming to the table, pulling up chairs, an breathing on everybody while you're tryin to eat. I don't know how Frank and Dean gets the food chewed.

All that Dean has to do at the studio is show up. No rehearsals, no nothing, and everything goes just as smooth as pouring oil. He just reads cue cards, just like I do, and you never see such a relaxed guy in your life.

Norma and me get together with both the Martin and the Sinatra families. Their kids are really whatcha could call beautiful people, polite 'n courteous like you never see. It's a real pleasure to be with all these people.

When Norma and me's getting ready to come back to New York,

Frank starts insisting he has his pilot fly us back in his own private jet. Man, was I thrilled! I wanted to be on that plane so bad!

You're right! Norma makes me ride all the way back on that dirty fuckin rattler, and if you think I was mad before, I tell her now, talk to me one time and I throw you right off the train. She comes back with things like, "Someday you're gonna go too far and I hope you stay there," and I come back with, "I don't know what I do without you, but I'm willing to try."

I tell her I never know what real happiness was until I marry her and then it's too late. I throw all kinds of zingers, but this kid is tough. She even hits harder than me. I think, I ever really hit her, it'd be in self-defense to keep her from killin me.

One day, to my surprise, Bernie Allen, the funny cab driver, looks me up, an I'm happy to see him. He musta known I was thinking about him when I read that Martha Raye divorced Bob O'Shay.

Bernie tells me he's doing a comedy routine in a small club out in Brooklyn, and I'm happy to hear it, knowing I had something to do with him takin that route. I tell the guy he did right, and show biz is just where he belong. I ask him what happened to the detective agency.

"Down the drain. Just like the poor kid's marriage," he says. "But Martha kept after me too, to become a comedian. She taught me routines, and showed me all the stage tricks. I opened at this club I'm at, two weeks ago for a one-week tryout, and they held me over. You gotta come out to see me, Rocky."

I go to the club, and when I see his name, Bernie Allen, outside the club, I get a special feeling. Inside, the guy's got me in hysterics as soon as he hits the floor. He even tells the audience he was gonna drive his car off the bridge just to give me a laugh. I send all my friends over to see him and this makes Bernie one of the happiest clowns in New York.

I could go on writing about guys who came into my life and sweetened it, from now till doomsday. If you're one of the guys who laid a little magic on me, and you don't find yourself in the book, you gotta know the special feelng I got for you. I only wish there was enough room to mention the names of every mother's uncle that ever crossed my path and didn't cross me.

In 1967 I gets a call to go on the Merv Griffin Show, and he was as big then as he is today.

First thing I say when I meet him is, "Merv, I think your show is fuckinfantastic!" Then Merv has this big talk with me about cursing on the air. He begs me, "Please, Rocky, whatever you do, don't swear while you're on the show. Even though they keep a word out when you hear it at home, they don't take it out for the people in the studio."

I don't want to swear but it was part of my street bringing up where I come from, part of being a tough guy, and then come one day, you find you're stuck with any words you use, and you can't get them out of your talk no more. Y'mean? Even today, when I'm with the guys, it's "fuckin" this an "fuckin" that. It's the way I talk. What could I tell you? A reporter once told me, very serious, that it sounded like poetry and he wished he could put it in his newspaper the way it flows outa my gapper. He says, he like to get it down, fuckin this, an fuckin that, specially because I ain't talking that way mad.

Anyway, I didn't do bad because they was always bringing me back to appear with the biggest guest stars in the business.

Arthur Treacher, a great fellow drinker, who useta play British butler parts in old movies, was Merv Griffin's "man Friday."

I always got a big kick out of Treach when we were on the show together. He always look down his nose at me, like he was smellin something, and what he's smellin is me. I never understand the guy and he can't understand me neither, but we could sure make people laugh.

Arthur got very sick one time and who they pick to take his place but me! I got the "man Friday" bit for four months, and man! did I have a ball. Best of all, I sure learn a lot from Merv and his great guests. Maybe they gotta bleep me once in a while, but one thing I always try to give the Merv Griffin show and everybody's show I go on, is their money's worth.

When Mike Douglas says, "I wouldn't have gotten anyplace without the love and confidence my family gave me. My family is my life," then you gotta know this makes Mike, one-a the toughest guys in the world. Don't laugh. Even though he still comes on like a altar boy, go try to hurt somebody near and dear to him. That's how strong he loves his family, but this kind of guy loves everybody. I know he loves me, otherwise why does he keep invitin me back on his show, over an over, even up to today.

You know where I come from and what I look like. Then you look at this apple-cheek Mike, with his own crockery and smile lighting up his puss like a hunnerd-watt bulb, and then you hear he's the only Irishman around who don't tip a glass even a wee bit, and he don't smoke or gamble, and you gotta come up with, "Ey! Who's kiddin who?" But it's all true.

Mike and me look like forty-eight t'ousan miles apart, but not so. He just sings better than me. This guy come up the hard way, just like most of the other guys I tell you about in my book. And as far as his career goes, Mike also had his share of ups and downs. But, by 1967 he's on top of the world and nobody shook him off since. It was during this same year I was on the Griffin show that I got my first call to go to Philly to appear on Mike's show. The guy's the smoothest natural you ever seen. Right away he got me at ease, and we're laughin and kidding like we know each other all our lives.

All I gotta say is something like, "My dumb, stupid wife blew all my racetrack money on the rent," and Mike breaks up more than the people watching in the studio.

One time, I says about Danny Thomas, "This guy's got so much religion he can't get fire insurance. His house is full of candles." The tears run out Mike's eyes, an he can't talk for a minute.

He useta put me on the show regular, a shot every two, three weeks, besides seeing all his good people, and yeah, you should see all the Philadelphia Italians he got working for him in the studio, in the band and a lotta the technical jobs.

Like I was gonna say, besides seeing all the stars he invites, I use to get this beautiful hunnerd-mile ride from New York to Philly. It give me a chance to get outa my city an see all that pretty scenery going down the Jersey Turnpike. In fact, I'm so happy going to see Mike, and even getting paid, that I would jog the whole hunnerd country miles if I have to.

After the show gets taped, sometimes me and some of the people ride into South Philly for some Italian food, and there in South Philly it's just like back on the Lower East Side.

Mike even give me a one-week co-host bit a couple-a times. During this time, I crack jokes an tell the audience things about me, like I work conventions and I stay busy all the time, running my ass off doin all kindsa shows. I gotta tell them I think I'm good. I go all over, doin commercials, maybe four, five a week.

Mike could start me off with just a question like, "How are things in New York, Rock?"

I tell him I get in a cab, cab driver says, "Hey, Rocky, I seen you get knocked out by Tony Zale. Man! What a fight!" Another guy, "Ey, I saw you get knocked out by Ray Robinson. Boy! What a punch!"

I had a hunnered twenty-one fights and all these bums ever seen was the seven I lose.

Mike is a champ at the way he asks questions. He can always get out the best. He asks me about my Jewish mother-in-law and father-in-law, and he breaks up when I tell him they hated me. He wants to know if they ever stop hating me. I tell him, yeah, when I start making fifty G's a fight. I tell him my Norma loves me more too when the big money started coming in. She don't care then if I get kilt or nothing. I guess you gotta know I'm kiddin.

Mike also asks me on his show if I ever get mugged. I tell him, once, when I'm comin out this bar a little stoned, and my friend Albie Goldstein was a little slow in catching up. Two big guys, and you gotta know they don't know who I am, but I know what they are. They come toward me from different directions. One-a them says, "Gotta match, fella?" I nail the cat with shot and knock him out. Before the other guy could move, I t'row a second hammer an flatten him too. Wasn't I in the same business myself when I was a kid?

Mike's one-a the greatest I ever appear with. All I hadda do was talk to him just like he and me are in a neighborhood bar having a beer.

SEVENTEEN

T alking about throwing punches again brings back a couple of things I feel very sorry for. When Frank Sinatra sang "Regrets," that he'd had a few, but too few to mention. He did what he had to do . . . It gets me, just like it done you, thinking about things I regret, and like you, I got my share.

I was used to being called names like wop, dago, guinea, meatball, greaseball, sonofabitch, and even worse than that. But that was in police stations when I was a kid and in the ring when I grew up. In fact, in the ring I even had my face spit in.

A lotta of good strong punchers, who couldn't get at me, useta start calling names hoping I blow my cool and rush them wide open, anxious to kill them. I know this because I use it myself to make a guy mad enough to start swinging wild. Then I step in with one shot and I pulverize them. It's like that in the ring. Everything goes, but when it's over you shake hands, and sometimes even become best friends, even after some Irish or Black guy spit in your face an call you a guinea bastard.

It's the guys with three beers in 'em, who you sometimes meet in bars, that you gotta know how to handle so's you don't kill 'em. Maybe they took a slap in the face from a mean wife who they afraid to hit back. Could be anything. You see these guys coming toward you and you know they looking for trouble. In a bar these kinda guys look for the toughest, meanest looking character to pick an argument with. This tells them they ain't yellow for letting some skinny ass, little five-foot broad beat the shit outa them. If they get hit they could cry like babies, and accept it like they got punished.

Guys like this coming up to real tough guys happen all the time and if it happen to me, I could usually sweet-talk them out of their belligerency, so's I don't have to paralyze some idiot.

It could even be a famous celebrity who knows you, choosing a fight, and go find out why?

One time, I'm in Toots Shor's and taking a lot of good-natured ribbin from Toots, but nobody never pay any attention because Toots would rib his own mother to death, but Jackie Gleason jumps into the act, and even though we know each other and talk a lotta times before, all of a sudden I begin feeling a lot of belligerant. Maybe it's the liquor talkin, an maybe it's somethin else buggin his ass, but I could feel the malicious. Next, he's callin me meatball an even worse, an tellin me I was all kinds of a bum when I was in the ring. He turns to people laughin at his talk, an he says, "This guinea never fought nothin but setups in his whole career. Who the fuck ever told this bum he could stand half a chance with a legitimate fighter?"

Some guys couldn't get a laugh if they walk down Fifth Avenue in their wife's underwear an wearing her best summer bonnet, but this guy's murder, and here he's dishing it out at my expense. He make Don Rickles look like a choir boy. When he sees he's got a big audience laughing he poured on the coal and I'm standin there grinning, looking like a big idiot. Jackie Gleason ain't a heckler, he's a pro. What good's a

line like "Ey, you look the same as you did twenty-five years ago—old."
What good's a line like that gonna do with this guy? He just eat you up. I
got only one way to go. When I know for sure that it ain't all for laughs, I
point a finger in his face, look him cold dead 'n the eye, an I tell him just
once, "Quit this fuckin shit right now, or I knock you right on your big
fuckin ass." They guy's goin' so strong he can't quit. He gets worse.
That's when I bring down the curtain with a short right hook to the jaw.
The guy scares the shit outa me when I see they can't get him up. He's
out cold for a good half hour.

I see Gleason at Toots Shor's again after that, and he calls me, "Ey!
Rocky, baby! How sweet it is! Come on over and have a blast." Just like
nothing ever happen, and that's the way I wanted to feel because my kick
for punchin guys out left me when I hung up my gloves.

I know Jackie is one helluva good guy and we're still friends today, but
go figure what triggers a guy off, liquor, bad broads, who knows. I
happen to know about the hard way Jackie Gleason hadda go as a kid
trying to make it out of that Brooklyn ghetto he was brung up in, how his
mom hadda go out slaving to buy bread to feed him, sick mosta the time
she go to work.

When Jackie Gleason was a little kid, his Irish pop once went out to
the corner to buy a newspaper and he never come back. All his life this
bugged Jackie, who was brung up very religious by his mom. When
Jackie was fourteen he was already out hustlin poolrooms, just like I was,
and then when he got a little older the show-biz bug hit him because, like
I always says, where else a guy from those streets gonna go? Jackie's start
came on a amateur vaudeville show they were always puttin on durin the
old days in neighborhood movie houses. His comedy routine went over
and, like they say, the rest is history.

I like to think Jackie was tryin to hit back at his own troubles when he
was a kid, troubles I just happen to remind him about by just bein' on the
scene.

Lots of people fight in show business. Could be the heavy competition,
and could be the way you gotta always be keyed up for this action, or
maybe because you're in big lights today and tomorrow somebody puts
all the lights out. Could be all these things together. But I seen lots of

people fight, and sometimes brothers an sisters, and next day they maybe cry, and make up, and kiss, and everybody's happy again. I think the makin-up an forgettin the bad is what it's all about, ain't it?

As the years go passing by, now I got nothing but beautiful memories left over from them. I got picture albums an scrapbooks two-foot high. All the fun Norma had filling them up is now giving me fun going through them once in a while. And, I can see right away who her favorite was. She's got pictures of me and Frank Sinatra everyplace you look. Most of the Sinatra pictures, wouldn't you know, was taken at tables in nightclubs like it's the only time there's ever a camera around. Every once in a while I haul out the pictures, nod my head, and treasure our friendship.

Whenever I go by where the Paramount Theater used to be, I wonder why there's these stores there instead of the big marquee, and I know we all gotta lose something while that steamroller of progress passes over us.

I'm having dinner at a high-class joint on East Fifty Fourth Street called Jimmy Weston's. Friend of mine, Jimmy, owns the joint. I'm there with just my Norma and Burke Zanft, when who should surprise us, walking in all alone, but Frank Sinatra. When I see him, I know it took quite a job for him to dodge his bodyguards, and everybody else that's around him all the time.

Me and Burke jump up, leave Norma alone at the table, and we run up front to join Frank at the bar. Goes to show you what happen when he makes the scene. I forget my food, my wife, my house, the restaurant, and maybe even who I am.

We bullshit away like mad, old times and things like that, when Frank says, "How about Norma sitting in the back alone?" Like a half hour's gone by. I hit myself in the head, like how come I forget. Frank says, "Let's go back and join her."

Anybody else, Norma woulda been mad enough to kill me, but when we go back to her and the cold food, like she always does when Frank's around she swoons all over the table. Frank kisses her on the cheek polite like, orders himself a steak, and then he pays more attention to Norma than he does us.

That was a great night for Norma, and she never forget it. When we ask for the check, the waiter tells us Frank got it already. And then I see him passing out tips to everybody, which gotta be ten times what was on the check. How ya gonna beat this guy?

Before you know it, here it was 1973 and the thing that makes it a special bad year is, I hear my boyhood idol, Jack Healy, a guy I really love, passed away.

It was 1954 when the doctors discovered his cancer and give the guy eighteen months to live. Jack just went on smoking up a grass storm, and the guy went a few more knockout routes too.

During the years a lotta his show business dreams came true. Nat Hiken wrote a series for Phil Silvers, "Sergeant Bilko," and he got Jack Healy on as one of Bilko's regular soldiers. This kept him in action for a few years, and he had parts in Hiken's "Car 54," and a lot of other shows through the years. Jack Healy made it through nineteen big years, and during that time the prosecutor who convicted him in the grass case died, the judge died, his doctor died, and even his own lawyer died. And like Jack had insisted, he was gonna beat the big "C," and he did. Jack Healy died of a heart attack.

It seems like old home week whenever Mike Douglas has me back on his show. It was a bunch of years since I had last seen George Raft, my lifetime idol, and here he was on the same show with me. Talking about bad breaks, here's a guy who scooped every one of them out of the bottom of the bucket an you never hear him squawk once. A lot of people who made it owe this guy.

On this Mike Douglas TV show, where I'm a regular guest, I meet George Raft on the same level, but I'm still thrilled. Before the show we talk over old times and about Jack Healy. Rest in peace. Raft is telling me how thrilled he was when he see me beat Zale, an he tells me he made a bundle betting on the fight, an he watching *me* like *I'm* the big shot.

On the show he says things like he knew I was gonna make it first time he looked in my eyes down in Lanza's on First Avenue. And I tell him he's still my idol, and how I still get a thrill being in the same room with him. We kid around a little bit, an I call him king of the silver screen. This breaks him an the audience up and everybody's laughing good. The guy ain't like an uncle no more but like a brother. I can't tell you too good how it makes me feel but I'm sure you know. George Raft and his writer Yablonsky wrote a book on Raft's life not too long ago, and I'm sure it did his heart a lot of good before he passed away recent. Rest in peace. George always belonged to the Good Club of Life, and he paid his dues.

When I see the faces of the kids who chase me for my autograph while they yellin, "Hi, Champ," I know how I must've looked to George Raft first time I looked in his face, an I know how the guy must've felt.

The reason I say old home week on the Mike Douglas show is because he's getting old buddies outa my past one after another. In a 1975 show Shecky Greene is on with me. Again the laughs are fanfuckintastic, and the guy swears to me he ain't drinking no more because of the influence of his beautiful wife, Lilani. That kid's not only a doll, she's one pretty smark cookie. She loves the guy, goes all over with him, an right now she's on the same show with us, an she's tellin Shecky, "Yes, be crazy, crazy as can be, but only on a stage. Standing in Caesar's fountain, arguing all wet with the cops, may be funny to those who're watching, but come next morning in jail, it's not funny anymore to the guy with the hangover and dirty, unpressed clothing."

These are the kind of things they talk about on talk shows, an they get miles of laughs just remember the bad hassles, and talking about them like they're laughing at theirselves.

On this show with Mike, we just got sat down, and Mike gets through with the greetins, and Shecky says to me, "How come you never use your regular voice on these shows, Rocky?" He makes people laugh right off, kidding that I got one way talking off and another stupid voice for the shows. I gotta remind the people out front, whatcha hear is watcha got . . . me!

Some wise guy in the audience yells out, "Are you Shecky's brother?" Lots of people tell me I look like this bum when he's with me.

Mike Douglas says, "Yeah, why didn't you have them pick Shecky to play you in *Somebody Up There Likes Me?* That was hard to believe, that Paul Newman could look like you, Rocky."

And I says, "Yeah, I wanted a guy that looks like me. I wanted a guy what was handsome, and good looking, and that ain't Shecky." What could I tell you?

Next Shecky asks me, "How come most fighters wind up broke, and I happen to know you're in terrific shape financially?"

An I gotta remind the guy, I marry a nice Jewish girl that took all my money for safe keeping. In fact, she takes such good care of it, I ain't never gonna see it again. I says the only way I ever get it back someday is if I change my name to Aaron Weissman. That's my grandson.

Shecky wants to know, since Norma won't give me too much spending money, if I got charge accounts at bars. I tell him I don't need any because everybody's always looking to buy drinks because they think I'm a tough guy.

Just as we finishing the show, Shecky says, "What do you think of thespian endeavors?"

"Who?" I say. "Oh, yeah! Didn't I fight him in Detroit once?"

Besides Shecky Greene and George Raft, some of the other good buddies I appear on the Mike Douglas Show with is Gregory Peck, Red Skelton, Redd Foxx, Groucho Marx, Princess Grace, Hank Aaron, Bob Hope, Ray Charles, Billie Jean King, Sammy Davis, Jr., Bobby Riggs, Freddy Prinze, David Brenner, Liberace, Mac Davis, Muhammad Ali, and a lot, I'm sorry, I forget. What could I tell you?

Now don't put me down, like Mike's the only guy around. Me raving about Mike's show don't say it's the only way to go. I love talk shows, and all of them are great, even though I gotta tell you here, Merv Griffin ain't no slouch, and how you ever gonna top Johnny Carson's "Tonight Show." These guys gotta be like magicians, to come up with those winners, night after night. Even the greatest fighters in the world ain't gonna come up with winners every time out of the box. Sure they raking in millions. More power to them. When guys like Johnny Carson keep climbing up that ladder we all go up with him.

Johnny always likes to talk about how he hadda get off the sauce because it made him a little wild. All I say is it's too bad everybody couldn't see Johnny doing a show in Vegas with a little jug of sauce in him. The juice useta make him ten times funnier and with a wit could kill the worst heckler you could throw in against him.

Gettin' back to Mike Douglas, he gets me back on his show again after he's got Muhammad Ali on, he wants to know what I think about the Champ. I still tell him I believe nobody, noplace, ever gonna top Joe Louis, but Cassius hadda be the best boxer in the world during his prime years. He had speed, a long reach, and could make more moves than a watch.

Even though they say things like, "When Ali was born, he was a fourteen-pound mouth," you gotta know there ain't a guy around saying it that could shine his shoes when it comes to boxing savvy. I had my money on him all the way. My advice is to stay retired before another up-and-coming Ali turns him into a dummy.

This guy done more to bring back fighting as a top sport than any fighter since the days of guys like Joe Louis and Jack Dempsey. The guy'll tell you hisself, just like me, "I can't read or write a damn," but here he was recent, makin a address to Harvard University's graduating kids. You gotta give the guy a lotta credit.

I wanna also tell you about being on with Liberace once. I says, this guy working without his candleholders and those crazy lit-up jackets would be like a plumber without no tools. Right or wrong?

Mike had everything and anybody you could think of on his show. Machine gadgets, animals, tricks, cooking, and people from all sides of life. He even brought in a *paesan* of mine once to twirl pizza pies eighteen t'ousan feet in the air.

I even went into the pizza-pie business myself few years ago. A friend of mine from Jersey, Mike Losurdo, talked me into it. The guy owns a company called Capri Pizza Supply in Moonachie. How you like that name? He gives you everything you need. I don't wanna get too involved, so I go in with a sharp Italian kid called Joey Brown, and he runs the joint. You know what I mean? We even put a big boxin ring in the middle of the restaurant on Second Avenue, with tables in the ring. One night we had a big fire that almost wiped out our spaghetti and all the pizza pies, and that's when I let Joey take over the pizza pies. And me, I better stick to show business.

Mike Douglas had Barnum and Bailey on his show, and even F. Lee Bailey, the big Boston lawyer. The best was when I was on his show once, an he's got this chimpanzee on his show an Mike has one of those

Planted of the Apes get-ups on. The chimp took a look or two, flew up
into the ceiling framework and started to wreck the studio. They hadda
call the zoo, and the fire department to come and grab the kook chimp.

Mike read in a newspaper in 1970 that I make a speech to a finance
group, and he gets me started with this next time I appear, but I can't tell
the dirty jokes I use with the Wall Street group. On Mike's show, I say
things like about Norma, I say, I always get in the last word—"Yes,
dear." I also tell Mike, the only time my wife come to me on her hands an
knees I was hiding under the bed.

The newspaper story about the finance groups started, "Rocky Meets
Wall Street and They Both Get a Belt." I got paid good money to talk to
these ghees, and this was the first and last time I ever make a nickel offa
Wall Street. Everybody I was talking to was bankers and brokers. The
only thing I know about them is that when I was a kid we useta play a
card game called "Bankers and Brokers."

At this Wall Street stag bash, we eat up a ton of shrimp, roast beef, and
other good things, then everybody settles back, with a cigar or a drink, to
hear me talk about big finance.

First thing I do is loosen them up by saying, "Hey, you know what the
rooster says when he couldn't jump the hen? You're chicken!" Then
while I got 'em laughing, I tell them about the guy who got caught naked
in a bedroom closet when a husband come home not expected. The
husband says, "Eh, whatcha doing in my wife's bedroom closet?" And
the guy says, "Can'tcha see? I'm watchin the clothes."

I see they like these, so I hit 'em with another about a husband comin
home when he wasn't supposed to, and here's a guy in the bedroom with
his pants down around his ankles. When the husband says, "Ey, whatta
ya doin in my wife's bedroom with yer pants down?" The guy says, "Like
I just got through telling your wife, either you pay the plumbin bill or I'm
gonna shit right here in the middle of the floor."

Now I know I got Wall Street hooked good, so I says, "Betcha a lot of
you guys come from small towns and you was big shots there, so you'll
know what I'm talkin about. There was a town whore who turn madam
and open a big whorehouse in one of your burgs, where she done real
good. She made a ton of money in a few years so now she wants to do

something good, in return, for the town. She goes to the mayor with ten grand and offers it toward the new recreation building they plan to start building. The mayor, knowing who the hooker is, turns it down cold, but then he got second thoughts, so he brung up about the offer and his refusin at the next council meeting."

" 'Take it you jerk!' they tells him. 'After all, ain't it our money?' "

Soon as they quiet down, I tell them, "I don't know a goodam thing about your business. My wife keeps all the money, an she just gives me twenty bucks when I go outa the house in the morning. Before things started getting tight with inflation, she useta give me only ten. If you could make something outta that, you're welcome to use it all you like." I tell them too, "some days I want more money, because I feel like making a few transactions at the track. She don't give it to me, and I wanna kill her. So you see, she won't let me invest in nothing."

Even though I talk stupid, this breaks 'em up, and after it's over, all these big shots want to do is have their pictures took with the Rock.

EIGHTEEN

In April of 1975, one of our best friends, a member of Frank Sinatra's clan, died, and this broke up Conte's buddies more than anything in years. Richard "Nicky" Conte, who was sixty-one, had a massive heart attack and stroke, and he never came out of it. Like Frank, Conte was also an Italian kid who come offa the streets of Jersey. His pop was an Italian neighborhood barber in Jersey City, just like Dean Martin's father was a barber, and Dean was Conte's friend thirty years. Conte seem like he follow in Jimmy Durante's steps when he was first gettin his start. Not that he wanted to be a comedian. It just so happen that Durante's father was a barber too, and Durante started as a piano player. Conte got his start as a piano player for a small Jersey City band before he went on to make it big as a actor in Hollywood. He also done a few pictures with Frank, like *Tony Rome,* in which I'm with him, and *Lady in Cement,* and *Oceans Eleven.*

I'm gonna miss him like everybody else. Nick Conte, which was his real name, was always one hell of a friend to everybody.

If the legacy these guys are gonna leave is this, then take my advice, to any Italian kid who wants to follow in some of these guys' footsteps, is get your old man to become a barber, and if he could play some fair mandolin, that ain't gonna hurt nuttin either.

Since I mention my good friend of many years, and everybody's good friend, Jimmy Durante, no book that's got Italians in show business could ever be a hunnerd percent complete without something about our godfather, and I mean the godfather of us Italians in show business. I don't mean the one you saw in the movies and read from Mario Puzo. I mean our godfather, our *compare,* Jimmy Francis Durante. Jimmy was one-a the greatest guys I ever meet, anyplace, anytime, and the only guy they ever run out of genuine trophies and awards to give him.

The great "Schnozzola" was born and raised right down on the same Lower East Side I come from. This was way back in 1893, a little before my time, but his time was just like it was my time. Jimmy's first shot at earnin money came, just like some of the other Italian stars I got in this book, from shinin shoes and sweeping up hair.

The thing that put the show business bug in Jimmy wasn't a mandolin but, just like with Nicky Conte, it was a broken-down player piano that his folks bought second-hand. When Jimmy's mom 'n pop see him tinkering with the keys all the time, they decide to go for a few lessons.

While Jimmy's taking piano lessons, he quits regular school in the sixth grade so he could go out an earn some money to help out at home. Just like me, very few kids of Italian parents ever finish gramma school in those days. The word "help" was up in everybody's house. Jimmy Durante went out selling newspapers and grabbin any odd job he could find, just like all the other kids done.

I first meet Jimmy Durante when I was fighting. He useta see my fights, and always come back to the dressing room, or invite me to the Copa, or someplace important like that. Durante always ask me very serious if there was something he could do for me.

There's a lotta guys and girls who made it big that Jimmy Durante give breaks to. Frank Sinatra and Dean Martin could also tell you a ton of stories about this guy and his big heart. In Jimmy Durante's time there wasn't a place he won't go to help a friend or raise funds for a cause. Jimmy not only loved his work, he loved all the people he worked with, and millions loved him.

Jimmy Durante passed away recent. Rest in peace. They guy will always be *numero uno* to me an, I'm sure, to every barber's son ever have a spotlight t'rown in his face. How you gonna ever forget, "Inka dinka doo, a dinka inka dinka do. Now is the time for dreamin . . . "

One time when Norma and me's out on the coast for a Dean Martin roast, we get a chance to run up to San Francisco for a little sightseeing, and we go on one of those tours to closed-up Alcatraz.

I got my own memories of iron bars while we walkin along the cell blocks, but all the guide's talking about is Capone, an how he was their star guest. He calls the place Devil's Island of the United States. Then, we go by, an he points out the five by nine cell where Capone spent close to ten years, and this was before I met him. In the cell is a toilet bowl without a seat, an a steel cot. While I'm looking inside, I start to sweat good, so I take out my handkerchief and wipe my head 'n neck. I know that there but for the grace . . . *I* coulda lived out my life in this hole, or one like it. When nobody's looking, I fast make the sign of the cross. My mind was going off, and all over the joint and on the walls I see shadows of Al Capone, Machine Gun Kelly, George Raft, Jimmy Cagney, Edward G. Robinson, Paul Muni, and Wallace Beery, just like the parts the actor guys play in movies was real.

Imagin the balls on a bunch of Indians breaking in, instead of out, an holding that place for two fuckin years.

On the way out of Alcatraz, I don't wanna look back. On the boat going back to Frisco I look at the ring Al give me, which I still wear today. I blow on the diamond and polish it on my shirt just like making a genie wish, get me away from this fuckin place as fast you could.

To get back to the Martin roast, on one appearance the guy we're roastin is Danny Thomas. I tell everybody the guy is so good the saints go to him for advice. If he was a street cleaner, he'd be fired for not being able to keep his mind in the gutter.

Jan Murray says, "Here we are, mostly Jews, honoring an Arab." But Danny says he ain't a Arab, "I is Lebanese." He says it in a southern accent, like he's a Black man from the South, or something like that.

Another time when I was on, and they roasting somebody on the show, I don't remember who that time, but I remember me an Gene Kelly are on the same show. As him and me go by Dean up on the platform, I bend down and steal Dean's bottle which he got stashed there. I put the whiskey between me an Gene, who's sittin longside each other, and when we ain't on camera, we bend down an take slugs outa Dean's bottle. Dean keeps swinging his fist at us and the audience is roaring. They see it in the studio but not in your house. Like what they call an inside joke. By the end of the show, me and Gene is pretty stoned. I swear, if anybody ever try to make us guys feel this work was jobs, we might quit.

No matter where Dean and Frank are, they always keep in touch. They have me out with them when they around and they give me those nice shots on their shows. Mostly now, when they ain't making movies someplace, you catch them either playin golf, or appearing in Vegas and Lake Tahoe. If Sinatra's at Caesar's Palace in Vegas, chances are you'll find Dean right down the strip in the Riviera. And that Vegas hums like a buzz saw when these two champs are there.

My co-author, Ralph, tells me he was visiting friends in San Francisco couple-a years ago, when he reads in a Frisco newspaper that Dean's at the Riviera, Frank's at Caesar's, an Tom Jones is at another big hotel. Also there is Elvis Presley, rest in peace, Sammy Davis, Jr., Tony Martin, Shecky Greene, and other great names in show business. Ralph and his wife Vicki hop on a plane and spend one of the biggest weeks of their lives, seeing all these great acts. When they see Dean, Dean makes cracks about Frank and about Tom Jones's tight pants, saying the guy wears them out from the inside. When Ralph sees Frank, Frank makes jokes about Dean, and about Tom Jones's tight pants. And when they see Tom Jones, in between songs, he talks about how Dean and Frank are jealous of his tight pants. In some clubs they all get together real late and then you see the laughing sparks really fly. And when this kind of a line-up is in that town, just try to get a good room without a connection. You gotta end up looking for a sleeping bag, or spending the night on a bench in the bus station. It's truly amazin. Here's a bunch of guys who, like me, just came outa nowhere and leaves a mark nobody's ever gonna wipe out.

And what you call coincidence, my pop worked on the docks when I was a kid, and Sinatra's pop did too. My pop was a pro fighter when he was young, and so was Frankie's. Few years back, my daughter Audrey make me a grandfather and Nancy, Jr. make Ole Blue Eyes a proud grandpop too. I heard, at his granddaughter's christening you never saw such a happy grandpop, his blue eyes beaming like two spotlights.

Paul Anka couldn't have said it better than when he put words in Frank's mouth about how he'd lived a life that's full, an' traveled every highway, an' more than that, he did it his way!

Since I mention Ralph Corsel I gotta tell you a little bit about him. I put it on tape and I tell him print it or else.

You never believe this Ralph. Thirty-five years, forty years ago, near the end of the Depression, he was a bum, ridin' freight trains around the country, an workin washin dishes in hash houses, doin odd jobs and sometimes laborin with a pick 'n shovel like his father done most of his life. Before, after, and in between, Ralph was a pretty bad guy, just like I was, when *he* was a kid.

What I need to say about this horse thief is I find out the hard way once that, with everything else, the guy is also a champ pickpocket. He stole my watch right offn my wrist and I never buy another. I could just imagin the ace whiz this guy was when he was movin real an not just for kicks. Houdini couldn't make your wallet disappear like this Ralph does. The only defense you got with guys like these is always make sure a half a block at least is between youse.

I wore boxin gloves for over ten years, but believe me, it's Ralph who shoulda been wearin boxing gloves . . . all the time. But, I'll tell you something, you gotta know I'm kidding, about the gloves.

Ralph, just like a lot of us, straighten out, went legit, and made a bundle in a great business, representin' big firms like Prince Gardner, Kayser-Roth, and Piedmont Shirt. Then he become a writer and his kicks now comes from writing about hisself, and guys like us.

Don't get me wrong, he still dip your pocket or lift your watch, just to keep his hand in, but now he does it for laughs and always blows back with the swag. I remember the days when his old friends useta call him "Ralph the Dip," and some of them still do. But around Elmer's and P. J. Clarke's, all us guys now call him "Ralph the Plume." Ya know, a plume like a writer's feather pen.

Today, I never be afraid to let Ralph hold my wallet, and I wouldn't even count my money before I give him the poke.

And since I'm tellin you about Italian neighborhood guys like Ralph, who made it up the hard way, I gotta tell you about Pete Petrella, another friend I know for years. Pete's a big guy who was also a pretty good pro light-heavyweight fighter in his younger days. Only Pete didn't fall in the road like a lotta other punchies I know when he hung up his gloves. He become a sharp young bookmaker and numbers man in the Fordham Italian section of the Bronx. When Pete saved enough loot, he quit that racket and went into the dress-manufacturing business with a couple of small contract factories. The guy was always a mover, a good hustler. In fact Ralph Corsel wrote quite a bit about him in his first book *Up There the Stars,* put out by Citadel Press.

Pete made some big money in the rag business, and even put a lot of his family in action helping him run the business, but Pete's heart was never in it. The guy's a big, rough, handsome guy with a terrific deep voice, and maybe that's why his head was always in the clouds, always thinking how he could someday be somebody by busting into show business.

Pete read all kinds of books about show biz and making movies, and he hustles around talking to people who was in the game. When he figures he's got enough film smarts, and the loot to put together a package, he changes his name to Peter Savage, takes on my old friend Hammerhead Jake La Motta as his co-star, an they go to Italy to make his first movie. Pete produces the movie hisself. He also stars in it an directs it. The story was, two veterans, him and Jake, stranded in Naples after the Second World War.

Since then, Pete produced quite a few fair movies, some of which he had me do parts in. Pete has a good heart for ex-fighters, because he knows too what happen to most of them, so he makes a picture, which he wrote hisself, called *Cauliflower Cupids.* The star was Jane Russell, but in it he also puts five ex-World Champs. Me for one, Tony Zale, Jake La Motta, Paddy De Marco, and Petey Scalzo. He even gave my old buddy Bernie Allen the cabbie a cameo funny part in it.

In another film, *Woman of Fame,* he starred me, Jake La Motta, and Betty Bruce. This was the last picture Betty made before the big "C" hit her, rest in peace.

Pete wasn't satisified with just seeing the name Peter Savage up there on light bulbs, so now he becomes a writer, serious, and decides to write hard-luck Jake La Motta's life story. He called the book *The Raging Bull,* and when it got published it become a pretty good seller. Pete then went on to hustle the book to Hollywood for some pretty heavy bucks for him and Jake, with Pete one of the producers and with Martin Scorsese of *Mean Streets* directing. Robert De Niro is playing Jake, and Jake spent months in a downtown gym teaching De Niro how to fight and make all his moves. Jake says he could throw De Niro into a ten-rounder and he'd beat most of the good fighters you got aroun today. The icing on Pete's cake was when Bobby De Niro goes up to accept the Oscar for best actor of the year and says he owes it all to Pete.

When the downers are telling some of you kids, you can't come up outa those basements once you're born there, just tell them about some guys I know, like me and Ralph and big Pete.

And how you gonna top this for a broken-down umbrella like me who come off the street? Ronnie Reagan sent word recent that he wanted me to have lunch with him an a few other guys at the Waldorf Astoria Hotel. You know it, baby, I showed spiff and spat, and right on the button. And, one thing I gotta tell you, I go because I love the guy. I ain't never gonna get accused of having bad breath because I kissed the boss's *ring.*

Reagan says to me, "You know, Rocky, I like to keep in shape too, but I do it chopping wood and riding my horse 'Little Man.' You can't believe the view when I'm on his back up in the mountains, looking down over Santa Barbara and the Pacific Ocean." He got that far look in his eyes when he's telling me this, and I know it make him a little sad.

'I tell him, "Why don't you go ride him if you miss the nag so much?"

"You ever try riding a horse down Pennsylvania Avenue?" he says with a grin.

So, I tell him, ain't you the boss? Aaah. I couldn't bet on his bangtail anyway. He tells me his horse got seventeen years on his hide and he's still going strong. Just like his boss.

While we're having our coffee, I tell him I read all about how big his ranch is. I told him, "Ronnie, if you put your ranch in El Salvador it would *be* El Salvador and we would never have all that trouble down there."

He still laughs up a storm every time I say something, and I know we're gonna have lots of happy times ahead for everybody.

It don't matter how many years me and my Norma been together, we're still making those toe-to-toe scenes once in a while. And, like I say, I get so fucking mad sometimes, I wanna kill her, but when I cool off I gotta laugh. I seen some kids carrying signs once, "Make Love Not War," and I think here I'm doing both. It's usually the old thing that does it, like I'm out having a few drinks with the boys. I keep tellin her how much "Marcus M.D." can a guy watch on TV, an how much painting pictures can a guy do, cooped up in the house, before going daffy. Thing is, I love to paint, and my walls and my closets are loaded with my oils. I just ain't got no place else to put them. I was always hoping someday somebody comes up with an offer to give me one-a those fancy gallery showings, so I can take the extras out-a the closet and maybe, thank God, that now I just make it three big careers in one lifetime, an this too finally happen. Some of the people who seen the paintings in my house for the first time make me an offer to buy one but I never sold. If you're real special to me, then I give you one for nothing.

To get back to Norma, go put a dent in this kid. Maybe I tell you before, but I tell you again. There's only one big thing sets me off, and that, you guess it, she won't give me no money. My own fuckin money! Man, does this get me mad!

Some couples celebrate all kinds of anniversaries like fifth, tenth, silver. Norma celebrates an iron anniversary, because sometimes that's what she's made of.

Somebody offer to give us a piano once and even though nobody play it, we took it. I knew it come in handy if we give it a chance. It did. One day, I hauls my ass home a little bombed, with Phil Kennedy and Frankie Gio, my two drinkin buddies who were supposed to be takin *me* home.

When my little five-footer knew we were coming, she pushed the piano right up against the door. I tell you one thing she never bring into my life, and that's boredom. What I gotta worry about is, she hits harder than me. I'm afraid a punch from her could straighten out my nose and put me out of this actin bit I'm now in. There's times when I like to put my Norma on a train and forget about her. What good it do? When the train reaches the last stop it turns around and comes back.

Here's something I gotta tell you too. This is good. I sit around Elmer's with the boys some afternoons, and one day, who we got sitting with us but a famous psychiatrist. He looks at me kinda funny once, after I'm tellin' everybody how I love my New York and there ain't no place in the world like it, and he says, "You know something, Rocky, guy like you'll never need a psychiatrist. You've got no identity problem. You're you, and you love you just like you are." So ain't that beautiful? What the hell did the guy mean? And what I really wanna know is what the fuck's my wife yelling about? Y'mean? Even though I complain, there's one thing I know for sure. I know my wife. I know how she thinks, an I know what makes her happy.

The last big argument we have, I don't talk to her for three days. This time like always, it's the money, my money. I ask her. You know how much? Twenty bucks! I don't need money. All I need is ten, twenty dollars when I go outa the house. Maybe, thirty dollars, so I spend it. What the fuck's the big deal? The one fuckin tag I ain't lookin to get pinned on me is "slow pockets." I tell Norma, if I go someplace, take a cab, there's five bucks right there. I told her, you kiddin me, you won't give me twenty dollars? I get so mad fire's coming outa my eyes, and I say, now I want a hunnerd dollars, but still she don't give the money. She's gotta be savin it, knowin its gonna be valuable again someday.

You know I ain't the kind of a guy t' hit a dame, so I storms outa the house. I tell you somethin, if that little Jew of mine can buck me, and I holler pretty good, she could buck City Hall and win.

But, the way she act with me over money is wrong, dead wrong! It's my own fuckin fault for lettin her break herself in like that. It's dead wrong! Here I am, making t'ousans, and I gotta go outa the house without a twenty-dollar bill in my pocket. I really don't need the money because I could sign tabs anyplace in town but that ain't the point. And you know something else? If I don't ask her for money for a few days she accuses me of holdin out. How you like that? Holding out my own fuckin money! Here I am, ex-middleweight Champ of the World, and big star, and look at what I gotta go through to try to get my five-footer to come up with twenty lousy bucks. Why can't a guy's wife understand? All I gotta do is think about a few ex-fighters, and other ex-sports figures around who think the world owes them. They never in their lives pick up a tab or buy one guy a drink, even though they drink up everybody else's money. I hear people talking about 'em, calling them mooches and leeches, and I swear this ain't never gonna happen to me. *No sir!* Of course Norma remembers when I drop that ten thou' gamblin' in Miami.

All this bullshit with my wife comes from those days when we had nothin an I'm sure somethin like that could scare a lotta people. There was even that "religious" difference when we got married. Norma worshipped money, and we didn't have a dime. I gotta remember, when we moved to Brooklyn we pack everything we own in a cigar box. You gotta look at the other side of the coin sometimes. Even though I got a lotta friends, you gotta know, my three best friends is my wife, my dog, an *our* cash. My Norma keeps a nice, clean classy house for us. She's a terrific cook an hostess, we got a house fulla plants, an, yeah, the *tumult* is still there, but there's a lot of love too, and in my house you could see it bouncin off the walls.

I was very, very lucky with my two kids. Both married stand-up Jewish boys . . . with money.

Getting back to *tumult*, lemme tell you what she did to me last summer. Lucky the kids was married an gone.

This story has to do with dogs, my best friends. The dog I had before Aljo was called Plumber. Perry Moss, a guy in the plumbing business, give him to me and for respect I name the dog that. Plumber was just a lil puppy when I got him but ya hadda see him six months later. Grew as big and fat as a elephant, and he tore up the house racing around the rooms. All Norma ever yelled was, "Get that damn mutt outa the house."

Every day, come five, five-thirty, I gotta leave Elmer's or wherever I am, and I race home to walk my best friend. Plumber's pulling me along the curb on the end of his long chain one day, an a big truck turns the corner and kills him. You gotta see this fuckin dago go crazy. I throw a flurry of punches and drop the truck driver in the street, then I start crying—I'm trying to get over it for a couple of weeks, and even Norma's telling me she misses him. Then, who comes into P.J. Clarke's one afternoon but my good friend, Albie Goldstein, guy owns Key Foods and big piece of Elmer's. In his arms he's carrying the heaviest puppy you ever seen, a bull mastiff, and his head's already bigger than Jake La Motta's. Albie says, "He's yours, Rocky, and ya got the papers too with this one." I run out of the joint with the puppy cause I'm cryin an I find out later, Albie go for about seven an a half bills. That's another kind of a friend for you. Anyway, we name my new dog Aljo, after Albie and his wife Joan, and I brung the mutt home.

Norma goes along with the action for a few months, and now she can see this dog's not gonna stop growing until he's two-foot wide and four-foot tall. Aljo starts racing around the apartment, and if she thought Plumber was bad this dog makes him look like an amateur. This bull dog is even eating up the wooden furniture. Aljo even tore up the toilet seat, and I hadda go out and buy a new one.

We supposed to go out to dinner that night but I show up home smashed. Norma says, take a shower an maybe you sober up. I take off all my clothes and I come next to the terrace door where she is and I wanna grab her. Norma pushes me out on the terrace, balls, ass-naked, and she slams and locks the door. I must-a cursed my ass off out there for over an hour but she won't let me in. I swear I was ready to kill her when she finally let me in but I just go to bed and sleep it off. Thank God, it was summer because if it was winter she coulda let me freeze to death. Whatta ya gonna do?

The more I mellow, the more I'm getting to do like my wife pleases. It's a free country, ain't it? In fact, a few things changed as I'm getting older. When I bought Norma a new fur coat for last winter, one-a my daughters says, "Don't you know an animal has to suffer for that?"

And my wife says, "Shut up and don't talk about your father that way."

And another thing, she gotta be getting jealous in her old age. Norma don't let me go out alone at night anymore after dark. She's always telling everybody, night air can kill a man.

When Roxie was growin up, she don't understand why we name her Roxie. She hates the name, says she feels like she's named after a theater. One day she picks a name outa the hat and tells us from now on it's "Linda," an that's what we gotta call her. And wouldn't you know, the kid laid the law down, stubborn like her mother. Yeah, what happen to all those left hooks that I useta get in the way of, when my pop didn't like what I did or said.

And, you know something, when my other daughter, Audrey, give us our first grandson, we figures finally we got a new and up and coming Rocky in the family. They name the kid *Aaron,* Aaron Weissman. Could you imagin when the kid's growing up and he tells other kids his grandfather is Rocky Graziano? The poor kid's gonna get hit with more punches . . . I don't have to tell you, both Norma and me started teaching that kid how to fight as soon as he jump down out of the cradle. Norma teach him how to hook, jab, uppercut, keep throwin punches, and never back up. I teach him how to duck, bob, and weave, and give a little ground when he has to.

We got four grandchildren, all boys now, two in each family. They hadda go show me up, because all I could make was girls. Anyway, we teach all these kids how to fight, and they're all squaring off pretty good. And you know something, I'm the only one who calls 'em Rocky Juniors. They still didn't put it down on paper for any of them. *I wonder why?*

There's a little bar an restaurant I like to go into once in a while, an it's called Johnny Squeri's, after the owner. It's got an atmosphere you never believe. The atmosphere ain't the way the joint is set up. It's Johnny and his wise-crackin sister Jeannie, who's the waitress, and his mom an pop, and some of the people who come in as customers. The atmosphere is, Johnny's wacky, his sister's wacky, his folks is wacky, and some of the customers is wacky. Sometimes when I'm there, I'm not even too sure about me. I gotta tell you too, even though a lot of customers go there to dig Johnny and his family, and all the funny things they come up with, they're all real nice Italian people.

Don't get me wrong, this joint ain't a joint. They got the best Italian food you ever get anywhere, anytime.

I meet a lotta my ex-fighter buddies there, like Jake an Joey La Motta, Frankie Gio, Freddie Russo, Mike Colluci, Billy Graham, Vinnie Ferguson, Lou Fugasy, Maxie Shapiro, an Joey Scarlotta, who tends bar up the block at the Maganette. Besides wise guys like me, Johnny's got a lot of show-business people, writers an agents, and a lot of good stand-up business people who hit the place for lunch. The only guy of any importance who might have missed this joint is gotta be Earl Wilson. No matter what I tell you, keep in mind you can't beat their cookin. Durin heavy lunch and dinner business hours everything is busy and on the ball. But it's during those off hours that things get crazy.

Being Johnny's wacky, he attracts a few others like 'im, like some of the guys always come looking for me. One-a them is Maxie Shapiro, who fought all the greatest fighters of his day in his weight, including the champs. Maxie walks into Squeri's a late hot summer afternoon, and he's got a hat on but he's bare chested, carrying his shirt bunched up in his hand.

Jeannie sees him, runs to the door and stops him with "C'mon Maxie, you can't come in like that. Put your shirt on. This isn't a dump. This is a *family* place, with my *family* in it." Maxie turns around and goes away.

They also got a woman going into the place most every afternoon. Phyllis. She spends hours at the bar, friendly with everybody who walks in, and she do or say anything come into her mind, buy you a drink or ten, and go for her loot like a drunkin sailor. Phyllis musta fell into a pit one day and come up with a ton of diamonds, because she goes for a bundle, and never runs outa money.

One day when it's quiet, she gets into a big argument with Jeannie, and she's calling Jeannie all kinds of hooker and things, when Jeannie, who's a pretty healthy-looking broad, blows her top, grabs Phyllis by the throat and almost wrestles her to the floor. Just then who should walk in but Maxie Shapiro. He puts his hands on his hips an says, "My, my, Jeannie, this is a *family* place. How could you act like that?" Broke everybody up, and the two girls stopped maneuvering and got hysterical laughing. Then, when everybody's calmed down, Phyllis starts yelling somebody stole her blackjack outa her purse.

Another time, during those quiet late afternoon hours, Phyllis did a strip-tease right down to the brush, just because somebody dared her and says she wouldn't do it.

I come in one afternoon an there's Phyllis arguing with Johnny, toe to toe, cursing like a longshoreman. Seems like she butt in when he was having a serious discussion with somebody and he blew his top. The guy acts like he don't care what she goes for in his joint, and he's even ready to t'row her out. I know she spends a good buck there, and everybody likes to see her around, so I put my two cents in and try to make the peace, but she's saying, "Rocky, I want you to spit in my face if you ever see me walk inside this fuckin joint again." I can't tell you some of the words she t'row at Johnny, but you could imagin. The mother this and the mother that shook the front window. Then she starts crying and Johnny starts saying, "Now you gotta go cry and make me feel bad, like it's all my fault."

"Fuck you!" she says. She grabs her coat. "I hope they break my legs if I ever walk through that fuckin door again." She blows out the door like a storm, and that's that.

I walk in Squeri's a few days later and there's Phyllis at the plank, just as sweet and happy as could be. She's sweet-talkin Johnny, and everybody else in the joint, and even Johnny's sister Jeannie, who she call a hooker few days before. To look at them now, you never believe anything ever happen ever to spoil this beautiful customer/owner relation.

Johnny Squeri's mom and pop useta own the place before they retire and make Johnny take over. Then the old folks can't get it out of their system so they keep coming in all the time, cooking, running the kitchen, getting in the way of the chef, and cleaning up, just like they never retire, and they love to drink wine.

One Saturday, I go by round twelve noon. I know they're closed but they're inside, so I knock on the door and they all come to see who's there, and they let me in. Saturday, sometimes, they're closed till five, but I know they're cleaning the joint so I go over to have a beer with my pal Johnny.

When Johnny opens the door and I see him and his sister, and his pop and mom, I tell him, you know your place shoulda been named, "The Four Roses."

The four of them are all talking loud and at the same time, like one guy once call the dialogue of the deaf, and they're all stoned, drinking wine. I look at this small old dog, which belong to his mom and pop, and I see the dog is stoned too. The dog's swayin all over the joint and you could see it ain't from old age. The old man takes a bottle of beer from the bar and pours a little in a bowl he got on the floor. The mutt laps it up and goes dancin off, fallin against the furniture.

There's a sign over the register that says, "if you drink like a fish, swim, don't drive," but I don't see no pool in the joint.

The old man talks to me in Italian, but I can't understand him. They don't talk *Nopooliton* like me. They talk that northern Italy stuff. I just keep nodding because I could hardly figure one word. Johnny's folks come from so far north in Italy, they gotta be Swiss.

The old man sees me in the joint all the time, but he still don't know who I am when he's stoned-like. He keeps asking, "Who's he? Isn't the place closed?"

Johnny says, "Rocky, Rocky Graziano, my friend!" He holds a fist in the air. "Champion, Champion of the World!"

The old man just shakes his head, puts more beer in the dog's bowl, and half staggers off whacking the tops of tables he passes with a big napkin.

"Come on, pop," Johnny slurs, "will ya cut out giving all that beer to your mutt. He's gonna fall right on his ass."

"*Imbecile!*" the old man calls out.

Johnny says, "Rocky, if you ever need a friend don't buy a dog."

You know I got one, I tell him. Aljo, and he's my *best* friend.

All of a sudden, the old man breaks out singing some kind of an Italian anarchist song and he bangs hard on the top of table when a line in the song calls for it.

Johnny pours some beer from a bottle into a glass for me, and he spills some on the bar. "Jesus, Rocky, I'm sorry", he says, like it's a big catastrophe. "Gotta be their influence," he tells me. "You know, I never smoked, drank, or made it with chicks until I was ten years old."

Jeannie sneaks another drink and for the tenth time, she says, "You know we're closed today, Rocky. What brings you around?" and she lets out this loud crazy laugh.

And for the tenth time, I say, I just come by to see your brother and say hello.

Johnny says, "You know something, Rocky? I gotta quit this drinking. I can't remember what I'm trying to forget."

Johnny's mom comes out of the kitchen, a little stoned, goes behind the bar, and when she figures nobody's looking, she slips a bottle of wine under her apron and starts back to the kitchen.

Johnny says, "C'mon, will ya, ma!" then he comes back to me with, "Tell me, Rocky, how could I make a million dollars without going to jail?" He pours more beer in my glass and on the bar, and again he's sorry.

I figure I better get outa here before I join them in self-defense. I take a few more sips and start to leave. I call out goodbye, take one more look at the mutt staggerin around and I think, the family that drinks together sticks together. The mutt's part of the family, ain't he?

NINETEEN

Bernie Allen came looking me up at P. J. Clarke's like he's done every time he comes to New York. That's because he's out in Vegas most of the time now. He come a long way since those cab-driver days, and he's been my friend about twenty years.

When he looked me up, he says, "Frank Sinatra is now number three, because he's been going out of his way, right and left, to help me get bigger and better bookins."

I'm so happy for the guy that I gotta yell out, "Fuckin great!"

Once in a while I even play a little golf with Bernie. I even got him a few show-biz shots that make him a few bucks. Bernie keeps telling me he loves me even better than a brother. For a long time he was teamed up with Steve Rossi, who by a coincidence was, before Bernie, teamed up with another Allen, Marty. It was like some kinda magic made Bernie and Steve come together and click right off. They finish thirty-two straight weeks at the Silver Slipper in Vegas a short time ago.

I read a column written by Forrest Duke, and he says, "Bernie Allen and Steve Rossi, long a strong music/comedy act in the Sahara Casbah's levity lineup, are now at the Silver Slipper where they make the famed showroom come to life like it was in the good old days. Allen, who handles the hilarity, is the funniest ever, and the perfect partner for handsome singing star Rossi."

I tell Bernie how happy I am for him, and he says, "I get a lot of laughs out of those old gambling stories of mine, just like you said I would. Could it be that God put me there to give me the experience for today? Anyway, God came to me once and said, no more heavy gambling, Bernie, and I give him my word, for as long as I live."

Like Bernie is reminding me of the days when I could resist anything but temptation.

It took a big piece of my life to discover that fate is fate, and that everything bad that happens to you can't be blamed on nobody, that the way you're brung up, good, bad, or whatever, is something only God can explain. Not only that, it could have really been bad for me, specially when I think of how a lotta other fighters I know end up.

When the Marquis of Queensbury put down the rules for the ref to give you in the center of the ring, he never tell you what could happen when you hang up your gloves, how you might turn into a slob on Bughouse Square or get lost for good in any of the hundred skid roads around the country. Y'mean?

Take my old horse-thief buddy, Terry Young, for instance. When his boxing days were over for good and he ain't got penny one in the bank, he tried to buck the mob, using muscle to declare hisself in, but the big boys don't work things out with a chip on the shoulder like we done when we was kids. Terry wound up dead in the street, right on our own Lower East Side, the place where your fists made you a king when you was a kid. The last blood that poured out of Terry, rest in peace, came from holes that bullets ripped through him, and the last guy that boxed him was the undertaker. This was the end that everybody had once picked for me.

Terry Young wasn't a bad guy. He was just lost, just like I was once, but nobody ever found him. The guy was there when I needed him. Ain't it funny how a guy could show you your way but can't get out of their own?

Terry's cousin, Lulu Constantino, a guy who never cross nobody, I hear died recently after a long illness. I hate to start telling you what happened to a lot of other kids I run with in those days.

When I got important, after I quit boxing, a lotta other guys who fought durin my time were still fighting long after they shoulda quit. So, a news guy interviews me about this, and he puts in his paper, "Open Letter from Rocky," an article he starts, "Hang up your gloves, suckers ..." I tell Ezzard Charles, Willie Pep, Ray Robinson, Joey Giardello, all they could end up with now is scrambled eggs in their coconuts.

So, lemme tell you about some of the great champs, and other great fighters of my time or any time, and here's how I hear they wind up. Joe Louis and Willie Pep was chasing around for years near broke and trying to come up with some kind of a break. In fact, I run into Willie Pep not too long ago. He's just a short little skinny guy, but he made a bundle as Featherweight Champ of the World. I ask Willie how short he was, and he says, "After my last divorce about twenty grand."

And a guy like Joe Louis died broke, rest in peace. Didja know he held the world heavyweight boxing title longer than any other boxer in history, eleven years, eight months, and seventeen days by the book.

And, when a guy asked me on a TV talk show recent, "Who's, in your mind, the best all-time heavyweight fighter?" I hadda tell him Joe Louis. Not only was the guy the top fighter but he had nothing but class, in and out of the ring. Y'mean? All his moves was smooth and clean. Sure the guy was rough. How else he get to be champ? But everybody'll tell you, always a gentleman, professional all the way. He's the one guy every fighter since him gotta respect.

And talking about respect, for my division, the middle-weights, the greatest fighter ever lived, in my books, is gotta be Ray Robinson. Ray's also one of the few ex-champs who manages to stay in there floating, far as his financial department is consoined. He picks up a nice buck as an occasional half-ass actor, like me.

Tami Mauriello, I heard, was working in a warehouse or driving a truck. Beau Jack, one-a the great fighters of my time, who fought for the championship in '48, same year I did, last I heard he been shining shoes in a men's room in the Fountainebleau Hotel in Miami Beach for quite a few years. Kingfish Levinsky, who fought the top heavyweights of his time—guys like Dempsey, Jack Sharkey, Primo Carnera, Max Baer, an Joe Louis, is the guy who's been selling ties on the streets of Miami, the guy I played in Sinatra's *Tony Rome*. Joey Maxim, a great light-heavyweight Champ of the World, was driving a cab in Las Vegas last time I seen him there. Ezzard Charles, who was World Heavyweight Champ from 1949 to 1951, died a couple-a years ago at fifty-three years old, after being in a wheelchair nine years. The guy made two million from his fight career but was dead broke when he sat in that chair to live the last years of his life in it.

And, if you're curious about what happened to good-looking Steve Riggio, *the track star,* I'll tell you. After fighting me, he stayed in the ring for another four, five years, and you know this guy couldn't get hurt. He stayed in the ring because he was raising a family and needed all the bread he could earn to buy table bread for his wife and kids. And I gotta say here, I'm glad I never fought this guy for the title. I'm sure he would have run off with it.

After quitting the ring, Steve Riggio started pushing a cab, and the guy hacked it for twenty years so he could send his three boys through college. You gotta give this guy a lotta credit. Today, Steve is one of my good friends, and I know he had to be doin somethin right. Specially when he taught his kid Lenny to run with a stack of books under each arm.

Lenny Riggio worked in the college bookstore to help earn his way through the New York University, and today Lenny makes his pop one of the proudest ex-fighters to ever leave the ring. Even though Steve gave his son Lenny his start in life, the kid did it all on his own. Today, Lenny Riggio is the owner of a multimillion dollar bookstore chain called Barnes & Noble.

And if you're innerested in what happen to Joe Wander, the guy who pull me out of Steve Riggio's dressing room, I'll tell you. Joe got off the streets of the East Side and also made it through NYU. Today, Joe Wander is a big Hollywood producer and right now he's trying to put together a film, *The Man Who Robbed the Pierre.*

Another big show-biz success was raised poor with me down on the East Side is Walter Matthau. In fact, he tells anybody who'll listen, how he beat me up in a couple of street fights when we were kids. So you see, you guys trying to fight your way up, coming off those mean streets, don't mean you gotta end up in the tank.

And quite a few ex-fighters went the show-biz route. There's me, and Frankie Gio, Ray Robinson, Jack Palance, Maxie Rosenbloom, Max Baer, Tony Canzoneri, Ken Norton, and some I forget.

You gotta know how lucky I am when I tell you what happen to some other great fighters of all time.

Take "Bummy" Davis, another great of my time. Shot and killed trying to fight holdup guns with his fists in a bar he was managing. Marcel Cerdan, Rocky Marciano, and Tommy Tucker died in plane crashes. Kid McCoy and Billy Papke, two former middle-weight champs, committed suicide. Primo Carnera, another popular heavyweight Champ of the World, wound up sick and broke back in his Italy, where he died. Irish Bob Murphy and Johnny Greco were killed in auto accidents. Chalky Wright drowned in a bathtub. Billie Bello died of an overdose. Al Guido was shot an killed by a close relative. Terry Young and Frankie De Paula tried to move in on the big guys an got bumped off. An you know what happened to Nick Bob, my pop.

Some guys done better 'n that, though. Tony Zale become a bouncer in a Gallagher's downtown New York sports bar. Kid Gavilan, somebody tell me, was on welfare for a while. An Paddy De Marco, an ex-lightweight champ, is dealin blackjack at Caesar's Palace in Vegas.

These were some-a the biggest fighters of my time, and look what happen to them, to say nothing about all the other fighters who wound up broken bums after making thousans.

An lemme tell you somethin else, I don't hear no bells when no bells is ringing. And since I started with nothing, every single thing I got today is profit. But, I also got one big regret. Just when I started making some big money and coulda tried to wipe away some of those buckets of tears, my mom passed away. I wish today I coulda had a chance to fill all those buckets with gold. Ain't it something how when you finally got money to burn, the pilot light goes out?

Couple-a years back, I read that when Dutch Schultz, the big racketeer, got pumped full with lead, he didn't die for twenty-four hours. The cops sat by his bed all that time, trying to pump him for info but nothing come. Just as Schultz is breathin his last, he opens up with just four words, and they was his very last words, "Mom's your best bet!"

Like I say, there's a list a mile long of boxers who ended up in the tank. Since I started there, where could I go but up? And as long as there's more television sets than bathtubs I ain't never gonna take a *bath*. Right now those beautiful commercials that I make national, or for local setups, have me shooting aroun the country like a hobo with money. And I make the bucks only because I talk broken English.

"The contract includes residuals." First time some boss told me, I ask, what the hell is that? They film thirty seconds or a minute, and you're through, but then come the beautiful clincher. Everytime it shows on TV you get another check in the mail. Didn't I tell you I hadda shrewd up in this business? Today commercials beat everything—movies, stage, TV shows, everything! Unless you could be in Paul Newman's class, gettin up to three million dollars a picture, you could, like me, have it made with the commercial action.

My old beer-drinking buddy Paul Newman and me still get together once in a while when he's in New York, and we always manage to crack open a few beer cans together. The one thing about him didn't change was the way the guy like and guzzle beer.

A lotta years have gone by since we palled out in Stillman's gym and down on the Lower East Side. Today he tells me, "Rocky, I don't like my privacy fucked with strange people knocking on my door, or stopping me in the street, camera guys, autographs, that kinda bullshit.'

Anyway, that's Paul's bit. He paid his dues and he's entitled if that's what he wants. Whatcha got was the entertainment when you planted your bucks in the ticket winda and saw pictures like *The Hustler, Butch Cassidy,* and *The Sting.* Ain't it funny how a guy'll bust his ass to become famous so people'll recognize him, and then when he makes it, he quick gets a disguise with dark glasses so nobody know who he is.

Me, I'm so happy some of my folks took the boat. I love people, and I love 'em stopping me on the street. It's like I'm now getting the love I lost out on when I was a kid. Nothing makes me happy like a smiling face running, looking for me to ask me for my autograph to take home to their kids. When I was a little bittie kid, playin hide 'n seek, the other kids didn't even come looking for me when it was my turn to hide. And today I love people talkin about me. I think one of the worse things for a guy in the light is when nobody talks about you no more.

All I gotta say now is, cab drivers, waiters and waitresses, office workers, grocery clerks, cops and robbers, bartenders, butchers, shoemakers, bakers, conductors, doormen, walkers, joggers, janitors, elevator operators, factory workers, and anybody else you could think of keep askin me for autographs. I'll steal a few more pens.

And while I'm talkin about Paul Newman, wouldn't the guy be great playin me again in a film sequel to the one he starred in as me? The guy could even use film clips from the first movie and bring me up to today through all the entertainment years. Almost like it was his own life. He shoulda got the Academy Award the first time around. This time I promise it to him poisonally.

Gettin back to commercials, the thing I hadda get over was some of the outfits they put me in. Lately, I do one for Lee Myles Transmissions, who I do a lot for, and they put me in a solid white tuxedo with tails, and a white top hat. Hope you seen it. That wasn't hard to take, specially lookin at the show girls they t'row in with me.

Some of the other outfits I gotta wear is women's clothes, blonde ladies' wigs, Arab outfits, Indians, cowboys, bums, mechanics, hard hats, aprons, you name them. All I say is, long as those checks keep hittin my mailbox.

One time I get a check from a company who look like it may go under. "You better give me cash," I tell the guy. "I don't trust those New York banks. They could end up robbing both of us."

Let me tell you. I love bein a TV salesman almost more than anything

I ever done. I got so good at it that I betcha I could sell some of those Texas oil millionaires the Pacific Ocean and make 'em believe they was buying the biggest swimming pool you ever seen.

Lately, I even started producing my own commercials for some pretty good companies, I'm doing great at it.

Through the years, my New York grew and grew. Reminds me of the comb I carried in my pocket when I was a kid. When you held it teeth up, they was all broken at different length, an that's what our skyline look like today. But even with all that shit I hadda buck when I was a kid, I still like to go back to my roots. Today, my idea of a good time is getting away from those skyscrapers to some Little Italy neighborhood, with a bunch of Italian guys in a bar like downtown Puglia's on Hester Street or the Leading Tavern in the Bronx, and laugh it up over old stories, while we load our stomachs with things like cheese, *prosciutto,* salami, *pasta e fahzool,* sausage and peppers, tripe, *capozelle,* everything flavored with garlic, big Italian salad, Italian bread, and strong wine. These are about the only places left where you can eat like a king and get your money's worth. The shit really hits the fan when you walk into a high-class joint today. You gotta ruin a hunnerd dollars jus bein there, and no violins neither, and what's more, the eats never compare with what I was just talkin about. And you useta only have to go for a thin one, or two bits, to bail out your coat. Today, if you don't come up with green pictures of presidents just watch the dirty looks and zingers you get. But, like I mighta said before, when you finally able to set the world on fire you either don't wanna go for the action no more or the pilot light goes out.

Me, I got nothin to squawk about. I hope every kid in the world come up out of the streets like me, an get the breaks I finally got. I once heard a poem with religion in it and there was this line I never forgot, "My cup runs over."

Today I could be walkin, along the street, and run into all kindsa important people what knows me. Like, couple-a weeks ago, when I spot Governor Carey gettin out of a limousine on Third Avenue, with his guard detectives surroundin him. I yell out from across the street, Ey, Carey! and he leaves his guys, runs across the avenue, and we're huggin and shoutin and laughin in the middle of Third Avenue while cars are going around us. When I had a summer house in Long Beach, Carey was my next-door neighbor. His kids played with my kids, and him and me useta go fishin and clammin an lookin for *scungillis,* and the fun we had was just great. You know something, he become governor of our state, but he's still the same guy today. Fanfuckintastic, in my book. What could I tell you?

I once watched one of Carey's kids climbing his pop like Carey was a backyard clothes-line pole. The kid made it to his belt an used it to pull hisself higher. Carey give his kid a fast assuring squeeze, and the kid got almost to his pop's shoulders before Carey grabbed him and sit him up on a shoulder. Then Carey stood the kid up, with one foot each side of his head while he held the kid from behind the ankles. Carey made the kid go as high as he could on his own, and the kid was trying to reach even higher maybe to try to grab an armfulla stars. I remember feelin glad and even sad. I punched my fists together just as if I had gloves on 'em. Because, well because, everytime I see fathers playin with their kids I see a pair of boxin gloves. I know I sometimes come back to these things like they some kind of obsession. But I don't think so. I think it's a message somebody keeps throwing in my way to go help pull other kids outa the gutter. Maybe it's the way my life was told to turn.

When I finally made it big, and somebody asks me to come and talk a little at a orphan home, I can't wait to do it. I say, Hi, kids! But after that I don't know too much what to tell 'em.

I know I wanna do this again so I go around to show-biz friends an ask them to give me lines for some kinda routine I could use on kids. I work on it just as serious as a big-money score, even though these shots are zilch shots, on the arm. But they pay you off in something you can't buy for no money.

I talk to the kids tough, and I make 'em laugh when I act like they're a buncha wise guys. I tell a few kid jokes and I close with songs that say that if I was a millionaire I'd buy up every schoolhouse an there'd be two six-month vacations twice a year.

I don't sing that good. I almost talk the song, but everybody says, the song is me an it come out good. When I see how happy I make these kids, looking to tear the house down and all, I know I make these kinda appearances even in Timbuktoo if somebody ask me and I got the time.

I also been asked to help raise money, and for every cause you could imagin. I've been even asked to raise funds for a crap table somebody wanted in Brooklyn. I've talked in orphan homes, hospitals, police kid clubs, and all kinds of kids' detention homes and reform schools like the ones people tried to talk to me in when *I* was a kid.

I don't think there's any real bad kids who can't get straightened out before it's too late. Most of these kids are sick and starved, and it makes them go bad. They're sick because they don't see no hope, and what they starved of is a little love and affection. If they could make penicillin outa old moldy bread then you gotta be able to make something of these kids. Didn't it happen to me? They got a chance too. When they see that a dog like me made it, they know they can get outa the bottom of the barrel too.

When I open up to young kids in reform school, I loosen 'em right up saying, kids, if I had a good lawyer and a good alibi, when I was a kid in trouble like you, I wouldn't be here today. Then I joke about the beans and things they gotta eat. I know every plate. They whistle and yell like they gonna tip the mess hall over, which is where I usually talk to them. I tell 'em remember when your mom and pop fell behind in the rent and it was the biggest catastrophe in the world for them? No sir. The biggest catastrophe is when you fall behind in life. But wait a minute, just like your mom 'n pop caught up on the rent, you can catch up on life. The answer is pure and simple. You never give up! You hear me? Never!

Then there's talkin to the junkies. With mosta them it's the toughest thing in the world to break through. Some-a them don't even know who they are, let alone who you are, or what the hell you're spouting in their ear for. But you get through to more than you think. The main thing is you gotta try to impress 'em with, don't be a drop out! And I mean a dropout in life.

Private industry decided to do something about the drug menace couple years back and they got my friend Paul Corvino and made him National Chairman. Paul ask me to help and I jump right in I ask 'em "Where you want me, what I gotta do?" Paul says he needs me and sports guys like me because the young kids chippyin with the weed and junk will listen to a great sports figure before they listen to Jesus Christ. Paul says it's a duty I gotta do because I got that second chance and now I gotta try to give it to others. As if he hadda tell me.

Some-a the people I appear on the Drug Rehabilitation Program with was, first, President Nixon, my fifth President. This was before they say about him, there was two sides to every question and he take both, and before that Watergate thing. Other guys that give their time, that I appear with, was Sammy Davis, Jr., a right-there first guy, and at that time, Duffy Dyrer of the Mets, Jerry Philben of the Jets, Vida Blue of the Oakland A's, Governor Malcolm Wilson, Ed Cranepool of the Mets, Vice President "Rocky" Rockefeller, Bobby Murcer of the Yankees, Ricky Thompson of the Giants, Jackie Robinson, rest in peace, Walt Frazier of the Knicks. Attorney General of New York State, Louis Lefkowitz, and a lotta others I forget.

In no time I'm in, an I got a speech for parents and one for the kids. First thing I open with makes the parents all loose and laughing, and this loosens up their troubles a little. I say, "I tell you how much I know about dope. Guy ask me what I know about L.S.D. once, and I tole 'im, 'The guy was a good president. He never hoit nobody.' I tell them then, we all gotta chip in because the kid you save could be your own. And when they see that message on TV 'Do you know where your kids are tonight?' they better know. Sure, marijuana ain't that dangerous, but the ghee sells it is the same ghee who pushes the stuff for the vein department. If you find a supply of glue and you know your kid don't go in for model airplanes, or you find a jar of pills and they don't look like marbles, or you find "roach holder" or "hookay," which is a pipe, or even worse, the needle, in your kid's belongins, I know you gotta get frantic and blow your top, but don't t'row the kid outa the house. Talk and keep talking to them and try to bring them back with love, even when you know they ain't listening to word one. Maybe someplace along the way you made them feel you didn't care what the hell happened to them.

And don't go thinkin it can't happen to your family because you're important people. It's happened to politicians' kids, ministers' and teachers' kids, and big shots in my own business. Go ask two of my best friends about heartache. They also figure, like you, they give their kids all the love and everything they could to keep 'em straight. Carol Burnett's daughter was hittin the stuff at twelve years old. How's a kid that age gonna know they just ruined their life? And my *man*, Paul Newman, and his gorgeous wife, Joanne Woodward, how many of youse know what a couple-a kids put them through? Scott, Paul's oldest boy, twenty-eight, was on his way to becoming a big star like his old man. The kid overdosed and killed hisself. When you see Carol Burnett, or the Newmans on film or TV all you see is the laughs, a good story, or a lot of money. Nobody ever see them in their home, crying like babies because their kids broke their hearts.

An you folks who don't have the problem because you think your kids are too small, I say, they found kids already hooked on heroin who was nine years old. And those of youse who don't have the problem because you don't have kids, or the ones you got never go that route, then how about pitchin in an helping somebody who ain't as lucky as youse? It ain't hard to spot when you know what you lookin for. If they don't look drunk and sleepy like they in a daze, glassy-eyed, scratching too much, maybe you hear them talking to other kids, outside or on a phone. Listen for words like twisted, bent, high, acid, spike, decks, nickel bag, hit, downs, ups, dead, grass, speed trip, turned-on, an horse. Y'mean? I ain't playin' like Robert Preston in *The Music Man,* but I'm sure as hell talkin' about trouble.

What could I tell you? I'm sure most of you don't need a guy like me to tell you what to do with your kids. Me, I love mine and I let 'm know it in some way everyday of their life.

And this I finally gotta tell you too. That third career finally give off some beautiful fruit. Yeah, somebody, sometime back, make a contact with me for just that. Right now, while I'm putting this down, my paintings are on exhibition at the Spectrum Galleries on Fifty Seventh Street off Fifth Avenue. How you like that address for an old horse thief? People come in and say, "Rocky, they're beautiful!" When I was a kid and somebody told me something was beautiful, I quick say, how could it be beautiful if you can't put tomato sauce, *ooo soog* on it. And one newspaper guy who come to the gallery to write up the show tells me I could get a scholarship with the work I put out. I remind him I got scholarships before but they were to reform schools.

All this action about my paintings is what Lou Gehrig done for me without knowing it. And all those things happen way back then was the road the Guy up there made me travel to get where I reached today. I got a million thanks for the Somebody up there, an for all those somebodies down here who like me too.

Lou Gehrig, rest in peace, would not only turn over in his grave but spin in it like a top if he ever know I got to meet, shake hands with, and do things for eight Presidents of the United States, starting with good old Harry S. Truman, to my smiling t'espian buddy, our great president today, Ronnie Reagan.

I don't know where I'm gonna go from here, but I sure ain't gonna hold my breath waitin for the beautiful job our president promise me years ago. You remember? "Secretary of Education." I love the guy, and I know he's gonna make one hell of a president. Maybe, the best that ever walked that White House floor. I, for one, knew it all the time and I broke my *ass,* yeah, helpin in that campaign. We got us a winner, and don't forget, the guy coulda never made it without my diction lessons.

Like I say, it's a dice toss for what's up ahead, but if I gotta start someday on still a fourth career, or even go back and start again, I do it all just like before. I know a lotta people could bore the shit outa you with the same old stories but I hope this is the first time you heard mine. Do me two favors. First, if your kid needs a friend, buy the kid a dog. And second, in the years to come, if you see me making my way down First or Second Avenue in New York City, please don't kick the cane out from unner me. I never really hoit nobody.

FIGHTERS' NICKNAMES

Coupla places in the book I put how a lotta fighters took on Irish names. I t'ought you might like to know about a lot of fighters who you just knew their fightin names, Irish or whatever, but never knew what their real names or any other names they had was. These are some of the famous fighters with odd nicknames, that go back to like seventy-five years.

My Pop	— *Fighting Nick Bob*
Myself	— *Rockaby, or The Rock*
Lou Ambers	— *The Herkimer Hurricane*
James Ambrose	— *Yankee Sullivan*
Henry Armstrong	— *Hammering Hank*
Okon Bassey Asuquo	— *Hogan Kid Bassey*
Max Baer	— *The Livermore Larruper*

Joe Louis (Barrow)	— *The Brown Bomber*
Christopher Battalino	— *Battling Battalino*
Giuseppi Antonio Berardinelli	— *Joey Maxim*
Paul Berlenbach	— *The Astoria Assassin*
Tony Bombace	— *The Bomber*
James J. Braddock	— *The Cinderella Man*
Aaron Brown	— *The Dixie Kid*
Bobby Brown	— *Bust 'em up Brown*
Joe Brown	— *Old Bones*
Noah Brusso	— *Tommy Burns*
Primo Carnera	— *The Ambling Alp*
Georges Carpentier	— *The Orchid Man*
Ovila Chapdelaine	— *Jack Delancy*
Cassius Clay	— *Muhammad Ali*
Mike Colucci	— *The Crotona Kid*
Billy Conn	— *The Pittsburgh Kid*
Gerald Cooney	— *Gentleman Gerry Cooney*
James J. Corbett	— *Gentleman Jim*
Joseph Corrara	— *Johnny Dundee*
Gus Corsalini	— *The Ring Master*
Nick Corsalini	— *Dempsey's Protege*
Arnold Raymond Cream	— *Jersey Joe Walcott*
Al Davis	— *Bummy Davis*
Pat De Marco	— *Paddy*
Jack Dempsey	— *The Manassa Mauler*
Angelo De Sanza	— *Terry Young*
Jack Dillon	— *Jack the Giant Killer*
Roberto Doran	— *I Think I Go Home, or, No Mas*
Samuel Engotti	— *Sammy Angott*
Jim Ferns	— *The Kansas Rube*
Jacob Finkelstein	— *Jackie Fields*
Luis Firpo	— *The Wild Bull of the Pampas*
Robert Fitzsimmons	— *Freckled Bob*
Frank Fletcher	— *The Animal*
Tiger Theo Flowers	— *The Georgia Deacon*
Tony Galento	— *Two-ton Tony*
Kid Gavilan	— *The Hawk*
Ralph Giordano	— *Young Corbett the Third*

Frankie Gioseffi	— *Fury the Anvil*
Francisco Giulledo	— *Pancho Villa*
Billy Graham	— *Fighting Billy*
Harry Grebb	— *The Human Windmill*
John Gutenko	— *Kid Williams*
Andrew Haymes	— *Fireman Flynn*
John Heenan	— *The Benicia Boy*
Dick Ihetio	— *Dick Tiger*
Morris Jabaltowski	— *Ben Jeby*
James Jackson Jeffries	— *The Boilermaker*
Verlin Jenks	— *Lou Jenkins*
William Jones	— *The Gorilla*
Georgie Kaplan	— *Cappie The Whiz*
Stanley Ketchel	— *The Michigan Assassin*
William Kilroy	— *Billy the Killer*
Jake La Motta	— *The Bronx Bull, and the Raging Bull*
Joseph La Motta	— *Tiger Joe*
Sam Langford	— *The Boston Tar Baby*
Samuel Lazzaro	— *Joe Dundee*
Benjamin Leiner	— *Benny Leonard*
King Levinsky	— *The Kingfish*
Leonardo Liotta	— *Tony De Marco*
Charles Liston	— *Sonny Liston*
Kid McCoy	— *The Corkscrew Kid*
Terry McGovern	— *Terrible Terry*
Jimmy McLarnin	— *Baby Face*
Samuel Mandella	— *Sammy Mandell*
Rocky Marciano	— *The Brockton Blockbuster*
Gershon Mendoloff	— *Ted Kid Lewis*
Dave Montrose	— *Newsboy Brown*
Battling Nelson	— *The Durable Dane*
Jack O'Brien	— *Philadelphia Brown*
Carl Olson	— *Bobo Olson*
Jack Palance	— *Kid Brazzo*
Willie Pep Papaleo	— *Will o' the Wisp*
Billy Papke	— *The Thunderbolt*
Henry Pearce	— *The Game Chicken*
Al Pennino	— *The Voice*

Natale Peregine	— *Preacher Nat*
William Perry	— *The Tipton Slasher*
Pete Petrella	— *Pete Savage*
Tony Pilleteri	— *Tippy Larkin*
Phil Rafferty	— *The Battling Mick*
Bill Richmond	— *The Black Terror*
Steve Riggio	— *Kid Lightning*
Joe Rivers	— *Indian Joe*
Maxie Rosenbloom	— *Slapsie Maxie*
Barnet Rosofsky	— *Barney Ross*
Freddie Russo	— *The Dynamite Kid*
Joe Saddler	— *Sandy*
Eligio Sardinias	— *Kid Chocolate*
Joey Scarlotta	— *Rigger*
Max Schmeling	— *Maximillian Adolph*
Tony Sciortino	— *Poosh 'Em Up*
Maxie Shapiro	— *The Blade*
Babe Simmons	— *Irish Babe*
Martin Sinatra (Frank's father)	— *Marty O'Brien*
Billy Smith	— *Mysterious Billy*
Walker Smith	— *Sugar Ray Robinson*
John L. Sullivan	— *The Boston Strong Boy*
Charles Bud Taylor	— *The Terror of Terre Haute*
Johnny Thompson	— *Cyclone*
Carmine Tilelli	— *Joey Giardello*
Bob Travers	— *The Black Wonder*
Gene Tunney	— *The Fighting Marine*
Mickey Walker	— *The Toy Bulldog*
Sidney Walker	— *Beau Jack*
Chuck Wepner	— *The Bayonne Bleeder*
Jess Willard	— *The Pottawatomie Giant*
Ad Wolgast	— *The Michigan Wildcat*
Albert Wright	— *Chalky*
Archibald Lee Wright	— *Archie Moore*
Joseph Young	— *Tommy Ryan*
Tony Zale	— *The Man of Steel*
Joseph Paul Zukauskas	— *Jack Sharkey*

"Ya done good, Rocky"

Joey Adams	— *"Rocky has a lot of the qualities that my golden, late, Tony Canzoneri had—punchy."*
Ace Alagna	— *owner/editor of the* Italian Tribune—*"Rocky makes every man feel like a king, and every woman a queen. He can have my two-page centerfold anytime."*
Robert Alda	— *"It was a pleasure having Rocky on my show. His good smart moves will always keep him in action."*
Mohammad Ali	— *"If I could talk like Rocky, I'da quit boxing long before I did."*
Bernie Allen	— big *Las Vegas comedian—"If it hadn't been for Rocky, I'd still be driving a cab today."*
Steve Allen	— *"Rocky's my boy—I hope."*

Woody Allen — *"I'm glad Rocky wasn't one of those dark-hallway encounters in the days when I could barely come up with fourteen cents."*

Paul Anka — *"You can't say he didn't do it his way."*

Lauren Bacall — *"No! Rocky cannot play the part of Humphrey Bogart if a movie is made of his life. Why did he ask?"*

Burt Bacharach —*"I'd write a song for Rocky, but he's liable to punch the hell out of it."*

F. Lee Bailey —attorney—*"When I was on the Mike Douglas Show with Rocky, he asked me, 'Where wuz ya when I wuz lookin through the bars yellin, I wanna see my lawyer!'"*

Charlie Baio — *of P. J. Clarke's*—*"If Rocky lived in the town I come from on a mountain in Agrigento, Sicily, his fists wouldn't be worth a nickel, but give him a jackass on a mountain pass and he could hold off an army with just that jackass."*

Lucille Ball — *"Rocky is a ball even if he wasn't born one."*

Rowland Barber — *Rocky's co-author of* Somebody Up There Likes Me *and* The Rocky Road to Physical Fitness—*"I don't know how that Ralph ever tied him down. If staying on the run is Rocky's secret of success, would somebody tell me what I went to college for?"*

Milton Barry — *Vice President of Faberge Perfumes. "Rocky couldn't understand how it was my brother George and not Cary Grant who was president of Faberge."*

Charlie Bates — *restaurant entrepreneur—"The ring is not the only place where Rocky cracked skulls. He cracked up a few* capozelli *in my joint too. A* capozelli *is a goat skull, an Eyetalian delicacy."*

Warren Beatty — *"We could certainly have used Rocky in* Bonnie and Clyde. *In fact, Bonnie and Clyde could have used him."*

Freddie Bell — man about town—*"If I ever find my money, I'll make us all millionaires, Rocky. You'll never have to do a commercial again."*

Johnny Bench — *"Rocky benched me after I missed a ball thrown by a girl on the Mike Douglas Show."*

Jack Benny — *"On our first meeting, Rocky said, "Eh! Ain'tcha the guy what's got long-pockets an arthritis of the elbows?"*

Polly Bergen — *"TV is the wonderful media through which I met Rocky. A joy to work with. I'd better say that."*

Milton Berle — *"When I started on TV as Mr. Television, everything was black and white. Then Rocky got into my act, and for a while it was black and blue."*

Yogi Berra — *"I was playing golf with Rocky one day during the Knapp Commission hearings, when Rocky said, 'Wonder why they don't make one of these things on boxing?' Take eighty years to figure out the dialogue, I told him."*

Whitey Bimstein — *"I trained Rocky right to the championship and everybody called me the Miracle Man. Shoulda been him got tagged with that handle."*

Joey Bishop — *"Watching Rocky being prepared for a show is like watching someone putting makeup on roast beef."*

Humphrey Bogart — *"Always a sweetheart!"*

Pat Boone — *"If Rocky had ever walked down First*

Avenue wearing my lily-white buck shoes, he'd have probably stopped a dozen ball-bats within a block."

Ernie Borgnine — *"Why didn't I get the part of the father in* Somebody Up There Likes Me?

Marlon Brando — *"I know for a fact that Rocky was a wild Indian as a kid. Perhaps he'll consider joining us now. We could use guys like him at the pass."*

Keefe Brasselle — *"I couldn't figure out how Rocky could get me to lean anyway he wanted when we once worked together. Turn the guy loose in Calcutta with a flute and a covered basket, and if it's under the lid, he'll charm it to the sky."*

Teddy Brenner — *Fight promoter—* *"Among white fighters, Rocky Graziano has been the biggest attraction since World War II."*

Jimmy Breslin — *"I could have used him in* The Gang That Couldn't Shoot Straight.*"*

Lester Bromberg — *sports—"If, as Rocky said, he never wanted to be a boxer, then Columbus never wanted to be a discoverer."*

Yul Brynner — *"Rocky was Champ of the World when my son was born. I named him after the Rock, and today they are both champs."*

Al Buck — *sports—"The most lethal punch in or out of the ring, anytime, anywhere."*

George Burns — *"What Rocky and I had in common as kids had to do with pennies. He swiped his off newsstands, while I had mine tossed into a peaked cap while singing in saloons."*

Richard Burton — *"How could they ever pass up Rocky when casting a Shakespearian play?"*

Rocky Buttons — *a button manufacturer with a penchant for track and games—"I asked Rocky if he knew a shylock who suffered from*

	amnesia or a bad heart, and he come up with the name of one of the biggest consumer-finance companies that advertises on TV"
James Caan	— *"If you've got to fall on your ass, go all the way and let Rocky put you there. Nothing like a hammer of his to send you in class."*
Jimmy Cannon	— *sports—"I once wrote that fighting had given Rocky an interesting craggy face. When I ran into Rocky soon after, he said, 'I like it just like it is. If I looked like you, I'd be carryin a briefcase."*
Al Capone	— *"Don't let us down."*
Rich Carey	—*"I asked Rocky to invest in my coal mine. To prove he already had coal he brought a bucketful to the mine."*
Carmine Caridi	—*actor—"Rocky baffles the imagination—three illustrious careers in one lifetime."*
Rocky Caridi	—*proprietor of Friar Tuck and La Maganette in midtown Manhattan—"Come summer afternoons, Graziano and his pals take over several of my outside tables, faces toward the sun. I renamed my outdoor cafe Rocky Graziano Beach in honor of Jacobs' beach."*
Art Carney	—*"Rocky's one guy always welcome to come down my sewer and break some bread with me."*
Johnny Carson	—*"I went off the sauce."*
Bill Carter	— *actor and now Ambassador to the United Nations—"One of the sweetest people I've ever known. He'd give you his last cigar."*
Jack Carter	— *"Rocky, it's still a free country, so go on doin as your wife pleases."*
John Cassavetes	— *"Rocky told me he was lecturing kids on*

the evils of breaking the law. He tells them, if you don't have a strong alibi, be sure you get a good lawyer."

Charo — *"Goochy, goochy, Rocky ees a pussy-cat."*

Angelo Cheesecake — *"If you could get Rocky to move into your house you wouldn't have to put up the barbed wire."*

Steve 'Bath and Tennis' Chirash — *"Watching Rocky put away a pound and a half of macaroni and sausages made me wish I was Italian."*

Irving Cohen — *"Managing Rocky's prize-fighting career was the greatest thrill of my life. I cannot tell you how it felt to watch him drop a seasoned fighter, making him splash on the canvas like an egg from a tall chicken's ass."*

Myron Cohen — *"Any argument, he can settle ... long as his Norma isn't a part of it."*

Dr. Joseph E. Colaneri — *"No, his sidewise moving posture isn't a physical handicap. He just walks with that kind of a balance."*

Mike Colucci — *ex-boxer turned bartender—"The bar I'm workin in could be dead, but it hums and comes to life as soon as Rocky walks through the doorway."*

Perry Como — *"He may not sing well, but his voice, like his smile, is genuine."*

Bob Considine — *"Rocky Graziano was once invited to speak to the mentally disturbed at Creedmoore Hospital. When he arrived and saw the dazed look on many faces, he assumed they were addicts, rather than disturbed. He opened his speech with, 'Ya gotta stop takin drugs. Do it for me, Rocky. Get off the junk an you'll straighten right out.' Rocky didn't real-*

*ize that most were sedated with tran-
quillizers to keep them calm. What he
said didn't matter. They were, for the
most part, beyond understanding, the
important thing was that he was there."*

Freddie Corrado — *president of Port Electric. "Rocky's the
only man I ever met with more friends
than he could handle, and not a one
would he do without."*

Tony Corrado — *"Only a few of us left to remember.
We're thinning out."*

Barney Corsalini — *"I ran into Rocky at the track once and I
asked him to give me a horse. He said,
'I'd have to steal one for you but I don't
steal nuttin from nobody no more. I'm
gettin a lil too old to do time.'"*

Gus Corsalini — *Merrill-Lynch broker—"Must be true
about wife Norma holding all the cab-
bage. He hasn't invested any at this
office."*

Nick Corsalini — *ex-pro singer, boxer, cop—"I took-
Rocky fishing on my small boat once
and as we passed the entrance to an
inlet, he said, 'Let's try there.' 'We can,t,'
I said, pointing to a sign, 'Fish and
Game Preserve. No Fishing.' 'Don't
worry about it. Go there.' I followed his
instructions and in a short time we had
a pail full of fish. Another small boat
pulled alongside and the man said, 'Any
luck?' 'Yeah,' Rocky told him, 'we got a
whole pail full of beautiful bass.' 'You're
Rocky Graziano, right?' the man said.
'Yeah, who are you?' 'I'm the game
warden.' And Rocky shot back with,
'An I'm the biggest fish-story liar you
ever run into.'"*

Candy Corsel — *"While attending an affair, I asked Rocky if he would dance with me. He said the only step he knew was the box step. I said okay, let's try it. Rocky answered, only in the ring, and besides, the only girl I box with is my Norma.*

Vicki Corsel — *"I could never understand how my husband, Ralph, compiled all that grief to do with Rocky's early life. I've never come across a more docile pussycat."*

Ralph Corsel — *"I was visiting Rocky once when he put a plate of left-over potatoes on the terrace for his dog, Plumber. The dog raised a leg and pissed on them. 'You think he's tryin to tell me somethin?' Rocky asked. 'He did the same thing the other day when I tried to feed him a raw onion. I had even chopped it up for him.'"*

Howard Cosell — *"Rocky Graziano, that puissant hunk of masculine pugnacious pulchritude, had the defial audacity to inform me, 'If I talked like youse, I wouldn't be woit' a nickel.'"*

Bing Crosby — *"The worst thing I ever did in my life was put a baseball suit on a statue of Saint Joseph when I was an altar boy, and I got caught. I'm certain Rocky topped that."*

Xavier Cugat — *"They tell me the man had marvelous footwork. Still, I've never see him do the rhumba."*

Tony Curtis — *"We weren't that far apart as kids. Me from a Bronx ghetto, and Rocky from the Lower East Side. So how come I can't talk like him? When I try, it comes out like Cary Grant."*

Sammy Davis, Jr.

— *"Rocky has a rat pack too. Ran into them at Second Avenue Elmer's. Unlike Frank's, Rocky's clan consists of a society of bent noses."*

Robert De Niro

— *"Jake La Motta trained me but Rocky charmed me into believing I could book and win a ten rounder in Madison Square Garden. What he's not aware of is that I'm satisfied with the face I have just as it is."*

Bo Derek

— *"Yes, he is my male #10."*

Vittorio De Sica

— *"On a visit to America, I had the pleasure to be on the Merv Griffin show with Rocky Graziano. Merv ask him to speak to me in Italian. When he say a few words, I say, "You speak Italian like you speak English.' "*

Joe Di Mono

— Co-author of The Ends of Power—*"I spent almost twenty years in school. Rocky got thrown out of the fourth grade. Now he's written a book. If it sells better than mine I'm afraid I might have to kill myself."*

Kirk Douglas

— *"Bad or good, the seeds Rocky sowed must have been right for him."*

Mike Douglas

— *"Just being himself, one of the funniest men in the business, and a hell of a golf player."*

Faye Dunaway

— *"Did someone else say he would have been a natural with me in* Bonnie and Clyde?*"*

Irene Dunne

— *"During a break in a rehearsal for the Martha Raye Show, while I chit-chatted with Rocky, a man went by supporting himself on two metal canes, painfully moving his two braced legs. 'Ey! ya wanna go a couple of rounds?' Rocky*

called to him. The broadest smile crossed the man's face. Rocky seemed to
know what the man's reaction would
be."

Dunninger — master mentalist—"I once read Rocky's
mind and had to consult a specialist to
have the findings decoded."

Jimmy Durante — "One punch in the schnozzola from
Rocky an he'da put me outa business."

Leo Durocher — "For almost all of my adult life I have
been quoted for something I once said,
'Nice guys finish last.' How come Rocky
came in a winner?"

Robert Duvall — "Was Rocky trying to tell me something when he fell asleep in a front row
during my entire performance of the
Broadway play Buffalo Nickel?

Clint Eastwood — "Rocky's answer to his opinion of show
business was, 'It sure beats lookin out
from behind a set of bars and yellin, Eh!
I wanna see my lawyer!' "

Vince Edwards — When Rocky and I appeared on a Dean
Martin Show, he learned of my Italian
background and spoke to me in Italian
when he intended something sotta-
voce. I understand and speak Italian,
but could not understand his. I didn't do
that well with his English either."

Elmer's — of Second Avenue—"We made sure
there weren't any bells around when
Rocky started hanging out here."

Con "Scamp" Erico — one of the greats of jockeydom—"I
wish I could trade places with Rocky
today."

Peter Falk — "Columbo might have solved it but he
couldn't understand the confession."

Marty Feldman — "On a show with the Rock, someone
suggested I resemble him. By Jove!"

Hugh Ferguson

— *sales rep extraordinaire: "Rocky taught me how to disco. He planted a punch on my stomach and said 'Dis go here,' followed up with one to my jaw and said 'dis go there.'"*

Totie Fields

— *"Rocky loves me. I'm sure he can't be the creep who said I've got more chins than a Chinese phone book."*

Ella Fitzgerald

— *"I was flying to Los Angeles for an appearance and who should happen to be on the same flight but Rocky Graziano. I asked him what he was doing there, and he said, 'I don't even belong on this plane. I was supposed to be on a nonstop to Chicago, an got on a nonstop to L.A. by mistake. Being they know me, they never even check my ticket. They tell me I got a free ride which I needed, right?' Rocky seemed to enjoy his goof, passing the time with laughs about other goofs. Once there, they put him on another plane back to Chicago."*

Errol Flynn

— *"My thanks to Rocky for his help in my portrayal of 'Gentleman Jim.'"*

Henry Fonda

— *"Rocky always knew where you could rent a guy to keep crows off your farm."*

Redd Foxx

— *"Had we met earlier, we might have become the perfect comedy team. Burlesque has suffered a terrible loss."*

Sergio Franchi

— *"Rocky criticized my singing. He said he preferred Jimmy Roselli because he had the real* napolitani *tone in his voice."*

Tony Franciosa

— *"When the Rock was a guest on my show he was the perfect gentleman with the females. I'm not sure they liked that."*

Walt Frazier — *"I've done several commercials with Rocky. There was one instance where I turned a commercial down. The script called for a jab to my body. His jab is right on eye level with my* poleens (balls).

Lou Fugazy — *public relations—"I was having lunch at Jimmy Weston's with Rocky Graziano and Doctor Louis Scarrone, when Rocky brought up* capozelles. *It's a goat or sheep's head that many peasant Italians consider a delicacy. It's prepared by halving the skull by sawing it between the eyes and down through the center of the mouth and jaw, separating it into two equal portions, distributing the brain equally on both sides. The halves are lightly salted and garlicked, and roasted inside up to a well-done attitude. As Rocky relates how he misses this delicacy, which can only be found in few Italian restaurants, Doctor Scarrone grimaces and says, 'They're no good for you, Rocky. They're poison. They'll kill you,' not meaning it literally. 'How could they kill me?' Rocky said. 'I ate 'em all my life an become Middleweight Champ of the World.' 'Without them you might have become heavyweight champ,' Doctor Scarrone retorted."*

Zsa Zsa Gabor — *"Rocky is a dahling boy, but why can't he speak English or Hungarian so I can understand him?"*

Bill Gallo — *sportswriter and cartoonist for the* New York Daily News—*"You need not identify to enjoy this wonderful account of a man's rise from one of our city's poorest ghettoes. Yes, a very sad beginning, but save the tears. Rocky Graziano is one ex-fighter that no one is ever going to have to throw a benefit for."*

Ava Gardner — *"My, my! Does he play the fool!"*

John Garfield — *"What stroke of fate kept Rocky from becoming a concert violinist?"*

Judy Garland — *"On a show with Rocky once, he was obviously bored while sitting in the balcony waiting his turn at rehearsal. He started sailing paper planes and high-jacked one out of the theater."*

Ben Gazzara — *"I'll bet he can do Shakespeare!"*

Lou Gehrig — *"Lock him up!"*

Frankie 'Gio' Gioseffi — *ex-pro heavyweight, turned actor—"I ran into The Rock once and told him I was suffering from too much cholesterol from the thousands of eggs my mom made me eat when I was fighting. My mom had insisted it was the healthiest thing I could put in my stomach besides Italian homemade wine. Now my heart was pumping like mad. Rocky's remedy was not medical. He phoned me the next day to say he got me a great fighter's part in Ernest Hemingway's 'Fifty Grand,' starring Ralph Meeker. That's how I broke into show business. Thanks to The Rock, I've enjoyed a great career, but why do they always have to cast me as a gangster or Indian?"*

Jackie Gleason — *"I was told I zinged when I should've zagged."*

Albie Goldstein — *president of the Key Foods chain and entrepreneur of Elmer's Restaurant—"Rocky cost the bouncer his job when*

The Rock and his fight mob started hanging out at Elmer's. We have a half-dozen bouncers now, and we don't have to put them on our payroll."

Robert Goulet

— "My 'O Solo Mio' doesn't cut much ice with Rocky, but one of my Italian wife's, Carol Lawrence's, Neopolitan dishes could turn him into a permanent guest."

Cary Grant

— "A few years back, Rocky and I were guests on a yacht belonging to an executive who was using Rocky in a commercial. As the yacht motored by Riker's Island Penitentiary, Rocky said, 'I spent a year there once.' 'What would a nice guy like you have been doing there?' I asked, and his answer was, 'Time!' "

Sonny Grasso

— Ex-cop turned film producer. "I'm glad I wasn't a cop during his day. Pistol-whipping was then in fashion and might have straightened him out, but it would have ruined his great future as a mumbling celebrity."

Grasso's mob

— At Puglia's Restaurant on Hester off Mulberry Street "It's a pleasure to watch Rocky put away four capozelles, that shoulda quit while they was ahead, six plates of pasta e fagiole, an all at one sittin. You gotta see the sparks fly off his knife an fork, an when he reaches the hard part, we gotta remind him that's the plate."

Norma Graziano

— "During Rocky's amateur boxing days, he got paid off in watches and medals, which he immediately hocked. And so, through the years he never really owned a watch. I decided to buy him one for a Christmas gift one day, one of the *best money could buy. The clerk assured me the one I chose was most unusual. He said it was waterproof, shockproof, unbreakable, antimagnetic, not a thing in the world could possibly happen to it. Something did happen to it. Rocky lost it."*

Shecky Greene — *"If I hadn't been suffering from a case of Dom Perignon while filming* Tony Rome, *I would have never thrown that couch off my room balcony just to give Rocky a laugh."*

Emil Griffin — *"How come The Rock got a five-minute standin ovation when he got innerduced in the Madison Square Garden ring before my fight? I'm the guy who hadda stop the punches."*

Merv Griffin — *"Getting Rocky to appear on my show with Arthur Treacher combined two incongruous people in a superb blend of humor."*

Buddy Hackett — *"In the days when I was crazy, drunk, and somewhat hazy, I'd have even chosen a fight with Rocky Graziano. The good Lord must have known what everybody else knew, and sent that man around some other way."*

Gene Hackman — *"Have they ever made* The Graziano Connection?*"*

Rex Harrison — *"Had Sir Bernard Shaw known Rocky, he might have made his* Pygmalion *a he instead of a she."*

Pat Henry — *"With Rocky on his side, my uncle wouldn't have needed the knife."*

Irish Johnny Heron — *P. J. Clarke's bartender—"Even though somebody up there likes you, Rocky, you'll never die. There's not room upstairs for you."*

Dustin Hoffman
— *"Due to our strong resemblance, I would love to play Rocky in a film."*

Bob Hope
— *"He's a comedian's comedian who does not have to rehearse and perform."*

Ralph 'The Bank' Jacobson
— *"I give 'im money anytime."*

Jim Jennings
— *sports—"Rocky hadn't become an actor yet when he was in that ring."*

Georgie Jessel
— *"Once a champ, and always a champ."*

Lady Bird Johnson
— *"I met Rocky in a Washington, D.C., bookstore where we were both autographing literary endeavors, and we presented autographed copies to each other. Do you think he read mine?"*

President Lyndon B. Johnson
— *"Try this hat on for size, boy!"*

Tom Jones
— *"Rocky can borrow my tuxedo anytime."*

Boris Karloff
— *"I once suggested to Rocky an idea for a show in which he could participate, called 'An Evening with Boris Karloff and His Friends.' I wonder why he turned me down?"*

Charlie Kelly
Lieutenant Detective—"Some years ago Rocky walked in on a crap game being raided. I recognized him and said, take off, the joint's being raided. He came back with, 'What'sa matta? Ain't my money any good?' "

Gene Kelly
— *"I think Dean Martin's whiskey is no good for footwork, Rocky's or mine."*

Phil Kennedy
— *ex-National League ballplayer—"Rocky Graziano and Babe Ruth had a lot in common. One made it with his fists, the other with a bat."*

Allen King
— *"Rocky was the kind of a fighter who could never sell advertising on the soles of his shoes.*

Jake La Motta
— *"The Raging Bull," ex-Middleweight Champ—"Rocky got me a personal*

appearance job once, which I thought was just outside Montreal, Canada. I fly to Montreal and find out I have to change planes there. I ended up in a four-by-four town, Ellesmere, which is almost to the North Pole. I didn't start figuring I was in trouble until I get off the little plane and find a dog sled waiting to take me to the job. If it wasn't for seeing a little yellow snow once in a while. I'd never known another man had been there before me. Do you really believe Rocky Graziano is my friend?' "

Burt Lancaster — *"Methinks The Rock has learned, 'tis better the fool than the sword."*

Abbe Lane — *"I would love to teach him to rhumba."*

Mario Lanza — *"If I had been born with Rocky's voice, I would have been a truck driver."*

Peter Lawford — *"Rocky's accent was definitely not British. What was it he said?"*

Jack Lemmon — *"Guys like Rocky may not add to New York's cleanliness, but they do keep it beautiful."*

Jerry Lester — *"When Rocky and Dagmar were on my show, they had one thing in common, large chests."*

Jerry Lewis — *"I had ten of the best years of my life with a fighter from Steubenville, Ohio. Go find yourself a singer, Rocky—and good luck."*

Lou Linder — *vice-president of Rosenfeld, Sirowitz and Lawson, an ad agency for whom Rocky has done commercials—"Rocky and I left Longchamps in a snow storm one evening. All transportation had stopped. Not a cab in sight. A patrol car pulled to the curb, and Rocky poked his head inside and said, 'How about taking* us to the Copa?' 'Hop in,' said the surprised cops on recognition. After getting deposited at the Copa door, Rocky said, 'Those same bulls woulda crushed my skull with their bats a few years ago.'"

Tony Lo Bianco — "I got a lot of fighting experience playing Rocky Marciano on a TV show, however, I'm closer to Graziano's weight. Do you think he might give me a second chance shot when they film this one?"

Bela Lugosi — "Could it be that Rocky turned down a spot on the Karloff show because I was one of the friends? I didn't like Graziano's tough, muscular neck anyway."

Paul Lynde — "I can't understand how I beat out Rocky for the title, 'Comedian of the Year.'"

Billy Mack — airline pilot—"It happened on New Year's Day. Some of the gang from P. J's and a couple of bookmakers were all in my bachelor pad, right down the street from Clarke's. We were watching the ballgames, playing some cards, when who rings the bell but Rocky Graziano. He hung around a while, made a few small bets, and tried to phone somebody. All of a sudden, and very pathetically, he said, 'You know, today is also my birthday.' We all yell out, 'Happy birthday, Rocky!' and I asked, 'How come you're not out in Long Island spending it with Norma?' 'I don't live there no more,' he said. 'We moved into an apartment over on Sutton Place. I hear about all the burglars workin the apartments, so I go out an get a big seventy-five dollar lock that even Jesus Christ can't budge. Here I am with all the keys in my pocket, an even me can't fuckin open it. Here it is, New Year's Day an my birthday an I'm locked out of my own fuckin house.' 'Why won't the keys work?' 'Norma's on the other side of the lock, an she's got it fixed so's I can't get in.' "

Shirley MacLaine — "No amount of explaining how I could be a member of Sinatra's clan was acceptable to Rocky. 'But youse is a goil!' he kept repeating, shaking his head."

Joe Marino — man about midtown—"The two best places to be with Rocky are the race-track and the dinner table."

Dean Martin — "The sonofabitch stole my whiskey!"

Lee Marvin — "Rocky and I had things in common before turning to acting. I was a plumber, installing lead and brass pipes. Rocky was the guy who hacksawed them out of empty apartments to sell to the junkman."

Marcello Mastroianni — "Un uomo incredible!"

Walter Matthau — "Rocky and I knew each other in the days when we were both growing up poor on the Lower East Side. We even had a couple of rough fistfights with each other. I'd hate to think of how he'd have scattered my brains and ruined me for my present career had we fought just a few years later."

Vaughn Meader — "Holding Rocky down is like capturing the wind."

Burgess Meredith — "While at Gallagher's once, Rocky sent me into a glass-doored room telling me I was wanted on the phone inside. He slammed and locked the door, and faced *me laughing through the inch-thick glass, while I rained panicked blows on it. He had locked me in the refrigerator."*

Sal Mineo

— *"The character I played in* Somebody Up There Likes Me *could really have been me. Rocky's to be admired for the transition he made."*

Gary Moore

— *"Rocky couldn't understand why he couldn't get on our show, 'To Tell the Truth.'"*

Perry Moss

— *of Savoy Brass—"I invited Rocky and his wife on my yacht for a weekend. During our cruising, he fell asleep in a chair and his testicles dropped out of his loose-fitting swim trunks. Norma made no secret of informing him of the catastrophe while she scolded. 'So what!' the Champ said, 'They're champeen balls, ain't they?'"*

Leroy Neiman

— *the famed artist—"I did a painting of Rocky sitting on a toilet bowl, and presented it to him with an inscription under it, 'Plumbing by Perry Moss.' Rocky asked, 'Where ya got my name, inside the bowl?'"*

Paul Newman

— *"Mentioning Rocky Graziano when I got flagged down for several minor traffic offenses caused the officer to snap handcuffs on me."*

Joe Nichols

—*sports—"Devastation in the ring!"*

Jack Nicholson

—*"I would have relished the part of Rocky Graziano in* Somebody Up There Likes Me. *It was just before my time."*

Dr. Walter Nicora

—*"Rocky never feared any man, in or out of the ring, but when he sat in my dentist chair to get his teeth worked on, he shit in his pants."*

Richard Nixon —*on meeting Rocky in conjunction with the Drug Rehabilitation Program— "Always remember, Rocky, others may hate you, but they can't win unless you hate them, and then you only destroy yourself."*

"Irish Jack" O'Connor —*P. J. Clarke's fizzical culturist—"The only thing musclebound about The Rock is the overly exercised hand that repeatedly tips our stemware."*

Al Pacino — *"How come you weren't in* The Godfather*?"*

Jack Palance — *"One could never believe the things Rocky and I have in common. We've both been professional boxers, we both became actors, we've each done numerous commercials, we both took ballet lessons, and we've both been on the cover of* Esquire *magazine with Raquel Welch."*

Bert Parks — *"A recent commercial portrayed Rocky as a flashy blonde, clothes, wig, and all. It caused me to invite him to appear on the Miss America Pageant. Why did he turn me down?"*

Johnny Peanuts — *"I once ran with the Rocky pack but I had good legs then."*

Valerie Perrine — *"I have always been fond of fighters, street, ring, for a cause, anything. Do you think Norma would mind my sending Rocky a nude from my picture* Lenny*?"*

Robert Preston — *"Believe me, there have been many instances when I could have used him."*

Vincent Price — *"I asked Rocky how to go about fighting a dilemma and he said, 'What's his ring record?'"*

Freddie Prinze — *"Ees not my yob to say it, but I think Rocky is America's and Puerto Rico's most charming guest."*

B. S. Pully — *"I gave Rocky a winner at the race track once, and I asked him to place a small bet for me. He did. He laid out and put me down for six cents across the board. The horse came in first and I owed money on the bet."*

Anthony Quinn — *"For a short period of my own life, I was also a boxer before turning actor. Had I been able to pack a punch like Rocky, I might have made boxing my career. Then, instead of starring in* Requiem for a Heavyweight, *it might have been the story of my life."*

Phil Rafferty — *ex-lightweight boxing contender and now bartender at P. J. Clarke's—"Rocky told me I was one of the greatest fighters in the country—but in the city they killed me."*

George Raft — *on the Mike Douglas Show—"I could have certainly used that horse you touted Mamie Eisenhower on."*

Martha Raye — *"I've collected doll clowns for years, but this one defies collection."*

Oliver Reed — *"Rocky will always be a champ. For me he has never lost."*

Burt Reynolds — *"That first centerfold was a toss-up between Rocky and me. It could have gone either way."*

President Ronald Reagan — *"Rocky Graziano becoming governor of New York State is not an improbable thought. I can think of several actors who took their acting seriously enough to run for office. Leo Carillo and George Murphy for two."*

of a tough top fighter. Now, who's there shootin crap but this kid, Rocky Graziano. I call him aside and I say, get the fuck out of here fast. I wasn't being fair to all the others that I locked up but that was the way the mop flopped in those days."

Jimmy Reardon — retired New York Detective, author of The Sweet Life of Jimmy Riley—"Just the night before a raid on this gambling establishment, I had been to the Garden and seen this dago kid whip the hell out

Robert Redford — "Many thanks for your consulting help on The Sting."

Sammy Renick — ex-jockey, now sportscaster—"You know I'm little to begin with. I was walking along East 57th Street with my head down and I see this big brown animal on the curb. Looked like a chestnut colt. I thought I was seeing Secretariat again. I look up, and see what this big dog is pulling along on the end of a leash is Rocky. He tells me his dog's name is Plumber. If someone would have thrown a saddle on the monster, I'da tried a comeback right there in the street."

Marco Ricardo — entrepreneur of Starbucks—"Believe me when I tell you, Rocky's one smart cookie. You may not be aware of it, but it's all in his head."

Don Rickles — "The only way for Rocky to keep his beauty is not introduce her to anyone. Putting makeup on him is like putting it on a meatball. He brought new colors to TV—black and blue. I'm kidding, Rocky."

Jilly Rizzo — *"Keeping Rocky away from Frankie Sinatra would be like trying to hold back a steamroller with your shoulder."*

Phil Rizzuto — *"I wish he wouldn't compete with me for the pizza and spaghetti commercials. Am I not Italian too?"*

Ray Robinson — *"I thought it was the end of the trail for Rocky when I beat him late in his fight career back in 1952. What I didn't know was, the guy was just getting started."*

Dr. Terry Robinson — world-famous chiropractor and author of The Mario Lanza Story—*"The man's body is in tip-top shape. It's the brain that defies medical science."*

Ginger Rogers — *"If your front isn't the clothes you wear, one would do good to have that special something you can't take away from Rocky."*

Caesar Romero — *"While Rocky and I were rehearsing a Martha Raye show, we went next door into a small snack restaurant. He ordered a hamburger and I a hotdog. The waitress took a frozen hamburger from a box and clamped it in her armpit. 'What're you doin with my hamburger?' Rocky wanted to know. 'I'm thawing it out,' she replied. I cancelled the hotdog."*

Murray Rose — sports—*"Synonymous in the history of boxing will always be the names of Stanley Ketchel and Rocky Graziano."*

Bill Ruocco — past or present Mayor of Springfield, N.J. *"No record of Rocky in any of our jails. Why were we snubbed?"*

Freddie Russo — an educated ex-fighter with flawless grammar that has not enhanced his fortunes—*"Rocky offered to teach me to speak the way he does. He guaranteed I would make a bundle."*

Peter Savage	— *writer, producer of* The Raging Bull—" *"Rocky, the incorrigible young hood, beat an environmental hazard with sheer determination.*
	Rocky, the fighter, fought his way to the middleweight Championship of the World, and on to the stars.
	Rocky, the entertainer, gave the world a moment of laughter and left them with his infectious smile.
	Rocky, the artist, painted a picture that brings hope to every under-privileged kid faced with having to break through the invisible walls of a ghetto."
	"I jestfully called Rocky a Malaprop and he almost belted me, assuming I had called him a fag. Just in time, someone explained."
Telly Savalas	— *"Rocky wanted the crook to get away."*
Dr. Louis Scarrone	— *"I'm writing a book too, Rocky, for people like you—*How to Study Brain Surgery at Home in Your Spare Time."
Joey Scoongeel	— *one hell of a guy—"I wanna know from Rocky, how I go about t'rowin out my mother-in-law, an he sez, 'Big guy like you should be ashamed, can't pick up a little old lady. So watcha better do is wait till she out, pack up her bag, an t'row it outta the door.' I can't, I gotta tell Rocky. It's her apartment."*
Ralph "Ironman" Serpico	— *"Friends and business associates call me the millionaire iron-man, but it's really Rocky who has the loot and the balls of steel to go with it."*
Maxie Shapiro	— *ex-fighter, recreation director.* "As a kid, Rocky was an honor student—'Yes, your Honor, no, your Honor.' And he

always went home with big marks—on his nose, a cut lip, black eye. He dropped out of school on account of pneumonia. He couldn't spell it."

Phil Silvers — *"Years ago, Rocky assured me I'd come out on top some day. He was right. I got bald.*

Frank Sinatra — *"Never in my life have I seen a guy start at the bottom and climb a ladder like the Champ. Rung by rung, one at the time, pulling himself up, working, sweating, struggling, right to the top of the ladder. I don't know too much about Rocky's success. But he could sure climb a hell of a ladder."*

Sidney Skolsky — *columnist—"Rocky Graziano was always a star even though he never rose above the title of 'second banana'."*

Paul Sorvino — *"While I was singing* Return to Sorrento *at Puglia's Restaurant one evening, Rocky never missed a beat with his fork."*

Sir Santo Spagnuolo — *"While setting up a commercial for men's cologne I asked Rocky if it would be proper to send his wife, Norma, a bottle of perfume with my compliments. He said, 'Send her a stack of hundreds instead. Her perfume has to be green and bear pictures of United States Presidents.'"*

Sly Stallone — *"Yeah. He's the Real Rocky! I picked his name for my film because of the tremendous impact Rocky made on my life."*

Rod Steiger — *"At the age of twelve, I delivered ice and coal from one of those corner-cellar icemen of the day. Rocky, who* *happens to approximate my age, said that cellar could have been the source for many of the pilfered sacks of coal which he dragged home to help keep the house warm."*

Rise Stevens — *"Rocky tosses a hell of a salad."*

Lou Stillman — *"Whenever anything was missing in the gym, we used to yell out, 'Ey! Where's Rocky?'"*

Barbra Streisand — *"When concerns make one sad, you need the Rockys to make you glad."*

John Cameron Swayze — *"Rocky turned down the offered watch saying he'd rather get the cash. He hocked or lost every watch he ever owned and was afraid Timex was unhockable."*

Sam Taub — *sports—"I hung on the ring apron with such intensity I forgot what to say."*

Elizabeth Taylor — *"A man! . . . for all seasons."*

Mark Tendler — *actor, pro-wrestler, and bouncer at P. J. Clarke's—"Nice to know Rocky is always around in case I need some back-up help."*

Lana Turner — *"I think his Norma really sings."*

Bill Uncles — *fabric distributor—"Whole cloth, a mile wide."*

Harold Valan — *ex-fighter and famous boxing referee— "I'm the kind of a horse player who studies all the sheets, the* Racing Form, The Telegraph, *and anything else with race-horse records. I went to the track with Rocky once and after a race he showed the winning tickets on a horse. 'Our Anniversary,' with ninety bucks across the board. The horse paid him nine hundred smackers. 'Jesus Christ! I says, "That horse hasn't showed in fifty starts. He was even left at the post a few times.' I like to went crazy. I says, 'What the fuck made you pick that cripple?' an he says, 'It's my anniversary today.' Now I know what they mean when they say, since Rocky's book,* Somebody Up There Likes Me, *come out, Rocky only bets on horses who start from a kneeling position.' "*

Dick Van Dyke — *"Rocky tried to clarify something for me. It didn't matter. He couldn't understand me either."*

Governor George Wallace — *and ex-prizefighter—"Unrecognized ability will always out someday."*

Joe Wander — *Hollywood producer—"Rocky will always have my admiration and respect. He rose above almost insurmountable odds."*

Gene Ward — *sports—"In my book, others are as good but none greater."*

Jack Warden — *"Pound for pound, none ever better"*

Dionne Warwick — *"Burt Bacharach and Rocky Graziano . . . Do I mention them in the same breath because they're both champs?"*

John Wayne — *"Could have used him at the Alamo!"*

Johnny Weissmuller — *Tarzan and ex-Olympic swimming champ—"I met Rocky at a poolside once and suggested we race the length of the pool for a drink. Rocky said, 'I don't take dives.' "*

Raquel Welch — *"While doing a cover picture assignment for* Esquire *with Palance and Graziano, I asked Rocky what he thought of women going into the fight game, and he replied, 'They always been. Ask any married man.' "*

Orson Welles — *"I asked where he was taking his speech lessons and he said, 'What make you think I can't talk Shakespeare as good as you?' and he continued to recite, 'Where art thou maiden, round of tit an foim of ass? Hasten to my savage chest.'"*

William B. Williams — *"Rocky and Norma came up to my 'Make Believe Ballroom' some years ago, and he walked up and down the halls looking for the ticket booth and dance hall."*

Earl Wilson — *"Met Rocky G. at one of those publicity parties I get invited to. While greeting each other, I detected the soft classical strains of Beethoven in the background. Making small talk, I asked Rocky what he thought of Beethoven. His answer was, 'Wrecked him in the fifth in Chicago once.'"*

Flip Wilson — *"I've suggested they refilm* Somebody Up There Likes Me *in living color, and consider me for the two starring roles. With Geraldine as my wife they would get two for the price of one."*

Jonathon Winters — *"First time Rocky and I did a show together, he wanted to know who all the other guys and the little old lady who looked like me were."*

Harry Wismer — *sports—"The fight game has never been the same since he left."*

Dick Young — *columnist—"Rocky confided in me once that he was both rich and broke. His wealth was all on paper, paper with Norma's name on it. And he was broke because she wouldn't give him any cash."*

Henny Youngman — *"Since Rocky made that show with the Coppola Marionettes, he won't make a move unless somebody pulls the right strings."*

PURE GRAZIANO

(GLOSSARY)

(only approximately in alphabetical order)

Afta	—	*Afta da rise come da fall.*
Ahm	—	*Da cop twisted my ahm.*
Amacha	—	*Before ya toin professional*
Anudda	—	*Annudda guy dit it.*
Areddy	—	*I seen him areddy.*
Arguin	—	*What's he arguin about?*
Arra	—	*I shot an arra inta de air.*
Oit	—	*It fell to oit, I know not waah.*
Ast	—	*Da cop ast me a lotta questions.*
Lotta	—	*He also give me a lotta warnins.*
Astoot	—	*Da chicks not only smart, she's astoot.*
Atual	—	*Da atual time is tree o'clock*
Auta	—	*Ya auta watch yerself gettin outa de auta.*

Bahs	— *What a judge puts you behind.*
Bean	— *Da guy's a human bean.*
Becuz	— *Becuz God made thee mine.*
Betta	— *No betta, no wois.*
Bigga	— *More than smalla.*
Boidies	— *They choip in the trees.*
Choipin	— *The canary is choipin to the fuzz.*
Fuzz	— *A ghee wid a badge.*
Ghee	— *A guy.*
Bootiful	— *That's my broad.*
Boitday	— *When ya bawn.*
Bawn	— *Foist time ya breed fresh air.*
Breed	— *When you stop doin it you in trouble.*
Bret	— *What most my opponents run out of.*
Cha	— *Anudda woid for ya.*
Champeen	— *Ain't got nuttin to do wit ballpeen hammer.*
Cherce	— *My cherce of companions wuzent always da best.*
Choich	— *If you got a prayer, you take it there.*
Chom	— *He chom da spots offn a leopard.*
Cleenas	— *I got taken to da cleenas.*
C'meer	— *C'meer wise guy.*
Coises	— *He coises wois than me.*
Wois	— *The guy keeps gettin wois an wois.*
Coitens	— *You hang em over windows, or, its coitens for a guy when he get bumped off.*
Commoishels	— *Keep 'em comin.*
C'mon	— *C'mon slowpoke.*
Consoin	— *I always have consoin for my friends.*
Contenda	— *A guy goin for da champeenship.*
Cupla	— *Two.*
Cuvva	— *Cuvva him up an don't let him catch cold.*
Da	— *spelled T-H-E.*
Dare	— *Off ta the side, or far off.*
Dat	— *Somethin ovah dare.*
Deez	— *Deez are da times.*
Dem	— *The udda guys.*
Doze	— *Da enemy.*

Den	—	*An den I tole him.*
Detts	—	*Somethin you gotta pay*
Didden	—	*I didden do it.*
Dis	—	*Dis is it, baby!*
Disoit	—	*I disoited da table just before disoit.*
Dun	—	*Somethin da guy did.*
Dunno	—	*I tole the cop I dunno nuttin.*
Eeda	—	*Eeda ya shit, or get off da pot.*
Family	—	*Da Mafia.*
Figger	—	*I figger she got a pretty good figger.*
Foist	—	*Comes before second.*
Fuh	—	*Fuh want of a lock, da boss got stolen.*
Gapper	—	*Dare's teet in it.*
Teet	—	*Whatcha chew wit.*
Getcha	—	*You gotta getcha self in shape.*
Gimme	—	*everything you got.*
Ginja	—	*I aks Ginja for a rye an' ginja*
Goil	—	*My wife is also my goil.*
Gonna	—	*Whatcha gonna do?*
Hadda	—	*I hadda figa a way out.*
Hafta	—	*I hafta go to da terl't.*
Helpa	—	*Somethin your mudda should have.*
Mudda	—	*She's ya best bet.*
Fodda	—	*The guy what help her make you.*
Histree	—	*That's what George Washington is.*
Hoid	—	*I taut I hoid a boidy choipin.*
Hoit	—	*It don't feel good.*
Hoofa	—	*A tap dancer.*
Howja	—	*Howja know I dun it?*
Huh	—	*It wuzent me, it wuz huh.*
Hunnerd	—	*Ten times ten.*
Hypatenchon	—	*Noivis blood.*
Novis	—	*Could come from hypatenchon.*
Imag	—	*Imag that cop takin me for a dope.*
Inna	—	*I be there inna minute, right afta.*
Innerduce	—	*I got innerduced in da ring.*
J'eat	—	*J'eat yet?*

Jools   — *The famly jools is in da guy's pants.*

Kilt   — *Ya could get kilt fuckin with* malandrines.

Kissa   — *My face.*

Leesha   — *I do it at my leesha.*

Letric   — *Da light.*

Letta   — *Letta go check da mail for a letta.*

Liddle   — *Like your liddle brudda.*

Brudda   — *Opsit of sista.*

Loin   — *Whatcha do in school.*

Luvva   — *Everybody luvs a luvva.*

Malandrines — *Bad guys.*

Manaja   — *Guy what tells you what to do wid your money.*

Matta   — *It don't matta no how.*

Naw   — *If somebody aks ya if ya dun it.*

Aks   — *Aks me a question I tell ya a lie.*

Nevva   — *Nevva say die.*

Noive   — *You got some noive!*

Numba   — *Age is jus a numba.*

Nuttin   — *What I had plenty of when I wuz a kid.*

Offa   — *Whatcha got to offa?*

Oil   — *A guy's name.*

Earl   — *You put it on a salad.*

Oily   — *Oily to bed an oily to rise makes a man helty.*

Oncet   — *upon a time.*

Twicet   — *Two times as much as oncet.*

Onnah   — *Yer Onna da judge.*

Oppsit   — *Da udder side.*

Ovah   — *How ya toin eggs.*

Toin   — *Ya gotta wait ya toin.*

Owny   — *I gotta go away owny for a liddle while.*

Picher   — *Dey took his prints and picher when he got booked.*

Plenny   — *I had plenny of nuttin.*

Poiches   — *I din swipe it, I made a poiches.*

Poils   — *I give my Norma a string of 'em.*

Poisonal   — *For me owny.*

Powa   — *Somethin ya gotta have in a punch.*

Poyse   — *A lotta poyse snatchers come out of my old neighborhood.*

Practly   — *I wuz practly safe when he caught me.*

Presha	—	*Ey, don't put no presha on me.*
Probly	—	*They'll probly spring him.*
Quata	—	*Twenty-five cents.*
Dolla	—	*Faw quatas.*
Radda	—	*I radda be here den dare.*
Ratchet	—	*Bigga then a mouse shit.*
Reconize	—	*I always reconize a good score.*
Regla	—	*He's a regla guy.*
Reltiv	—	*Everythin is reltiv, like da cousins ya hardly know.*
Rememberized		*Somethin dat comes back in ya head.*
Rider	—	*A guy like Ralph Corsel who makes books.*
Saboiban	—	*On da outskoits.*
Outskoits	—	*Away from downtown.*
Satidee	—	*Comes befaw Sundee.*
Scad	—	*I'm not scad of ghosts.*
Seesin	—	*What you put on food all seesins of da year.*
Sence	—	*The judge hit me wit a long sence.*
Aloigic	—	*I'm aloigic to long sences.*
Seprit	—	*Give us seprit checks.*
Shawta		*He's shawta than huh.*
Longa	—	*More than shawta.*
Shoit	—	*Da guy swipe da shoit offn ya back.*
Shudda	—	*I shudda, I wudda, I cudda.*
Wudda	—	*If I wudda went on that job I'da got nailed.*
Simpity	—	*I get no simpity from nobody.*
Sindikit	—	*Da Boys.*
Skeeta	—	*One t'ing I can't take is skeeta bites.*
Smackeroos	—	*I got twenny-five of 'em for my foist pro fight.*
Soicle	—	*What I run aroun in.*
Soiv	—	*Soiv me foist.*
Soona	—	*Oppsit of layta.*
Spect	—	*I spect you to show on time.*
Speshly	—	*Never cop out, an speshly if you didden do it.*
Strippa	—	*A goil what takes off cloes.*
Cloes	—	*Cloes make da wimmin.*
Sunly	—	*Sunly, who shows but dis cop.*
Tanks	—	*for da memories.*
Taut	—	*I taut she taut me da ropes.*

T'eat	— *I gotta get somethin t'eat.*
Teata	— *I pafawmed in dat teata.*
Pafawm	— *What I get paid for today.*
Tempamentel—	*She wuz so tempamentel, I couldn't say shit widout gettin her mad.*
Tention	— *I don't pay no tention to nuttin.*
Terl't	— *When ya gotta go.*
Tespian	— *Is what I am today.*
Theirself	— *Da other poyson.*
Thunk	— *Somethin you t'aut.*
Tin	— *You too tin.*
Ting	— *Like a tinga beauty.*
Tink	— *I tink I go home.*
Toinamint	— *Like in golf.*
Winna	— *Da guy what wins the toinamint.*
Toity	— *Ten times tree.*
Tole	— *I tole 'im nuttin.*
Tree	— *A number.*
Faw	— *Comes afta tree.*
T'rew	— *Somethin ya t'row. A way to go.*
Troot	— *Whatcha supposed say when ya swear on a bible.*
Useta	— *I useta be a wrongo.*
Waah?	— *Ovah daah.*
Wayja	— *You bet it on your cherce.*
Wanna	— *Maybe ya wanna dance?*
Watta	— *You can lead a hoss to watta . . .*
Hoss	— *Da one I bet on broke a leg.*
Waudin	— *Ya fodda when youse is shakin time.*
Wedda	— *Wedda or not, ya come in bad wedda, I be here.*
Welty	— *Helty, welty, an wise.*
Whatcha	— *Watcha see is whatcha got.*
Wimmin	— *are soft an pretty.*
Winda	— *Whatcha look troo.*
Winta	— *It gets cold.*
Summa	— *It warms up again.*
Wit	— *Who ya wit?*
Witcha	— *I ain't witcha no more.*

Woids	— *In udder woids, I luv you.*
Woild	— *Da place we live on.*
Woit	— *Da difference between whatcha pay an whatcha get.*
Wotsa	— *Wotsa big deal?*
Wrongo	— *Da oppsit of righto.*
Wunda	— *I wunda who's kissin huh now.*
Wuznt	— *It wuznt me.*
Ya	— *Da guy ya talkin wit.*
Yaws an ows	— *Like his an huhs*
Y'mean?	— *You know what I mean?*
Yoot	— *It's wasted on kids.*
Youse	— *Youse kids betta listen to The Rock.*

Index